FURIO DURANDO

ANCIENT
GREECE

*THE DAWN OF THE
WESTERN WORLD*

STEWART, TABORI & CHANG
NEW YORK

ANCIENT GREECE
THE DAWN OF THE WESTERN WORLD

Text
Furio Durando

Editorial coordination
Fabio Bourbon
Valeria Manferto De Fabianis

Graphic design
Patrizia Balocco Lovisetti
Anna Galliani - Clara Zanotti

Translation
Ann Ghiringhelli (text)
Studio Traduzione
Vecchia Milano (captions)

Drawings
Monica Falcone
Roberta Vigone

CONTENTS

1 *The Nike of Samothrace (190 BC), by a sculptor from Rhodes, rises atop the Louvre staircase.*

2-3 *The Parthenon of Athens (447-432 BC) symbolizes the perfection achieved by Greek architects.*

4-5 *All the mystery of the island sacred to Apollo is enclosed in this broad view of the Hellenistic Theater Quarter in Delos.*

6-7 *Segesta, the powerful city of the Elymians in Sicily, had a splendid Greek-type amphitheater.*

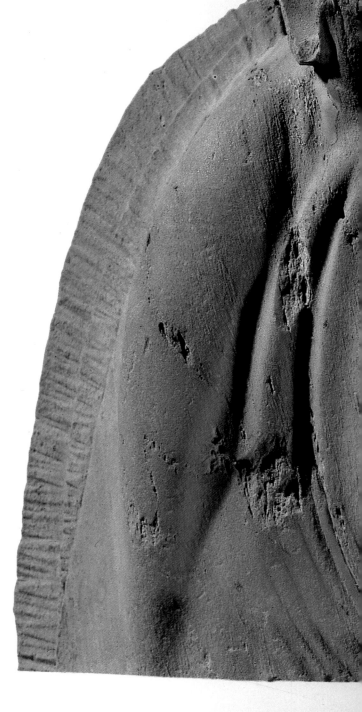

8 *These beautiful silver rhyta come from the Thracian cemetery of Borovo (Bulgaria, 4th century BC).*

8-9 *The vivid realism of Phidias' art can be seen in this marble horse head, from the east pediment of the Parthenon.*

10-11 *This broad and realistic painting of a port of the 16th century BC comes from a Minoan house of Akrotiri (Thera).*

12-13 *A symposium between Greek aristocrats painted on the wall slabs of the Tomb of the Diver from Poseidonia (480 BC).*

8

Published in 1997 and distributed by Stewart, Tabori & Chang, a division of U.S. Media Holdings, Inc., 115 West 18th Street, New York, NY 10011

Distributed in Canada by General Publishing Company Ltd., 30 Lesmill Road, D on Mills, Ontario, M3B 2T6, Canada

Library of Congress Cataloging-in-Publication Data

Durando, Furio.
[Grecia antica. English]
Ancient Greece: the dawn of the Western world / by Furio Durando.
p. cm.
Includes bibliographical references and index.
ISBN 1-55670-601-4 (hardcover)
1. Greece—Civilization—To 146 b.c. 2. Art, Ancient—Greece. 3. Mediterranean Region—Antiquities, Greek—Pictorial works. 4. Architecture, Greek—Mediterranean Region—Pictorial works.
5. Cities and towns, Ancient—Greece—Tours. I. Title.
DF77.D79513 1997   938—DC21   97-14192

Printed in Italy by Grafedit, Italy.
Color separations by Bassoli and Fotomec, Italy.
10 9 8 7 6 5 4 3 2 1

FOREWORD

The civilization of ancient Greece is the root, essence, and inexhaustible core of Western thinking, as well as, variously, the source, tributary, or delta of the numerous cultures in the Mediterranean basin. Over the centuries its power to fascinate each new generation has never waned. Tourists still flock to visit the splendid traces of Greek antiquity; museum exhibitions on the ancient Greeks still draw huge crowds. Evidence of the seminal influence of Greek culture on our world is plentiful: each year general and specialist studies by historians and archaeologists, on-site explorations, and laboratory-based research reveal whole new intellectual and aesthetic dimensions of our ancient Greek forebears.

Why add another book to this already almost infinite bibliography?

It is our belief—possibly immodest but nonetheless sincere—that no work intended for lay readers and no textbook for students has yet succeeded in capturing this fascinating and complex subject with concise narrative and discussion, precise scientific information, in clear, inspiring language, and high-quality illustrations.

Our objective is to take our readers on an amazing journey in search of ancient Greece and its civilization and to offer new insight into the classical world through outstanding pictures, many of them never previously published. The illustrations have been selected to reflect the narrative and place each topic addressed in its historic and cultural context. The summary but rigorously factual text is complemented by detailed captions.

While this book is intended for the lay reader, we hope it will also stimulate the interest of those who study ancient Greece and its civilization in greater depth. We follow the chapters on the

14 *Oedipus and the Sphinx, in the central tondo of an Attic kylix with red figures, from the late 6th or the early 5th century BC. The Oedipus story, of mythological origin, symbolizes the fight between man's thirst for knowledge and the unknown.*

14-15 *This beautiful black-figure amphora, signed by Exekias as potter and also attributed to him as painter, is dated between 540 and 530 BC. The scene, depicted with graphic realism, shows Achilles slaying Penthesilea.*

15 *The Homeric epics have been widely portrayed in Attic ceramic painting. On this splendid amphora with black figures, signed by Exekias about 540 BC, the heroes Achilles and Ajax are playing dice.*

history and culture of the Greek and Hellenistic worlds with an outline of its visual arts, as they developed from their Aegean origins to the Roman conquest. Here too the descriptions are brought to life by splendid and detailed illustrations, together with graphic reconstructions of the most significant monuments.

Completing the volume is a spectacular itinerary that directs the traveler to the most beautiful cities and colonies of ancient Greece. The last few pages offer a brief glossary of technical terms and a short bibliography.

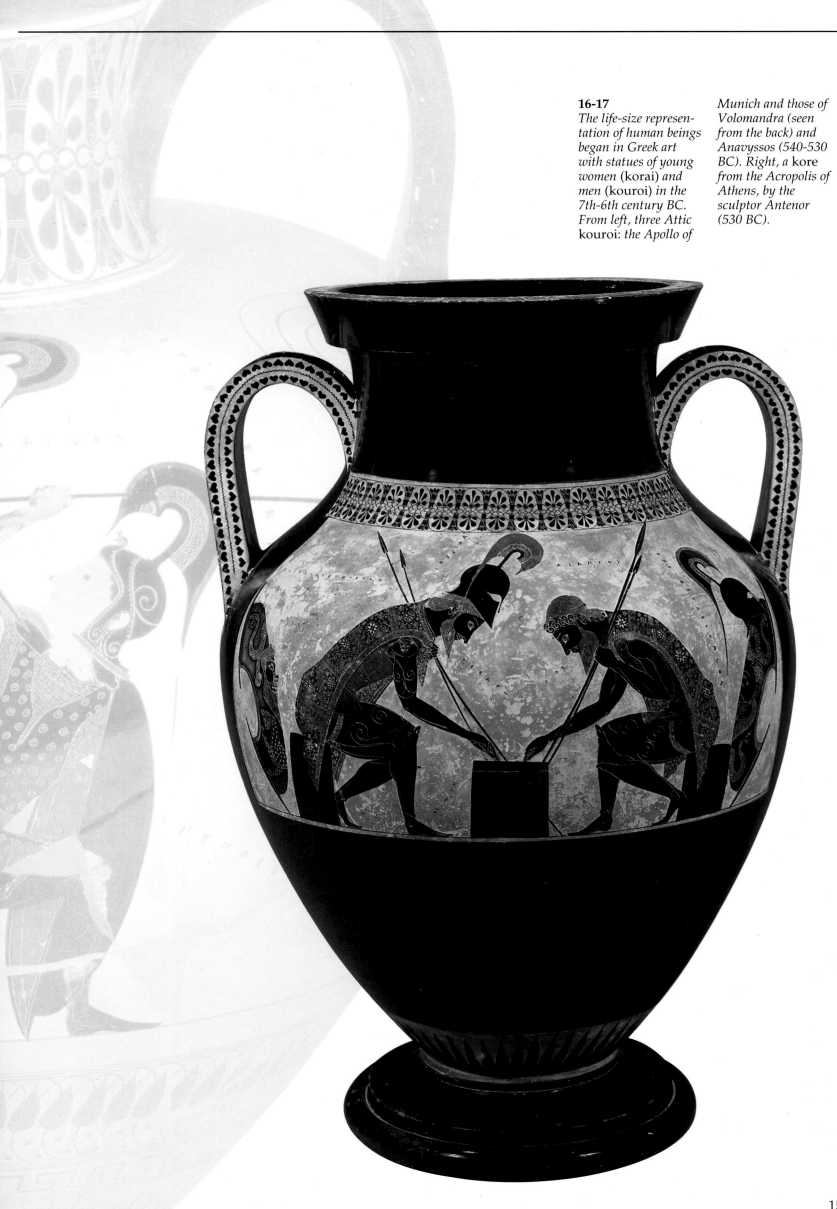

The life-size represen-
tation of human beings
began in Greek art
with statues of young
women (korai) and
men (kouroi) in the
7th-6th century BC.
From left, three Attic
kouroi: the Apollo of
Munich and those of
Volomandra (seen
from the back) and
Anavyssos (540-530
BC). Right, a kore
from the Acropolis of
Athens, by the
sculptor Antenor
(530 BC).

GREEK HISTORY FROM MINOS TO AUGUSTUS

18-19 *A scene of the late Archaic Ionic frieze (525 BC) of the Siphnian Treasury in Delphi shows a dramatic phase of the battle between the gods and the giants (the gigantomachia). Even at this early date, great skill is used in portraying dynamism and depth of space.*

GREECE BEFORE THE GREEKS:
PREHISTORY

20 *In this painted Neolithic kourotrophos (3500-3000 BC), from Sesklo, a woman nurses an infant. Scholars tend to recognize in her the primitive Mother Goddess, perhaps the most direct and persistent cultural reflection of Neolithic societies structured around matriarchy.*

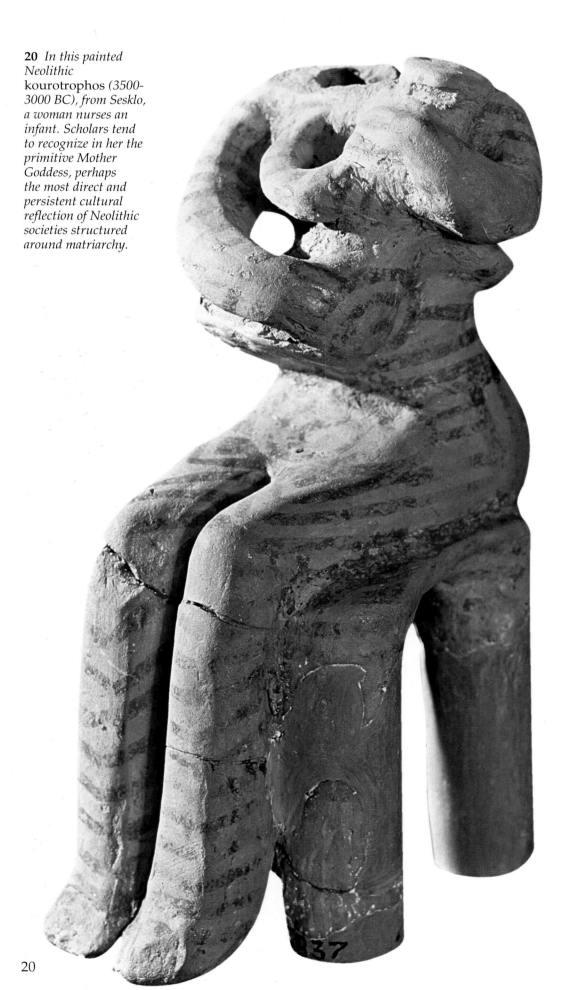

The earliest evidence of human habitation in Greece dates to the Upper Paleolithic period (45,000-13,000 BC), typified by finds in Epirus, Thessaly, and Argolis. The objects unearthed closely resemble discoveries elsewhere in the Balkans and in the Danubian region, where various cultures of the Upper Paleolithic appear to have been scattered. The focal importance of the Greek peninsula, even before its inhabitants can be called Greeks, becomes apparent around 6800 BC: the exceptional cultural development of the first agricultural communities in Crete, the Cyclades, the Peloponnese, and Thessaly indicate that it was from here—Europe's "gateway to the Orient"—that Neolithic civilization spread to the entire continent.

The first sea voyages across the Mediterranean—for the most part passing over the blue waters of the Aegean from one of its countless islands to another—were made by traders carrying surplus food from early human settlements. These same routes were traveled by traders carrying flint, to be chipped into tools, and obsidian, a black volcanic glass from the island of Melos. These items were gifts exchanged by notables of distant villages, indicating that diplomatic relations had already gained a footing.

In the middle and late Neolithic periods the largest villages had already attained amazing levels of civilization. As early as the fifth millennium BC, Sesklo and Dhimini, in Thessaly, were surrounded by defensive walls. Soon metals came into use, and the dissemination of metallurgy—by a process still not entirely reconstructed—got under way. As early as 4500 BC, metal artifacts had already made their appearance in the proto-urban community of Sesklo, with its flourishing farming and pastoral economy. Since metals were primordial source of wealth and progress, continuous conflicts arose over access to and control over sites where these precious raw materials could be found.

THE SECOND MILLENNIUM BC: PEOPLES OF THE AEGEAN, CRETANS, MYCENAEANS

A Andros   E Syros   I Siphnos
B Tinos   F Serifos J Milos
C Mykonos G Paros   K Thira
D Delos   H Naxos

21 left *This tiny Cycladic head from Antiparos, resembling Modigliani's works, reveals the delicacy of execution of Aegean artists in the second half of the third millennium BC.*

21 top right *The typical violin-shaped marble statvele is a synthesis of the human figure, as attested by this example from Paros, dating from the most ancient stage of Aegean art (ca. 3000-2500 BC).*

The Cycladic islands lie in the heart of the Aegean Sea, like a bridge across the water between Greece and Asia Minor. Their geographical position made these islands one of the preeminent areas of early civilization in the ancient Mediterranean basin. Between the end of the third and early second millennia BC, the urban societies to the east increasingly demanded valuable raw materials that were available in the Cyclades. Obsidian in Melos, marble in Paros, Tinos, and Syros, and copper in Siphnos attracted merchants from Egypt and the Near East who, in exchange, provided local communities with foodstuffs to make up for the archipelago's insufficient agricultural production.

The most flourishing period in the Cyclades, both in the south (especially Milos and Thira) and in the north (Tinos, Paros, Naxos, Syros, the "minor Cyclades" like Keros and Despotiko, Amorgos, Siphnos, Kythnos, and Kea), appears to have been between 2200 and 1700 BC. Thereafter the islands gradually became assimilated within the orbit of Crete and its maritime dominance. But in the golden age of Cycladic civilization, trade covered the whole Aegean Sea and extended throughout the eastern Mediterranean. Important settlements developed, and their inhabitants enjoyed great prosperity, as is evident from the varied objects found in their burial chambers.

21 bottom right *This female figure from Syros, with an indication of sexual characteristics, belongs to the mature stage of Aegean art (2200-2000 BC).*

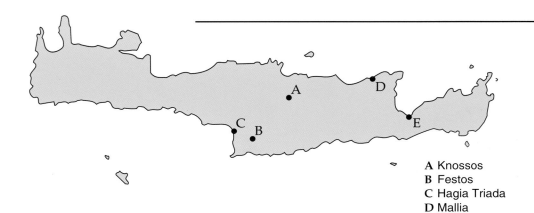

A Knossos
B Festos
C Hagia Triada
D Mallia
E Gournia

the absence of defensive walls suggests that the inhabitants feared no one—comprised hundreds of rooms grouped around a central court. In these complex architectural structures, symbols of the authority that rested at the apex of the social pyramid were mixed with the brightly colored frescoes that embellished the rooms and corridors.

Trade thrived, assuring steady inflows of foodstuffs. Exquisitely crafted objects were made by the most skillful potters, woodworkers, goldsmiths, and metalworkers, who were gathered together in the workshops of the palaces. Writing—in a script that has still not been deciphered, now known as Linear A—may well have served mainly for state accounting procedures. Its use, for whatever purpose, is testimony to the complex organization of Cretan civilization and the amazing efficiency of its palace-settlements.

Around 1700 BC the palaces were destroyed. The cause of their

22 top *The fresco of the Parisienne of Knossos (17th century BC) exemplifies aspects of feminine charm and custom in Crete.*

22 bottom
This rhyton, *or drinking vessel, comes from Zakros. Made of serpentine, it displays the Cretan rulers' symbols of power.*

As Cycladic civilization was at its peak, toward the end of the third millennium BC, Crete—the largest Aegean island—initiated its own amazing history. Great palaces that encompassed entire settlements, known as palace-settlements, were built at Knossos and Festos around 1900 BC. These imposing royal residences, about two centuries later, witnessed the definitive rise to power of the *minos*. Not unlike the pharaohs of Egypt, this ruler was endowed with both political and religious powers. (From the name comes the term *Minoan,* which is used as an alternative to *Cretan.*) Most

important, every *minos* helped transform the Cretan way of life from an agricultural and pastoral economy to a full-fledged thalassocracy, or supreme maritime power.

The military, territorial, and entrepreneurial supremacy of the Cretans over the Aegean eventually allowed them to control trade with Egypt and with the kingdoms of the Near East. Other Aegean peoples were increasingly influenced by Cretan civilization, which developed in ever more grandiose ways.

The monumental palace-settlements—

urban setting of the palace-settlement and to its surrounding landscape. Visual and scenic elements were clearly given priority over functional aspects, such as the road's destination (a temple or rural settlement).

The influence of Minoan culture in the southern Cyclades was especially strong in Thera, modern Santorini. Here at the Akrotiri site, archaeologists brought to light spectacular remains of a splendid town with buildings up to four stories high. Their ornately frescoed rooms are only one sign of the riches and prosperity wiped out forever by a tremendous disaster. Around the year 1450 BC the volcano from which the island had originated many thousands of years before erupted, turning Thera into history's first Pompeii, burying the settlement under fifty feet of ash. Fortunately the inhabitants had time to escape from the island—no bodies have been found in the areas excavated.

23 top This mysterious goddess, ruling the forces of nature, may be associated with magic (the snakes) and fertility (the large bare bosom). As the "Mistress of the Snakes," she is a cultural antecedent of the Greek Potnia theron. *She is preserved in this statuette in faience from Knossos (17th century BC).*

destruction is uncertain (a disastrous earthquake, perhaps). However, they were rapidly rebuilt, even larger than before. The so-called Period of the Later Palaces (1700-1450 BC) saw the construction of palaces in Knossos, Festos, Zakros, Mallia, and Tilyssos.

The earlier palaces had been agglomerations of living quarters and spaces used for administration, economic production, and commerce. They contained vast apartments, throne rooms, religious areas, artisans' workshops, and storerooms. The later palaces were flanked by large squares that were themselves overlooked by rows of steps, normally taken to be open-air theaters, where collective rites were celebrated or ceremonies performed.

This same later period saw the construction of country residences. A fine example is the splendid villa near Festos and the present-day village of Hagia Triada.

Paved roads also date to this period, like the splendid Royal Road in Knossos. The architects who built the Royal Road paid special attention to the

23 bottom This beautiful rhyton, made of steatite and shaped like a bull's head, is a masterpiece of Cretan sculpture. The golden horns, the jasper mucosa, the rock crystal eyes, and the mother-of-pearl profile show that great care was taken in creating this ritual vase. It may have been used to hold the liquid poured in a sacred libation—perhaps bull's blood.

24 left *Minoan painting was the first in ancient art to express a true naturalism, moving away from the stereotyped tendency of ancient Egyptian art. The smooth lines, rich and bright range of colors, and sense of nature are evident in this fragment of a fresco from the second palace settlement of Knossos. Its multicolored garden is populated by birds (partridges and a hoopoe), like similar figures of the Hellenistic and Roman age.*

24 right *Luxury arts attained a high level in Crete. An impressive number of jewels and other objects were produced by skilled craftsmen, whose workshops were located inside the vast palaces. This rhyton from the neopalatial period was carved from a single piece of rock crystal and completed with a fine added handle.*

According to archaeologists, this catastrophe triggered the decline of Cretan civilization: the entire southern Aegean was affected by a series of earthquakes and great waves; ash rained down on the Earth and darkened the skies; and climatic changes ensued. A debilitated Crete was left to face the expansionist ambitions of the Mycenaeans on the Peloponnese. In the Minoan religion, a powerful goddess of fertility occupied an important place. She was associated with the bull—the animal that symbolized Crete and its rulers—and the youth of the island performed initiation rites in her honor. These rites consisted mainly of a kind of bloodless bullfight in which boys with almost acrobatic skill leaped to avoid the charges and swerves of the enraged bull.

The artistic creations of the Cretans express the imagination and originality of an essentially peace-loving people. Although they were hard-working and highly productive, they appreciated life's pleasures rather than made displays of power or glorify weapons. Plentiful evidence of the their love of luxury and finery is found in the beautiful apparel worn by the figures painted on the walls of the palace-settlements and by the exquisite creations of Cretan metal-workers, goldsmiths, woodworkers, and sculptors, which send visitors to the archaeological museum in Herakleion into raptures. It is also seen in the presence of facilities otherwise uncommon among the populations of antiquity, such as bathrooms fitted out with private pools, toilets, and deluxe accessories.

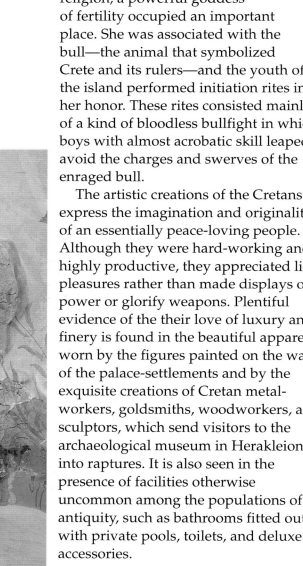

25 *The Cretans'
crucial relationship
with the sea comes
out in countless works
of art, especially in
frescoes like this
splendid and vividly
naturalistic one from
the 16th century BC.
It was found in a
house in Akrotiri, on
the island of Thera,
which was destroyed
by the eruption of its
volcano. The elegant
silhouette of a young
fisherman was caught
by the artist's eye
while he was carrying
the fruits of an
abundant haul. He is
rendered in such
detail as to identify
the fish—big
mackerels or perhaps
small tunas.*

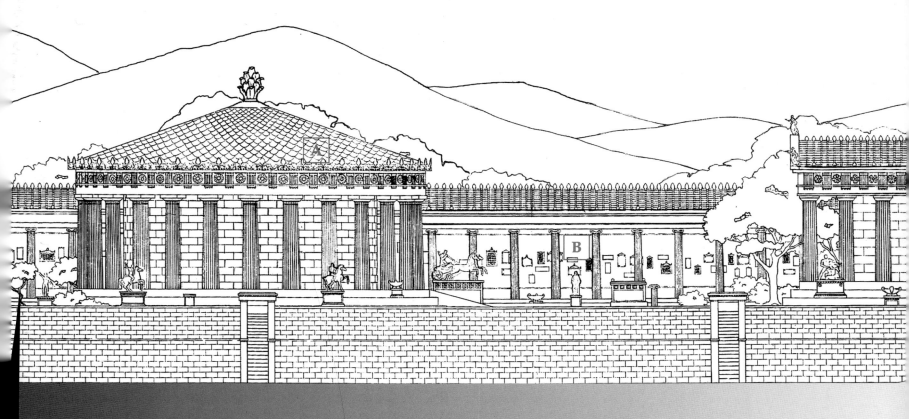

THE SANCTUARY
OF EPIDAURUS

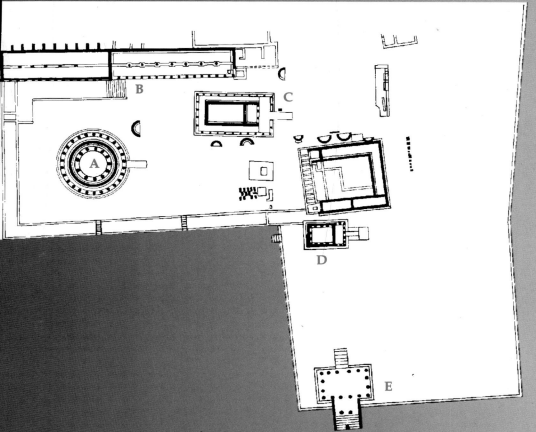

A Tholos
B Incubation Stoa
C Temple of Asclepius
D Temple of Artemis
E Propylaea

Epidaurus, a seaport on the eastern coast of Argolis, was the site of a famous sanctuary dedicated to Asclepius, the Greek god of medicine and healing. The lovely picture on pages 29–30 conveys how the splendid sanctuary—one of the best known in ancient Greece—must once have looked. At left is the elegant round Tholos; behind it is a portico used for incubation rituals. Moving right, we see the temple of Asclepius, then the temple of Artemis, which is partly hidden from view by the stately north propylaea (foreground).

The lost beauty of the Tholos is evoked in a short passage by Pausanias: near the temple of Asclepius "stands a circular building in white marble called Tholos, worth visiting: inside is a painting by Pausias depicting Eros, who has put down his bow and arrows and holds a lyre instead. There is also a painting of Inebriation, drinking from a crystal goblet: in this painting, also by Pausias, you can see the crystal cup and, through the glass, the face of a woman."

GREECE THROUGH THE AGES

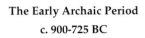

Prehistory	Protohistory	The Helladic Dark Ages	The Early Archaic Period	The Middle Archaic Period
c. 45,000-2800 BC	c. 2800-1220 BC	c. 1220-900	c. 900-725 BC	725-610 BC

Prehistory
c. 45,000-2800 BC

Evidence exists of sporadic human presence in the region (nomads, hunters, fruit gatherers; cultural affinities with the Balkans) in the Upper Paleolithic and Mesolithic periods.
C. 7000 BC: Europe's first groups of farmers/herders appear in Macedonia, Thessaly, the Peloponnese, the Cyclades, and Crete, probablly in migrations from the East. A thriving trade network is established, with land and sea routes extending across the continent (especially for obsidian, amber, salt).
6000-4000 BC: large settlements develop, several (Sesklo, Dhimini) with a proto-urban structure and fortifications.
C. 4500 BC: manufactures in native copper make their appearance; widespread use of the metal contributes to agricultural development and population growth, with more organized social structures.

Upper Paleolithic and Mesolithic periods
(c. 45,000-6800 BC)

Neolithic period and earliest use of copper
(c. 6800-3500 BC)

Copper age
(c. 3500-2800 BC)

Protohistory
c. 2800-1220 BC

With the Bronze age (early, middle and late Helladic) come the first waves of Indo-European migration. Cultural affinities emerge between mainland Greece, the Aegean islands, and the Anatolian seaboard. The Cyclades become a flourishing center of trade, hand-in-hand with the rise of a powerful elite. In c. 1900 BC the first Western state model is developed in Crete. Palace-settlements, built as residences for the *minos,* become centers of political power and economic production. After the destruction and reconstruction (1700 BC) of the palace-settlements, Minoans enjoy maritime supremacy over the Aegean. The disaster of Thera (1450 BC) prepared the way for the conquest of Crete by the Achaeans, who, by 1700 BC, had invaded much of Greece.
The splendid Mycenaean culture, with its vast fortified palace-settlements, dominates the Aegean region. In the 14th and 13th centuries BC, trade-oriented expansionism results in precolonial trading posts in the western Mediterranean, while the Trojan War establishes Achaean control over the Dardanelles.

The golden age of Cycladic culture; development of Minoan culture
(c. 2800-2000 BC)

First Minoan palace-settlements
(c. 1900-1700 BC)

Destruction and reconstruction of Minoan palace-settlements; Achaean invasion of Greece; the golden age of Mycenaean culture
(c. 1700-1450 BC)

Collapse of Minoan culture
(c. 1450 BC)

Hegemony of Mycenaean traders in the Mediterranean
(c. 1450-1250 BC)

Trojan War
(c. 1250-1220 BC)

The Helladic Dark Ages
c. 1220-900

The Sea Peoples bring devastation to the Aegean and eastern Mediterranean, and trade comes to a halt. At the same time another Indo-European race, the Dorians, invade Greece from the Balkans, triggering the demise of the Mycenaean political and socioeconomic structures in the 12th century BC. The long period known as the Helladic Dark Ages, is characterized by the breakdown of settled conditions, with extensive depopulation, economic crisis, and absence of urban settlements. Dorians, Ionians, and Aeolians determine the development of Greek dialects after over a century of migrations. With the aid of weapons or wealth, aristocracies based on families or clans emerge: they adopt the "heroic" funeral practice of cremation. Use of iron starts to spread. In the 10th century BC a general economic recovery leads to the foundation of new urban settlements, trade activities, and colonial expansion along the coasts of Asia Minor.

Raids of the Sea Peoples
(c. 1220-1180 BC)

Indo-European invasions and the end of Mycenaean culture
(1220-1120 BC)

Foundation of the first urban centers and early developments of the colonizing movement
(1100-900 BC)

The Early Archaic Period
c. 900-725 BC

Demographic and economic growth slowly strengthens the newly established cities, or poleis: Athens, Argos, Thebes, Sparta, Corinth, Chalcis, Eretria, Miletus, Smyrna, Phocaea, and others burst onto the Mediterranean trade scene and set about founding colonies and trading posts in both east and west, competing peacefully with the Phoenicians and Etruscans. Constitutional structures take root, with aristocracies firmly in control. Monarchies are abolished in favor of oligarchies (with Sparta's supervised dyarchy the sole exception). Script, adapted from the Phoenician alphabet, provides the means to preserve the poems of Homer—the *Iliad* and the *Odyssey*—for posterity. Production of fine pottery and metal artifacts and exports of oil and wine make Athens, Corinth, Argos, and the Euboean cities prominent.

First Olympic games
(776 BC)

Foundation of the first western colony, at Pithekoussai
(c. 770 BC)

First constitutions in Athens and Sparta
(c. 754-753 BC)

First Messenian war
(743-724 BC)

Colonies founded in southern Italy
(740-708 BC)

The Middle Archaic Period
725-610 BC

Trade between Egypt, the East, the Greek poleis (particularly Corinth), and their colonies thrives, and competition continues with the Phoenicians and Etruscans (who control important metal ore sites in the West). As a result Greece experiences notable economic growth. Cultural output also escalates in literature, philosophy, and art. Artists and craftsmen are much influenced by eastern wares, imported in great quantities to satisfy the taste for luxury of the dominating aristocracies. In Corinth, Argos, and Sicyon social tension between the nobles and the ordinary people brings tyrants to power. The religious and political importance of the Panhellenic sanctuaries of Delphi and Olympia is strengthened.

Further colonies founded in southern Italy
(688-648 BC)

Second Messenian war
(684-668 BC)

Tyranny at Corinth under the Cypselids
(657-583 BC)

Tyranny at Argos under Pheidon
(650-630 BC)

Foundation of Cyrene
(631 BC)

Law code introduced by Draco in Athens
(624-620 BC)

Archaic Period 0-510 BC	The Persian Wars 510-449 BC	The Classical Age 449-338 BC	Macedonian Rule 338-323 BC	The Hellenistic Period 323-146 BC

...a is extending its ...over the entire ...se (Argos alone ...ts autonomy), ...nomic conflicts ...e oligarchies and ...tive classes, who ...a greater say in ...ead to attempted ...he kind instituted ...Athens. The failure ...iatives results in an ...umber of tyrannies ...veep away the ...g aristocracies in ...Athens, Megara, ...axos, and Miletus. ...stablished colonies ...more and more ...s, found colonies of ...wn, and fight for ...egemony. Athens ...he leading economic ...er the tyranny of the ...ratids, who are ...ly banished. In the ...h century BC the ...extend their Eastern ...d threaten the poleis of Ionia.

Cleisthenes establishes a democracy in Athens. The Persian king Darius I threatens the poleis of Ionia, which react by revolting. Miletus and the other colonies fall and are harshly punished. In 490 BC the first Persian war ends, with the victory of the Athenian commander Miltiades at Marathon. The second war (480 BC) is declared by Xerxes I; after several victories and the sack of Athens, the Persians are defeated in the naval battle of Salamis. With Ionian support, the wars continue under the leadership of Athens, which founds the Delian League. The Western Greeks defeat the Carthagians and Etruscans. Under Themistocles and Cimon, Athens begins a period of military and economic imperialism, in a state of permanent conflict with the other poleis. Callias signs the peace treaty with Persia (449 BC).

Under Pericles Athens reaches the apex of economic success and cultural and artistic splendor. Its expansionist foreign policy triggers revolts throughout the Hellenic world. Rivalry with Sparta, Corinth, Thebes, and Syracuse leads to the thirty-year Peloponnesian War. Athens eventually capitulates and spends the last decade of the 5th century BC under short-lived oligarchic governments. The new century opens with the restoration of democracy in Athens; Spartan attacks on Persia; Carthaginian expansionism in Sicily; and other wars. Sparta dominates the Greek scene for several decades before being deprived of its hegemony by Athens and Thebes, the emerging power. In 356 BC Philip II of Macedonia begins his systematic conquest of Greece, completed in 338 BC at Chaeronea. With the Corinthian League, peace is imposed on the Greek states under the aegis of Macedonia.

Macedonian hegemony over the Greek poleis takes the form of an alliance that survives the assassination of Philip II. His heir, Alexander III—called "the Great" on account of his amazing conquests—takes up the plan to invade the Persian Empire, involving all the Greeks in the liberation of cities dominated by Persian satraps. His expeditions become a triumphant march of conquest across the Persian empire. Alexander reaches the banks of the Indus and present-day Afghanistan, establishing cities that bear his name. He founds the first universal empire in history, promoting the cultural Hellenization of the countries conquered. His death in Babylonia, at only 33 years of age, triggers fierce struggles among contending successors.

The imperial regent Antipater suppresses a revolt by the Greeks, but for forty years Alexander's Macedonian generals struggle to gain the upper hand. Eventually they divide the great empire into Hellenized kingdoms, starting long dynasties. Powerful states come into being, their political, economic, and cultural activities centered on splendid capitals. The Greek poleis found leagues, such as the Aetolian League, which routs the invading Celts in 280 BC and the Achaean League, which puts an end to Sparta's independence. But the hegemony over all Greece of the Antigonid dynasty remains intact. Likewise, the Seleucids in Asia Minor, Syria, and Mesopotamia; the Ptolemies in Egypt; and the Attalids in Pergamum continue to reign until the 2nd and 1st centuries BC, when Rome completes its conquest of them.

...e of Solon in Athens
...594-591 BC)

...phases of tyranny
...isistratus in Athens
...561-527 BC)

...t the sanctuary of
...pollo at Delphi
(548 BC)

...ates tyrant of Samos
(546-522 BC)

...sian conquest of
Near East
(559-513 BC)

...ion of the Pisistratids
...from Athens
(514-510 BC)

Democratic constitution in Athens
(508-507 BC)

Ionian revolt against the Persians
(499-494 BC)

First Persian war
(490 BC)

Second Persian war;
Battle of Himera between Greeks and Carthaginians
(480 BC)

Second Ionian revolt against the Persians
(479 BC)

Delian-Attic League
(478 BC)

Naval battle of Cumae between Greeks and Etruscans
(474 BC)

Third Messenian war;
wars of Athens against Aegina and Corinth
(464-455 BC)

Peace treaty between Greeks and Persians
(449 BC)

Hegemony of Pericles in Athens
(449-429 BC)

Peloponnesian War
(431-404 BC)

Oligarchic revolution in Athens
(411 BC)

Wars between the Greeks and Carthaginians in Sicily
(409-392 BC)

Surrender of Athens and fall of the Thirty Tyrants;
restoration of democracy
(403 BC)

Hegemony of Sparta
(404-379 BC)

Hegemony of Thebes
(379-362 BC)

Philip II of Macedonia overlord of Greece
(356-338 BC)

Corinthian League between Greeks and Macedonians
(338 BC)

Assassination of Philip II at Aegae
(336 BC)

Reign of Alexander III, the Great
(336-323 BC)

Alexander conquers the Persian empire
(334-329 BC)

Alexander's campaigns in India and Bactria
(328-327 BC)

Alexander dies in Babylonia
(323 BC)

Greek revolt against Macedonia
(323-322 BC)

Division of the empire and foundation of the Hellenistic kingdoms
(322-281 BC)

Absolute Macedonian monarchy over Greece
(276-239 BC)

Foundation of the Hellenistic kingdom of Pergamum
(240 BC)

"Democratic" revolution in Sparta; end of Spartan independence
(227-222 BC)

Rome frees the Greeks from Macedonian dominion
(200-196 BC)

Rome defeats Macedonia and divides it into four republics
(171-168 BC)

Rome makes Macedonia and Greece provinces;
siege and destruction of Corinth
(147-146 BC)

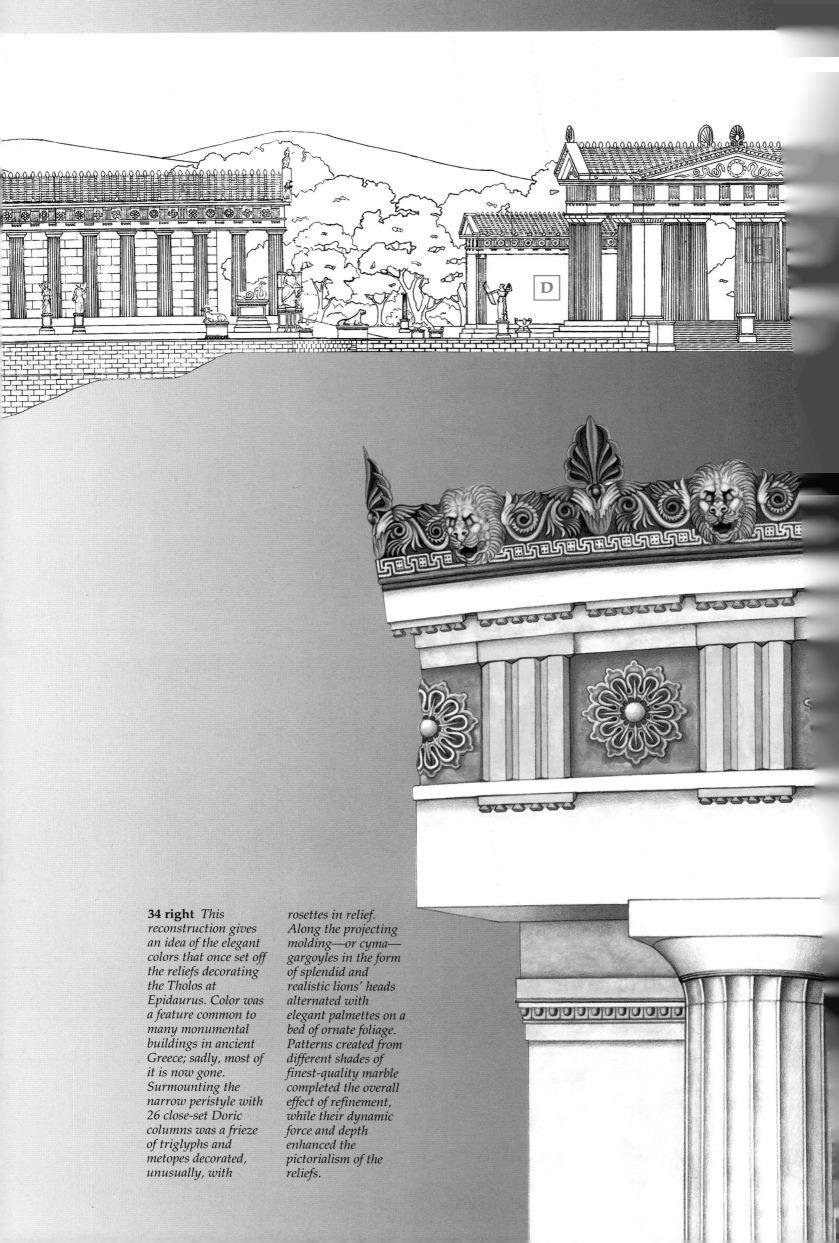

34 right *This reconstruction gives an idea of the elegant colors that once set off the reliefs decorating the Tholos at Epidaurus. Color was a feature common to many monumental buildings in ancient Greece; sadly, most of it is now gone. Surmounting the narrow peristyle with 26 close-set Doric columns was a frieze of triglyphs and metopes decorated, unusually, with rosettes in relief. Along the projecting molding—or cyma— gargoyles in the form of splendid and realistic lions' heads alternated with elegant palmettes on a bed of ornate foliage. Patterns created from different shades of finest-quality marble completed the overall effect of refinement, while their dynamic force and depth enhanced the pictorialism of the reliefs.*

A Mycenae
B Nauplia
C Tiryns
D Vapheio
E Pylos

During the same period when civilization was blossoming and flourishing, between 2000 and 16[mainland Greece and the Pelopo[were invaded and permanently occupied by an Indo-European pe called Achaeans, whom the Hittit called *Ahiyawa.*

The groups who had previously inhabited these regions appear to I been totally and forcefully absorbe these warrior-herdsmen searching fresh pastures for their herds. They settled in Thessaly, Boeotia, Attica, Argolis, and Messenia and rapidly abandoned their seminomadic lifes as they made their way down throu the Balkans. Their new home, proje naturally toward the Mediterranear had exceptional resources in terms cultivable land and animal life, whi they put to good use.

It was not long before the princes Iolcus, Argos, Mycenae, Tiryns, and Pylos—men at the very top of the Achaeans' rigid social pyramid—too advantage of the trade routes of the region. Not only did large quantities foodstuffs change hands, but preciou artifacts made of gold, silver, and bronze, fabrics, and fine pottery reac the enterprising merchants who trad throughout the Aegean and eastern Mediterranean. Since the late 19th century, when the importance of Mycenae was established by the excavations of Heinrich Schliemann (approach may now be considered amateurish, but his work was undeniably fruitful), the peoples who occupied this whole region have been generally known as the Mycenaeans.

36 top *The Nestor's Goblet was found by Schliemann in the rich Tomb IV of Funerary Circle A at Mycenae (16th century BC). It is a* kantharos *of gold leaf, embossed, engraved, and fretworked, weighing nearly 300 grams. It bears marks of inaccurate technical and artistic workmanship.*

36 bottom *These tablets of raw clay were burned in a fire that destroyed the Mycenaean palace of Pylos, in Messenia, in the 12th century BC. It is engraved with syllable signs of Linear B, the Mycenaean script.*

37 *An excellent example of Mycenaean metal-work, this beautiful lion's-head-shaped* rhyton, *also discovered in Tomb IV, dates back to the 16th century BC. Its form is derived from Cretan models, but the result is less naturalistic and shows the characteristic simplification and geometrization of Mycenaean art. Both in Crete and in the Achaean world the* rhyta *were vases intended for ritual ceremonies. They are provided with a inlet and outlet holes, suggesting that they were used in religious and funeral libations.*

Achaean society was centralized in its power structure but had a dual economic structure, with huge landed estates and at the same time entrepreneurial activities that relied on the work of skilled craftsmen and a network of experienced mariners and traders. The distinguishing feature of each Mycenaean city-state was a fortified palace and "town" surrounded by massive defense walls. At the top of its social pyramid was the *wanax*, a supreme ruler who represented the warrior and landowning aristocracies—*lawos* and *damos*—who, thanks to their huge estates, were enormously wealthy. At the right hand of the *wanax* was a military commander called the *lawaghetas*. A series of consultants and officials assisted with the political and administrative functions.

The village authorities, the *basilewes*, controlled the collective ownership of farmland that was not directly owned or used by the *wanax*. Little is known about the structure of the lower classes, seemingly comprising artisans and agricultural workers. There was certainly a caste formed of slaves.

Extensive information about Mycenaean civilization has been obtained from precious clay tablets unearthed during excavation of the destroyed palace of Pylos in Messenia; in the palace of Knossos, controlled by the Mycenaeans after the 15th century BC; and to a lesser degree in Mycenae, Tiryns, and Thebes. The tablets are written in a language of Indo-European origin that uses a syllabic alphabet derived from ideograms. This script—deciphered and interpreted by Michael Ventris and John Chadwick— is known as Linear B. As well as indicating the number and functions of personnel living in the palace, the tablets contain inventories, lists of tributes, administrative procedures, and property ownership records.

The Mycenaean economy was based on agriculture and livestock breeding. The production of oil, flax and wool furthered the development of manufacturing of cosmetics (ointments) and textiles. Overseas commerce continued to expand: the palace of Knossos alone exported no fewer than 30 tons of wool a year!

Since the 16th century BC, Mycenaean craftsmen excelled at creations in gold and bronze. Their activity was controlled

38 top *This signet-ring of gold, from Mycenae, shows a crowded scene at a religious rite, derived from a Minoan model.*

directly by the palace, which supplied their workshops with copper imported from mines in Cyprus and tin from central and western Europe. Precious metals, amber, and glasslike materials were used in abundance, testifying to wide-ranging Mycenaean trade routes that, until the 13th century BC, extended from Egypt to Syria, from Rhodes to Cyprus, and from Cilicea to Ionia. When the Mycenaean empire was at its highest point (14-13th centuries BC), its traders pushed farther and farther afield throughout the Mediterranean basin, especially in the western Mediterranean.

Some scholars have suggested there was Mycenaean precolonization along the very same routes later taken by the Greeks in the 8th to 6th centuries BC. Settlements sprang up along the coasts of Italy and southern Spain, for example at Vivara on the Gulf of Naples, in the southern part of Apulia; on the eastern

side of Sicily, and in the Lipari islands. But their merchandise traveled as far as the mid-Tyrrhenian basin and its hinterland, and it even reached the upper Adriatic to the Po delta (as proven by finds unearthed near Rovigo, in northeastern Italy). The level of prosperity and power attained during this period is attested by the enlargement and consolidation of the walls of centers like Mycenae and Tiryns. But the most significant sign of the Mycenaeans' power was their decision to resort to war in order to destroy competitive states and gain control of strategic points of the Mediterranean. The event that came to symbolize this whole policy was a war fought by Achaeans from all over Greece against the Phrygians of Troy, who had established a powerful kingdom. In particular, they controlled the Dardanelles, a vital strait between the Aegean and the Black Sea that was fringed by areas rich in ore deposits and

38-39 *Created by a Cretan artist but discovered in Tomb IV of Funerary Circle A of Mycenae, this outstanding dagger of inlaid bronze and niello in gold and silver, decorated on both sides, features the aristocratic and "heroic" theme of lion hunting.*

39 top left *This signet ring from one of the most ancient royal tombs of Mycenae (16th century BC) vividly illustrates a deer-hunting scene.*

39 top right *The subject of the war appears on this third ring, quite similar to the previous one. Strangely, it comes from a woman's tomb.*

by vast fertile plains. And into the Black Sea flowed a river of enormous importance, the Danube.

The Trojan War broke out around 1250 BC and was fought by an exceptional coalition of the most powerful Achaean cities, from the regions of Thessaly, Boeotia, Argolis, Messenia, and Laconia. As related by Homer in his celebrated epic, the *Iliad*, the enemy was defeated. But the war was also a last moment of glory for a civilization that would collapse and then disappear within only decades. After the lands of the Mediterranean basin were invaded by the so-called Sea Peoples, trade—the mainstay of the Mycenaean economy—came to a halt. All the major centers were attacked and destroyed. The outcome of these invasions was extensive depopulation, depression of cultural and material standards, and abandonment of settlements—events that marked the beginning of the period now known as the Helladic Dark Ages.

39 bottom *Mycenaean goldsmiths' art sometimes showed a clear Minoan influence, while other products were more oriented to the schematic naturalism typical of Achaean art. At other times it preferred the simple and elegant shapes of drinking vases, renouncing all decoration, as is the case of this* kantharos.

THE HELLADIC DARK AGES

The origin of the Sea Peoples, whose raids brought destruction and chaos to the Aegean and eastern Mediterranean, has not been clearly identified, although certainly prominent amongst them, in the 12th and 11th centuries BC, were Phoenicians and Philistines. But they were not the only cause of the upheaval. A further series of invasions were made by Indo-European peoples, the real founders of Greek civilization. Most prominent among them were the Dorians, who had descended from the impervious valleys of the Balkans and settled mainly in Epirus, Acarnania-Aetolia, the Peloponnese, and the southern Aegean islands, even reaching the southwestern coasts of Asia Minor.

Along with the Ionians and Aeolians, they contributed to the division of the region into cultural areas, identifiable by their use of three different dialects of a single language: Greek. The disappearance of urban centers and the absence of a state encouraged the development of a social model based on the *genos,* a kind of aristocratic family clan that gained power through bravery, the forceful appropriation of lands and riches, and the possession of material goods and weapons. In funeral rites, burial was replaced by cremation, which had "heroic" attributes.

On a political level the Mycenaean *wanax* was replaced by the *basileus,* the leader of a community and a member of its aristocratic elite, supported by other heads of households. The first embryonic city-state—the *polis*—developed as early as the 11 or 10th century BC among Ionian and Aeolian emigrants who had settled on the coast of Asia Minor. But on the Greek mainland the social and the economic dislocations had reached their severest point. In the 10th century BC signs of recovery were evident in the settlements at Karphi and Dreros, in Crete. Around the same time cities, rebuilt on the remains of ancient Mycenaean centers or clustered in areas never previously occupied, presaged the subsequent emergence of the polis: Athens, Argos, Corinth, and Sparta are prominent examples.

The epic past of the Mycenaeans became the cultural heritage of the aristocrats (regardless of whether Homer actually existed as a historic figure). Poetry transmitted orally was transformed into literature by the adaptation of the Phoenician alphabet to the dialects of Greek. The old Mycenaean settlements became cult centers that were precursors of sanctuaries—for instance, at Olympia, Delphi, Dodona, Isthmia, and Nemea.

40 left *This bronze of the 8th century BC, discovered in Crete, preserves the fascinating image of an Aedo, a bard of epic poems. A typical figure of the Achaean and Archaic Greek culture, he is symbolized by the most famous Aedo, Homer. Fashioned in the form of Geometric art, the bent profile of the ballad singer, his hands on the kithara, appears to be searching for suitable notes for the "winged words."*

40 right *The most evident signs of population increase and economic recovery of Greece in the Geometric period are the findings from burials. The prestige of the wealthier families is documented by funeral outfits of remarkable artistic value. This amphora, from the cemetery of Dipylon at Athens (c. 750-740 BC), is a fine example.*

THE ARCHAIC PERIOD

The areas in orange represent Greek territories between the 11th and 10th centuries BC.

A Greek polis (plural poleis) came into being in 1000-900 BC when a community of individuals from different socioeconomic classes decided to concentrate their activities in a place suitable for habitation, with possibilities for defense, available resources, and trade prospects. Rural settlements of the type that had prevailed in earlier periods—with economies based on self-sufficiency and with limited trade—lost their importance and very soon became subordinate to the new centers.

In the poleis artisans, merchants, and entrepreneurs grew in number and prosperity, and their wealth became a challenge to the absolute powers of the aristocrats. Cultivable land, horses, and herds diminished in importance as attention was increasingly focused on the value of goods produced, successful businesses, and services that were no longer offered to an isolated ruler but to an expanding and thriving community.

As population grew and prosperity increased, it was necessary to bring the political institutions into line with the new social structures. Members of the old aristocracy were nonetheless reluctant to share their power. Instead of surrendering the existing social order, they founded colonies in the western Mediterranean. This practice, initiated in the 8th century BC and systematized during the 7th century, reduced internal strife without giving rise to fierce and pointless wars of conquest with neighboring cities.

41 left *The famous Lady of Auxerre, the first important Greek statue, represents a goddess or maybe a worshipper in a devotional attitude. It was most probably made in Crete in the mid-7th century BC and is nearly the paradigm of Archaic Greek sculpture.*

41 right *Nothing represents the exceptional commercial escalation of Corinth between the 7th and 6th centuries BC better than a typical Corinthian vase—in this case an amphora of the 7th century BC. These products of high artistic craftsmanship spread to the whole Mediterranean area.*

Thus the Greek colonies in the western Mediterranean were mainly intended to strengthen the economic role of the old *emporia,* which they gradually replaced. The oldest of these existing trade settlements—like Pithekoussai on the island of Ischia, the very first (770 BC)—continued to operate as open ports, where merchants of varying ethnic origins gathered to trade. Many new colonies were also established for agricultural purposes. In southern Italy and Sicily, the Greek area was known as *Megale Hellas, Magna Graecia,* or "Great" Greece. An immense offshoot of Greece proper, it was intrinsically linked to the motherland by a shared culture, shared vocations, and shared needs.

In the space of mere decades after Pithekoussai, Greeks established colonies in Cumae (740 BC), Naxos (733 BC), Syracuse (732 BC), and nine other sites scattered on the shores of Sicily, Calabria, Apulia, and Lucania. By the 7th century BC, Greece had consolidated its political, economic, and cultural position in the Mediterranean region. It had secured colonies in the Levant, which was increasingly prey to the hegemony of the Assyrians, as well as in the West, competing with the expansionist goals of the Phoenicians. It also traded intensively with the eastern lands.

It was not only merchandise that traveled on routes linking far-distant cities. Culture, in the broadest meaning of the term, was also spread abroad, propagated by the dominating aristocracies, who indulged their tastes for luxury and were increasingly fascinated by the wares of civilizations to the east. By now colonies had also been established from the Bosphorus to the Black Sea, with its rich mineral resources, from the coastal regions of

43 *The victims of the wars between rival poleis and between tyrants and aristocrats were many, as testified by many sepulchral monuments, especially in Attica. This stele of Aristion, a work by Aristocles datable to c. 510 BC, shows the dead man with his own hoplite armor (cuirass, helmet, shin guards, lance). He is portrayed with the typical technical fineness of the Archaic style.*

Asia Minor to Macedonia and Thrace. These centers became outposts of both trade and ideology, offering an arena for political and scientific experimentation, fired by the ideas of philosophers, artists, scientists, and men of letters, and influenced by the cultural and material effects of trade.

Between the 8th and mid-6th centuries BC, trade and cultural exchanges between East and West escalated. There is every reason to believe that tolerance and even peaceful cooperation prevailed in relations between peoples, a supposition endorsed by the findings of archaeological research. For instance, an enormous number of amphoras—probably from the Etruscan city of Caere (modern Cerveteri)—have been found at the most ancient archaeological levels of Carthage, while vast quantities of western Phoenician products have been discovered along the colonial Greek seaboards of Italy and in the hinterland of Campania, Etruria, and Lazio. There was clearly a trade axis between Pithekoussai and the Phoenician colonies of Sardinia—probably only one segment of a vast trading network extending from the Strait of Gibraltar to the eastern Mediterranean.

We also have proof of the presence of Levantine "trade offices" in Greek urban settlements, and of a similar series of Greek trading outposts along the coast of present-day Tunisia. Evidence for a kind of "common market" is provided by a system of accounting tables that were designed for easy conversion of the units of weight and measurement used by the various peoples of these regions—all of two centuries before Pythagoras!

On the political front, conflicts within the aristocratic oligarchies brought tyrants to power. (The word *tyrannos*, of Anatolian origin, simply means "lord.") Although often of aristocratic origin, the tyrants gained control because they found favor with the new working-class members of society. The tyrants used their authority to put an end to social and political tensions. Some tyrants ruled with an iron fist, others by trying to gain popular consensus through demonstrations of "good government." These might take the form of economic incentives or public works on a grand scale, like the religious buildings erected in Samos by Polycrates (c. 540-520 BC). Corinth was the trading capital of 7th-century Greece and home of the highly popular Orientalizing pottery style, with which Athens, the Cyclades, and the Ionian islands competed in vain. Here the Cypselid tyranny overthrew the Bacchiad dynasty, assisted trade by developing the ports of Kenchreai and Lechaion, founded agricultural and trading colonies, and even built the pioneering *diolkos*, a stone causeway across the isthmus that allowed ships to be transported from the Aegean to the Gulf of Corinth and the Ionian Sea.

Elsewhere the problem of social conflict was addressed by lawmakers. In Athens, for instance, first Draco and later Solon introduced constitutional and fiscal reforms. To a large extent, however, they both met with failure, and tyranny was the eventual outcome. Sparta, founded on a constitution combining communism and nationalism based on ethnic origin and caste, was one of the few cities to remain united. During the period when the other poleis were in the throes of serious crises, it was successful in its conquest of Messenia and the rest of the Peloponnese, meeting with unsurmountable resistance in Argos alone.

The 7th and 6th centuries BC also saw the Panhellenic sanctuaries at Delphi and Olympia firmly established as religious centers, as well as venues for sporting events and literary/theatrical contests,

This little bronze statue represents a hoplite, or infantry soldier, armed from head to toe while launching an attack. It should be considered a quotation from Greece's "heroic" Achaean roots, as illustrated in Homer's epic, as well as a document of the unceasing resistance of the small Hellenic city-states to the far more powerful Persians. It symbolizes the eternal fight of the Western world against the Eastern world, of Greeks against barbarians, of good against evil. Just as the Mycenaeans defeated the Trojans, the Greeks defended their political independence against the imperialism of the Persian king of kings. The memory of the past became the propaganda of the present.

which attracted competitors from every corner of the Greek world. These sanctuaries also provided the poleis with an arena for the diplomatic resolution of tensions and conflicts.

The city-states tried to gain political influence over the aristocratic priesthood as well. They instituted ostentatious worship of the divinities and made magnificent offerings. On a practical level, they appropriated huge sums to erect splendid buildings, dedicating works of art to the gods and devoting one-tenth of war booty to their efforts, making a

lasting impact on the whole of Greece.

In 561 BC Athens got its own first taste of tyranny when control of the city was seized by Pisistratus. He promoted the growth of small landowners and small businesses, built a fleet, implemented an expansionist foreign policy—as did other tyrants—and reestablished harmony among quarreling social groups, with the sole exception of his personal enemies, the powerful house of the Alcmeonidae. The period of tyranny ended in 510 BC after a decade of fierce battles against Pisistratus' sons, Hippias and Hipparchus. In 514 BC Hipparchus was killed in a conspiracy by the nobles Harmodius and Aristogeiton; four years later Hippias chose exile. The Alcmeonidae returned in triumph, and under the leadership of Cleisthenes, Athens had its first experience of democracy.

But a new threat was looming, this one from the Ionian Sea. With the foundation of the Persian empire, first Cyrus and then Cambyses rapidly expanded its territories westward, gradually taking over all the ancient kingdoms of the Near East and gaining control—sometimes by force—of the western regions of Asia Minor. The flourishing city-states of the Ionian seaboard—Miletus, Ephesus, Phocaea, Smyrna, Samos—faced imminent conquest, primarily because certain pro-Persian tyrants had become confidants and tribute collectors for King Darius. The eventual outcome was the tragic series of Persian wars.

45 *This golden funeral mask, dated to 520 BC, comes from the rich Macedonian cemetery at Sindos, according to Thracian tradition. It is gold leaf, embossed in such a way as to suggest quite realistically the dead man's features, set in a helmet of Illyrian type.*

45

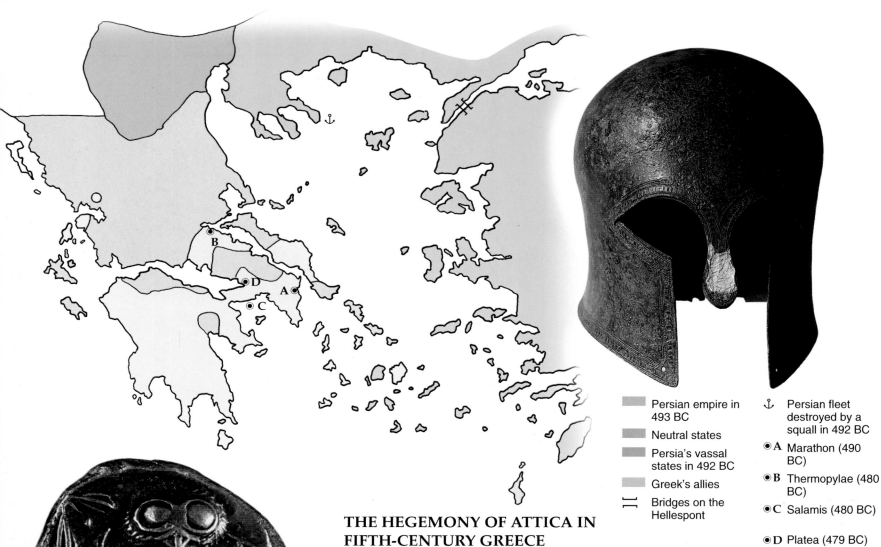

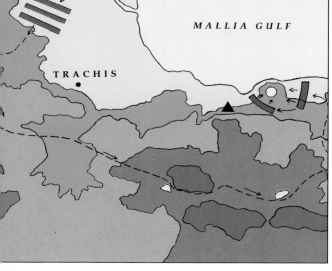

▬	Persian empire in 493 BC	⚓ Persian fleet destroyed by a squall in 492 BC
▬	Neutral states	
▬	Persia's vassal states in 492 BC	◉ **A** Marathon (490 BC)
▬	Greek's allies	◉ **B** Thermopylae (480 BC)
‖	Bridges on the Hellespont	◉ **C** Salamis (480 BC)
		◉ **D** Platea (479 BC)

THE HEGEMONY OF ATTICA IN FIFTH-CENTURY GREECE

Before the 5th century BC, a number of factors had contributed to a fragile equilibrium among the Greek city-states. One of these factors was the limited influence of Athens outside Attica, rarely threatening the hegemony of Sparta, Corinth, and Argos in the Peloponnese. In the Aegean archipelago, the prevalent political fragmentation enabled many bustling islands to focus their attention on trade. Countless inland areas, their economy still dependent on agriculture and pastoral activities, played a secondary role.

At the beginning of the 5th century BC, mainland Greece experienced a shake-up of unimagined proportions. An innovative political model was introduced that revolutionized Greek social and political life—and the history of the human race.

A democracy was established in Athens—the equation "state = citizens" materializing for the first time ever—as government of the polis was entrusted to the assembly of the *demos* ("people") and its elected representatives. With the various social and productive classes now directly involved in making political decisions, Athens and Attica soon became the leading economic, trading, and cultural center of the Mediterranean.

The new political model was exported from Piraeus, the city's busy port, along with Athenian merchandise and the products of its culture and art. The aristocratic oligarchs and the tyrants who held control elsewhere in Greece saw Athenian democracy as a very real threat. Divisions and conflicts increased, and violent struggles for

BATTLE OF THERMOPYLAE

▬	Persian forces
▬	Greek forces
↯	Great marsh
◯	Leonidas' last resistance
▲	Hot springs
▬	Mardonio's division
▬	Pausanias' division
– –	Path

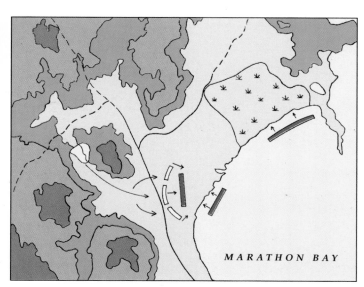

BATTLE OF MARATHON

power emerged between pro-Persian parties and "enlightened" aristocrats who had been won over—though to what degree, it is impossible to say—by the doctrines of equal rights and free trade implicit in democracy.

An immediate repercussion was the Ionians' revolt against the Persians in 499-494 BC. King Darius I crushed the revolt, and numerous prosperous poleis of Asian Ionia were overcome. Later thousands of spectators were moved by the tale of the conquest of Miletus, dramatized by the tragedian Frinicus and presented in the theater of Dionysus in Athens.

Darius next made an attack on Greece itself, its polymorphous city-states being considered too untrustworthy to be left independent. The Aegean was, after all, more important than the eastern Mediterranean as a crossroads of migration, trade, and wealth. In 490 BC his army, under the command of Artaferne and Dati, attacked Eretria and Athens. At Marathon, 10,000 men led by the Athenian strategist Miltiades routed the Persians, an extraordinary victory that brought the Persians' expansionist venture to an end.

But not for long. Ten years later, Xerxes I, son of Darius, attacked again, this time at the head of a huge army and fleet. Once again the Persians met with vigorous resistance and a forceful counterattack from Athens and its allies. Initially the allied city-states suffered huge setbacks: the Spartans under Leonidas were defeated at Thermopylae, a mountain pass linking the plains of Boeotia and Attica; the Greek fleet fought and lost at Cape Artemision; Athens itself was sacked and the sanctuary of Athena on the Acropolis defiled. Yet in a naval battle in the Strait of Salamis, the Athenians won the day. Led by Themistocles, the Greek ships even dared to chase the Persians as they fled in disarray. Throughout 479 BC Greek ships challenged Persian hegemony over Ionia, restoring independence in several cities.

During this period another rising power set its eyes on the flourishing colonies of *Magna Graecia*. From about 550 BC onward, the trading ambitions of the Carthaginians were transformed into Mediterranean imperialism. Their animosity toward Greece is attested by the de facto division of Tyrrhenian Italy between Carthage and the Etruscans.

The attempt to make Sicily a Carthaginian island nevertheless met with failure at Himera in 480 BC, at the hands of a coalition led by Gelon, tyrant of Syracuse. In 474 BC a new coalition of Western Greeks, led by Syracuse, ended Etruscan hegemony over Tyrrhenian Italy with a naval victory off Cumae, an old Chalcidian colony that subsequently became the most active trading center of the Western Greeks for over half a century.

Meanwhile, in 478 BC, the Delian League was formed, at the instigation of Athens. Its objective was to liberate more Greek cities still under Persian rule and to form a common front in the event of future aggression. Its political meeting-place and treasury were established in the sanctuary of Apollo on the island of Delos. They were moved to Athens in 454 BC.

In the second half of the 5th century BC in Athens, democracy enjoyed a unique level of popular consensus and participation. Athenian history developed along two main lines, of determining importance for Greek history as a whole. On the one hand,

47 *This beautiful Roman copy of a bust of the Athenian strategist Themistocles, the victory over the Persians at Salamis, is a wholly idealized version, created according to Greek canons.*

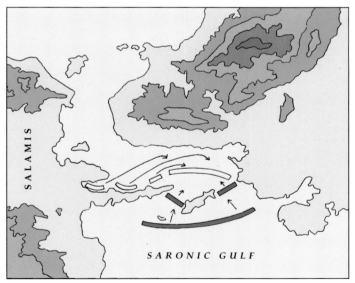

BATTLE OF SALAMIS

46 left *This silver coin of four Athenian drachms, minted at the time of the Persian wars, shows the owl sacred to Athena and the initials of the city that twice prevailed over the Persians.*

46 right *Corinthian-type helmets like this one, with typical nose and jaw guards, were used during the Persian wars. Countless examples, from the north to the south of Greece, attest to their wide diffusion.*

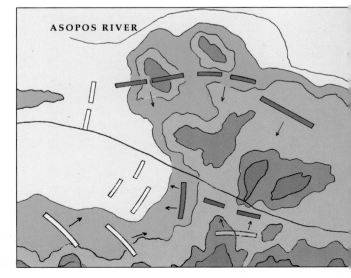

BATTLE OF PLATEA

strong figures played increasingly prominent roles in its government, while in both trade and military affairs, the city's foreign policy took on an aggressive slant that smacked of imperialism. On the other hand, Athens became the established capital of Hellenic culture, from philosophy and literature to art and science. These tendencies became particularly evident from the middle of the century, when Pericles—successor of the "conservative" Cimon—took over the reins of the democratic "party" and initiated a vast political program that eventually raised Athens to the greatest heights that the ancient world attained in terms of living standards, trade supremacy, and culture.

48 *This head of Pericles is a Roman copy of a portrait sculpted by Cresilas. A few citizens ordered a statue that could commemorate Pericles on the Acropolis after his death. (Athenian law prohibited portraits of living people as well as public tributes to politicians, even when well deserved.) This head lacks the subject's specific features, following Greek artistic tradition. Only Pericles's helmet, slightly raised on the head, lets us distinguish his "egghead," mocked by the playwrights of his time.*

49 *The Blond Ephebos, a masterpiece by an unknown Attic artist in severe style (c. 485 BC), still shows traces of the color that gilded the young man's hair. Perhaps he was an athlete or a warrior fallen in battle. The conventions of Archaic art have clearly become outdated.*

When the meeting-place and treasury of the Delian League were moved to Athens in 454 BC, the initiative, motivated by the need for greater security and by Athens's primary role in the alliance, met with a flood of protests from other members of the League. After the 449 BC, peace treaty with the Persians, the hegemony of Athens was further enhanced. Athens used its power within the League against its own traditional economic and political rivals, as in its victory over Aegina in 456 BC. But it still wanted to teach a lesson to Corinth, Megara, and above all Sparta, which wielded great power in the Peloponnese and did nothing to hide its strong anti-Athenian feelings. (They were more than matched by the Athenians' hostility toward Spartans.)

For Athens and to a lesser degree its allies, the Delian League brought many economic advantages. Its members formed a kind of "common market" and facilitated Mediterranean trade. In the space of mere decades Athens became enormously wealthy. It acquired unrivaled economic strength thanks to the discovery of silver, which was mined with slave labor, at Laurion (Sounion), and its privileged access to ore deposits in the northern Aegean. At the same time the entrepreneurial dynamism of working people working people and merchants was fostered by appropriate legislative measures. Before long the city dominated the Mediterranean scene, and its growing expansionism and aggressiveness were supported by popular consensus. Athens, in effect, had established its own "empire" in the Hellenized Mediterranean.

Initially its power was strictly economic, as demonstrated by its preeminence as an exporter of finest-quality oil and by the enormous demand for its red- and black-figured

50 *The outstanding development of philosophy in 5th-century Greece inspired art historians to name this beautiful bronze head, discovered in a shipwreck near Reggio Calabria, the Philosopher of Porticello. It is actually the most ancient example of a Greek physiognomical portrait (dated 460-440 BC). The skillful bronzesmith captured the real, specific features of a particular human face and reproduced their appearance almost photographically.*

pottery (by this time commonly found in all aristocratic and middle-class households in the ancient world), as well as other objects created by Attica's talented artists and craftsmen. The later political and military imperialism of Athens did nothing to increase its already flourishing commercial activities: on the contrary, it paved the way for a serious decline. The thirty-year Peloponnesian War shows the tragic consequences of empire-building ambitions that are based on annihilating the ideals and political identities of others, simply because they are considered weaker.

In the world of antiquity, however, imperialism was the course followed by all the most important geopolitical powers. When the territory, natural resources, and trading arena of a given state were no longer sufficient to sustain its growing population and its people's demands for prosperity—that is, when it was no longer possible to find new resources and increase production, to maintain consumption levels and extend markets—then forceful expansionism was the route inevitably chosen, regardless of political model. Wars were fought to colonize or annihilate rivals, and empires were created on the basis of political, economic, and military supremacy. Other powers that followed this course, before Athens, were Sparta (on the Peloponnese, in the 7th and 6th centuries BC) and Carthage (from 550 BC); much later—between the 3rd century BC and 2nd century A.D.—the same expansionist course was pursued by republican and imperial Rome.

In Athens, a general climate of euphoria led the majority of its approximately 40,000 citizens (women, non-Athenians living in the city, and slaves were not entitled to vote) to support Pericles' ambitious building program—his planned transformation of public architecture constructed of countless splendid monuments that eventually turned Athens into the first real "capital" of the ancient world. And yet in 431 BC this same politician involved Athens in the catastrophic Peloponnesian War, which lasted for thirty long years. Sparta and Athens first met on the battlefield in the last few decades of the 5th century BC and were at war with each other on and off throughout the 4th century.

51 This funeral stele of a rich Athenian woman, Hegeso, daughter of Proxenos, is one of the most impressive examples of a new melancholy that appeared in Greek art at the end of the 5th century BC, after the tragedy of the Peloponnesus War took much optimism and certainty away. In the quiet interior of a home, the woman, sitting on an elegant diphros, takes a necklace out of the casket offered by a handmaid. She is dressed in fabrics that reveal her still-blooming young body. The bride is preparing for her last, eternal, black wedding to the lord of the underworld, Hades.

At this point it is worth briefly considering the city that became Athens' archenemy in the Peloponnesian War: Sparta. The rivalry between Athens and Sparta is the aspect of the history of ancient Greece that many people recall most vividly. The two cities were very different in their political, social, and economic ideas and structures, not to mention their culture.

The cornerstone of the Spartan state was its celebrated constitution, traditionally attributed to the lawgiver Lycurgus (whose name, by no coincidence, means "bringer of enlightenment"). The city's institutions were certainly unique in the ancient world. Its class structure preserved its ethnic and aristocratic origins: only descendants of the founder-warriors had full citizenship status. The political structure was extremely simple—it was headed by two kings whose functions were supervised by *ephors* and who received advice from a council of elders *(gerousia)* and from a public assembly comprising Spartan citizens over thirty *(apella)*. The economy and state structure were based on an anomalous kind of communism (total equality, but only for Sparta's ethnically impermeable upper class) and on maintaining a colossal military machine to enforce law and order at home and bolster its aggressive policy abroad. From early childhood Spartans were trained for military service and citizenship, following a rigid disciplinary system that excluded the family from the education process.

Manufacturing and trade were handled by semifree citizens *(peroikoi)* who themselves had few rights, although their work provided considerable wealth for their austere community-state. Serfs *(helots)* were bound permanently to the soil, tilling the land and herding livestock from one generation to the next; they were the descendants of conquered peoples who had once populated this region, and of prisoners taken during wars fought in surrounding regions (most notably Messenia).

The Peloponnesian War began at the instigation of the Athenians: they had issued a decree that would have the effect of strangling trade by their neighbor and rival Megara, and they refused to withdraw it. Sparta rose to the defense of Megara. Well aware of the enemy's strength, Pericles ordered the entire population of Attica to take refuge inside the city walls, abandoning their fields and crops. His intention was to use a "hit and run" technique to put continuous pressure on the Spartans.

But Athens' strong financial position, its far superior fleet, and its supremacy

52 top *This funeral* lekythos, *with a white background, comes from Eretria and was painted by an Attic ceramist close to the Painter of the Cane Thicket, who in turn was inspired by the great classical painter Parrhasius. It dates to c. 430 BC and shows the achievements of Greek painting in that period: perspective, freedom of composition, smooth brush strokes, and the taste for naturalistic detail.*

52 bottom *This* lekythos, *also with a white background, is one of the best pieces from the Painter of Achilles (c. 440-430 BC). The theme it depicts alludes to death—a warrior taking leave of his spouse, a metaphor for a heroic leave-taking from life.*

over the Aegean (assured by allies who, on the whole, stayed loyal) served nothing in the face of a plague that, between 430 and 428 BC, killed one-fifth of the population, including Pericles himself (in 429 BC). In the early years of the war, the two sides experienced alternating fortunes: repeated invasions of Attica by the Peloponnesian forces were answered by fresh upsurges from the Athenians from 425 BC onward. But by 421 BC both sides were exhausted and more than ready to negotiate peace.

A new phase in the hostilities opened in 420 BC, with the rise to power of dangerous "warmongering" politicians like Alcibiades and Nicias. In the wake of the Battle of Mantinea (418 BC), Sparta regained leadership over the Peloponnese, while Athens lost the support of some of its allies and its own citizens because of its role in a massacre of Melos and a disastrous expedition to Sicily (415-413 BC). With the aid of Sparta, Syracuse inflicted a crushing blow on the Athenian fleet and army, killing thousands of soldiers and condemning countless prisoners to die of starvation.

The third phase of the war coincided with the period when democracy in Athens was temporarily overthrown by the oligarchs who sought peace with Sparta. But warfare was resumed as soon as full democracy was restored. Athens, although now isolated, scored several victories. Before long, however, the Spartans gained the upper hand (406-404 BC), led by their admiral, Lysander, who made a triumphant entry into Piraeus and ordered an unconditional surrender. The terms of the surrender demanded that the Athenian fortifications and fleet be destroyed, and that Athens become a member of the Peloponnesian League, which implied the abandonment of democratic government.

For a while Athens was ruled by tyrants. When democracy finally did return, thanks to a bold coup by Thrasybulus, Sparta did not oppose it, perhaps well aware that Athens would never again be the great power that had once held sway in the century drawing to a close.

53 *A painful testimony to the bereavement caused by the Peloponnesian War is found in this beautiful funeral stele of two young Athenian warriors, Chairedemos and Lykeas (420-410 BC), portrayed while going to war. The sober, classical naturalism celebrates the two hoplites, represented in perspective, as if in slow motion. The ideal features of "godlike" men, of heroes whose beauty is in their deeds and virtues, is translated into the harmonious shapes and in the fascination of their bodies, which echo Phidias in the treatment of their heads and Polyclitus in the definition of the rest.*

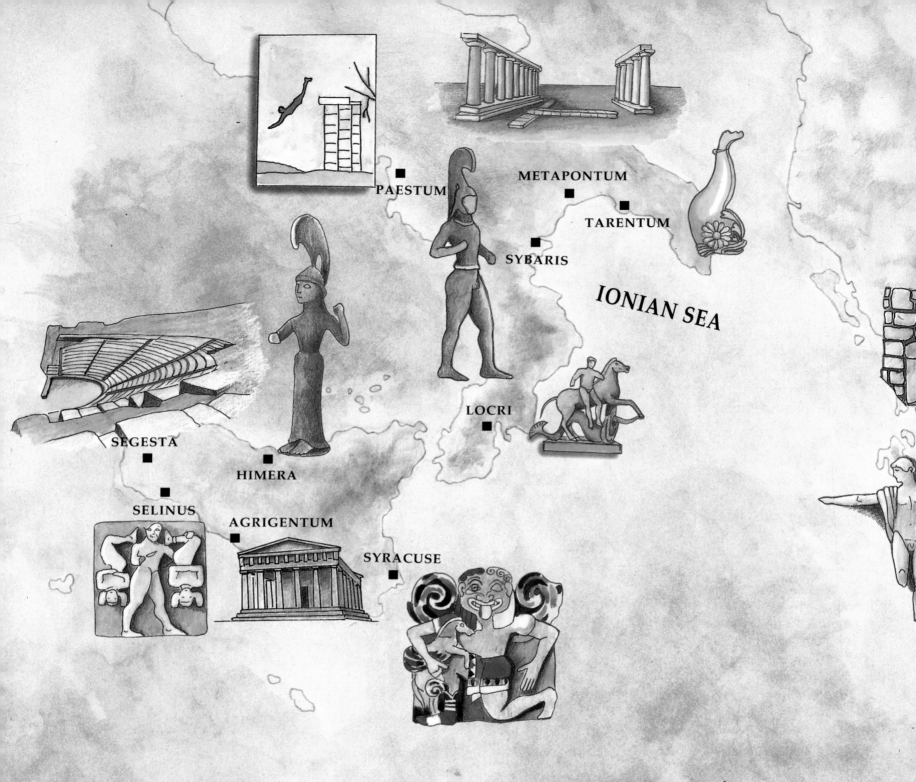

PAESTUM

METAPONTUM

TARENTUM

SYBARIS

IONIAN SEA

LOCRI

SEGESTA

HIMERA

SELINUS

AGRIGENTUM

SYRACUSE

Classical Greece
AND *MAGNA GRAECIA*

MEDITERRANEAN

AEGEAN SEA

ASSOS

PERGAMUM

MYCENAE   ■ DELPHI

ATHENS

EPHESUS

PRIENE

CORINTH

YMPIA

DELOS

HALICARNASSUS

SPARTA

EPIDAURUS

KNOSSOS

SEA

ALEXANDRIA

THE FOURTH CENTURY BC AND THE RISE OF MACEDONIA

56 *The beautiful bronze statue of Athena in the Museum of Piraeus (430 BC) is perhaps the most incisive image of the goddess of wisdom, adorned with a long peplos but armed and encircled with an aegis bearing the face of Medusa.*

With the tragedy of the Peloponnesian War not long concluded, 4th-century Greece faced new regional conflicts and tensions. These resulted in the short-lived hegemonies of Sparta and Thebes, the intermittent reemergence of Athens, and the rise of leagues of poleis (Arcadia and Acarnania-Aetolia, for example) who aspired to emerge from their economically and militarily peripheral positions.

In the Western Greek world, meanwhile, the long-established colonies had severed all bonds with their ancestral founders. A prominent example was Syracuse, which, after its victory over Athens (415 BC), embarked on a policy of aggression, from the Tyrrhenian Sea to the Adriatic. The Western Greeks realized they had to rely on their own resources to fend off the imperialist offensives of the Carthaginians, who had left many flourishing Sicilian settlements in ruins.

The Peloponnesian War and the state of permanent conflict in the first half of the century, kindled by the aggressiveness of the leading poleis, were either the cause or the effect—according to interpretation—of the retrogression of values that had been the mainstay of Hellenism for centuries. Gone was the profound sense of belonging to a community, the city-state; gone was the certainty of being part of an ontological dimension that got closer to perfection as spiritual and ethical values grew stronger; gone was the perception of self as part of a whole and "all of one part"; gone was love of knowledge (philosophy) as a logical process that made understanding the infinite its ultimate goal.

Their place was gradually taken by a short-sighted anthropocentrism, in which men came to see themselves as the measure of all things, individualism, and the cult of personality. People became even more aware of the precariousness of the human condition; reason was obfuscated by a turmoil of emotions that no philosophy or religion could placate.

Seen from a historical standpoint, the hegemony of Sparta occurred on a fairly general level only. When Sparta realized that its pro-Persian policy had left Ionia in the hands of a weak and unpopular emperor, Artaxerxes, Sparta opted to support his brother and rival, Cyrus II. Athens, however, felt tremendously threatened by the possible success of the people of Lacedaemon in regions traditionally under its own influence: it therefore courted the Persian king and helped thwart the Spartans' schemes, eventually obtaining financial support and control over the Dardanelles, a strategic point of access to the rich colonies of the Black Sea. The peace imposed by Persia (386 BC) was short-lived: Sparta attempted to install a pro-Spartan oligarchic government in Thebes, triggering a reaction that, in the space of a few years, resulted in Theban hegemony over the whole of Greece, until 362 BC.

In an increasingly complex political situation, with cities ideologically at loggerheads, it was practically inevitable that the expansionist moves of Macedonia, a monarchic power emerging from the northern periphery

57 *The superb bronze head of Satyros—who, in about 330 BC, won the Olympics in boxing—was made by Silanion, pupil of great Lysippus. The athlete's face is frightful and punch-filled, marked by swelling, wrinkles, and a thick, bristly beard of great realism.*

of Greece, should succeed so handsomely. A vast mountainous region sloping down from the impervious valleys of the southern Balkans to the northwestern shores of the Aegean and as far as Mount Olympus, Macedonia was inhabited by peoples of the Doric race, who had been in contact with the Mycenaeans in the second millennium BC. And yet they had long remained on the fringe of Greek history.

The ruling dynasty of the Argeads, in power since the 7th century BC, was based in the old capital city of Aegae; in the 6th and 5th centuries, it made several attempts to unify the region and gain control of Thrace. During and after the period of Persian hegemony (513-480 BC), it made friendly overtures toward southern Greece. And Alexander I eventually made an expansionist move toward Pangaeum and its silver mines, east of the river Strimon.

In the second half of the 5th century BC, Macedonia moved cautiously into the Greek arena, forming alliances variously with Athens and Sparta and gaining control of the region east of the river Axios. King Perdiccas II extended the sphere of Macedonian influence to the peninsula of Chalcidice, an important crossroads for trade in the north Aegean, previously within the orbit of Athens.

In the 4th century the Argeads bided their time and prepared to intervene in the ongoing struggles for leadership among Athens, Sparta, and Thebes. The outstanding military tactics with which Macedonia was to conquer the world—based on a special combat unit, the Macedonian phalanx—had already been perfected and tested.

Philip II (reigned 359-336 BC) was astute in his foreign policy, adapting it to suit regional political situations. He brought the whole of Macedonia and the northern Aegean together under his rule, establishing a protectorate over neighboring Thessaly. Meanwhile, the poleis of southern Greece were still divided into ephemeral leagues whose policies varied from short-sighted regionalism to politico-economic lobbying. Diplomacy was the key to Philip's initiatives to establish Macedonian hegemony. He operated, for example, through traditional Panhellenic associations like that of Delphi. Later, he offered Macedonian support to political forces and regimes that could further the cause of Philip's leadership within their own regional ambit.

After years of warfare, during which the poleis entered into terminal decline, the Macedonian victory at Chaeronea (338 BC) settled things once and for all. At Corinth, Philip II promoted the formation of a Panhellenic league that allowed the cities to retain their autonomy and institutions. He imposed peace upon all the Hellenes and laid plans for resuming war against the

58 top *Philip II is represented in this ivory head, 3 centimeters high, found in the Macedonian king's tomb in Vergina.*

58 center *This splendid gold quiver belonged to Philip II. Some scholars hypothesize a Scythian origin for it. It is decorated with the bloody scene of a plundering.*

58 bottom *This* larnax *of thick gold leaf contained the cremated remains of Philip II. In this masterpiece skillful Macedonian goldsmiths gave free rein to their decorative imagination, marrying elegance and delicacy with sumptuous material and high function. The lid bears the symbol of the Macedonian Kingdom, the sixteen-point star, while the sides are finely decorated with rosettes and friezes in gold and* pâté de verre.

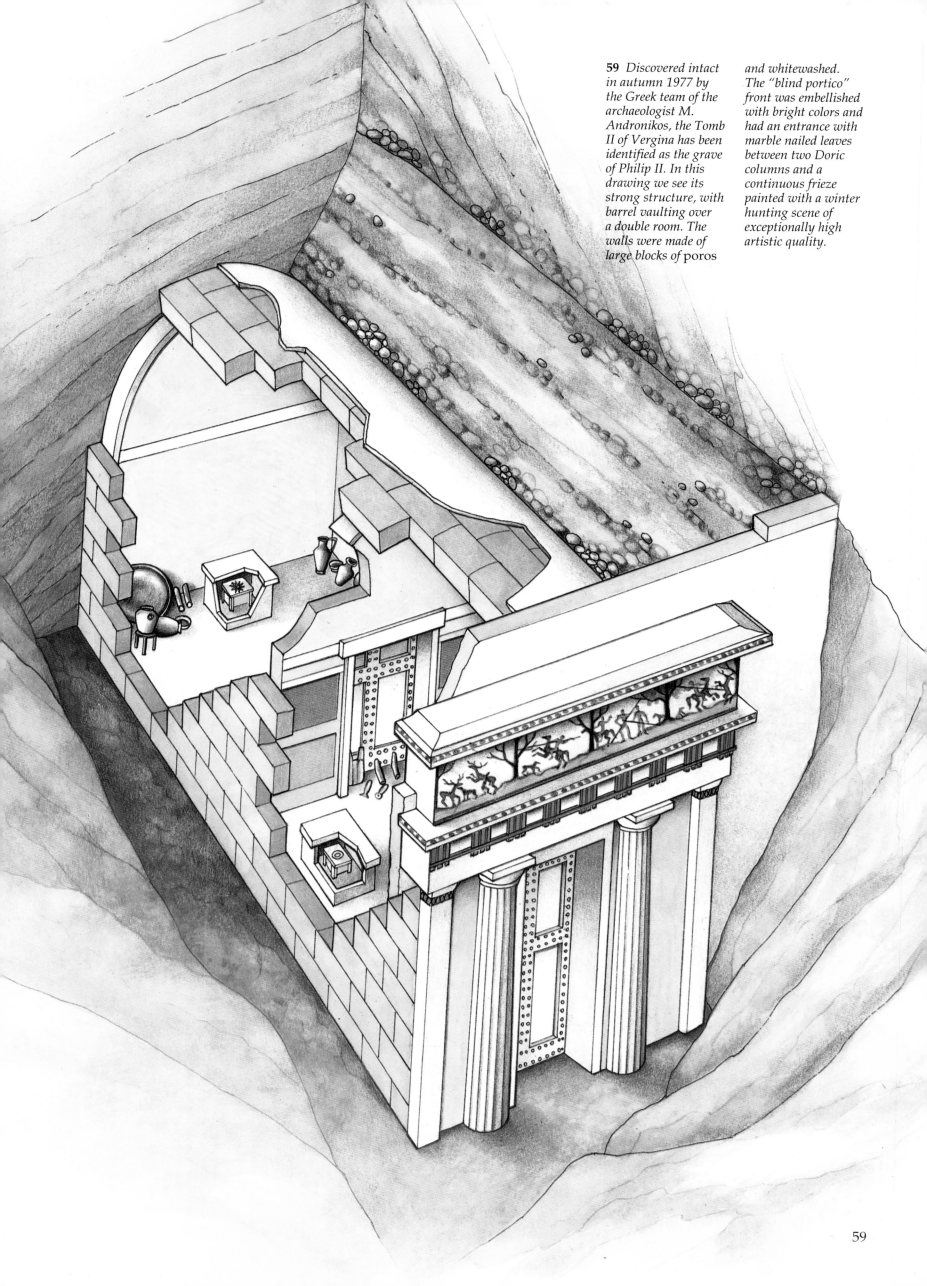

59 *Discovered intact in autumn 1977 by the Greek team of the archaeologist M. Andronikos, the Tomb II of Vergina has been identified as the grave of Philip II. In this drawing we see its strong structure, with barrel vaulting over a double room. The walls were made of large blocks of* poros *and whitewashed. The "blind portico" front was embellished with bright colors and had an entrance with marble nailed leaves between two Doric columns and a continuous frieze painted with a winter hunting scene of exceptionally high artistic quality.*

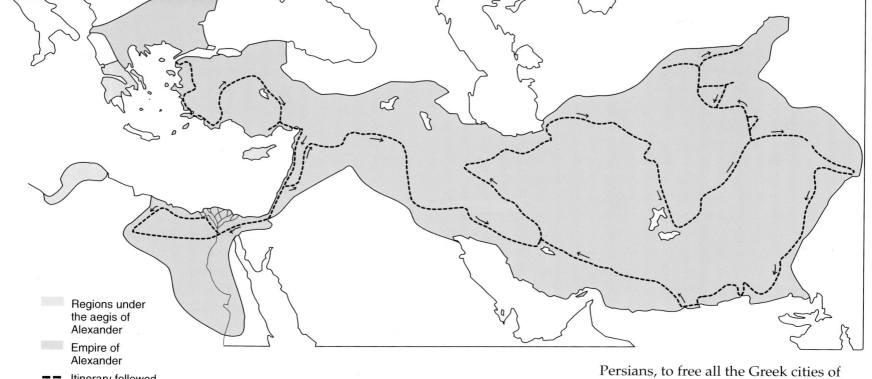

Persians, to free all the Greek cities of
Asia from the dominion of imperial
satraps.

On the eve of the expedition against
the Persians, Philip II was assassinated
in the theater at Aegae. His place on the
throne was taken by his young son,
Alexander III, whose amazing exploits
eventually earned him the name *Megas*
("the Great"). One of the greatest figures
of antiquity, Alexander did honor to the
political legacy he received from his
father—he transformed the plan to
free the Asian Greeks into a vast and
devastating military adventure, as a
result of which, between 334 and 329
BC, the great, age-old Persian Empire,
with vast provinces stretching from
Egypt to Syria, from Ionia to
Mesopotamia, was brought to its knees.

Having felled this colossus, in
328-327 BC the conqueror marched
relentlessly on, advancing as far as the
Caspian Sea and the shores of the Indus,
at which point his army refused to go
further. Attesting to his successes were
tens of Alexandrias—cities named after
him in the East, as in Egypt and
Anatolia before them.

Next Alexander initiated a policy of
ethnic intermingling, designed to join
Greeks and Macedonians with the races
they had conquered. A whole new
political idea—reaching far beyond
the limited worlds of the *poleis*—made
its mark on Greek history. It was the

60 *Alexander the Great
was the first western
historical figure to be
the subject of a real
personality cult while
still alive. The myths
surrounding his feats
generated several
idealized images, but
only Lysippus and
perhaps Leochares were
allowed to portray*
*the emperor officially.
This beautiful image
of Alexander in his
youth is attributed to
Leochares. The
anastole of hair on his
forehead, a sort of tuft
divided in two, is
typical, while the deep
and penetrating look is
ideally fixed on distant
and glorious horizons.*

idea of universal Hellenism, "Greece wherever Greeks have set foot," far greater than *Magna Graecia.* Greece would be the homeland of culture and civilization for a world that, having overcome ethnic and regional barriers, would bring together thousands of different cultures and civilizations and give them new life.

The early death of Alexander at the age of 33, in Babylonia in 323 BC, while his Persian wife Roxane was still carrying the heir to the throne, interrupted this amazing adventure. But Alexander's achievements had introduced to Western history the idea of a universal, quasi-divine monarchy, capable of gathering humanity together under a single flag and within a single splendid and variegated culture.

The end of the journey and the conquests of Alexander the Great did not mean the demise of the Greek world: on the contrary, "universal Hellenism" made Greek culture part of the heritage of all the races who came into contact with it, far beyond the boundary walls of the hundred poleis. Hellenism, in other words, originated with Alexander.

61 top *The mythic deeds of Alexander the Great were illustrated in countless works of art produced in the territories he* conquered. *This impetuous image of the young king appeared on a sarcophagus found in Sidon (Lebanon).*

61 bottom *A detail of the famous mosaic of the Battle of Issus between Alexander the Great and Darius, found in the House of Faun in Pompeii. It is* considered a faithful copy of an original *fresco by Philoxenos of Eretria, made for the Macedonian King Cassander (end of the 4th century BC).*

THE THIRD CENTURY BC AND "UNIVERSAL HELLENISM"

Not long after Alexander's death the *diadochoi*—the Macedonian generals who participated in his triumphs—threw themselves into a fierce power struggle for the succession. But Hellenism was already making its mark as new centers of outstanding economic and cultural vitality became established outside the traditional Greek world. Athens, Rhodes, and Syracuse were joined by the new capitals of the

kingdoms into which the empire had been divided: Alexandria, Antioch, Pergamum, and Pella, the Macedonian capital under the Antigonid dynasty.

As the struggle over the succession continued, a revolt by the Greeks was quickly stamped out by Antipater, ruler in Aegae (322 BC). The struggles for power—involving Cassander, Antipater's son Lysimachus, Antigonus the One-Eyed, Seleucus, and Ptolemy—continued for some forty years. Finally the empire was divided into kingdoms, some of them immense, some smaller. Cassander initially gained control of Macedonia (which was later taken over by Antigonus Gonatas, conqueror of the Celts, who invaded Asia Minor in 277 BC). Seleucus became master of Asia Minor, as far as Mesopotamia and the Iranian plateau. Lysimachus received Thrace (until he was ousted by Seleucus); Ptolemy acquired Egypt and founded the dynasty that bore his name. In 240 BC the independent kingdom of Pergamum entered the Hellenic sphere of influence under the Attalids, who zealously encouraged trade and patronized the arts. Antigonid Macedonia retained its hegemony over a now-declining Greece. Athens alone

62 *The great frieze of the Altar of Zeus at Pergamum is almost the symbol of Hellenistic art. Here the theme of the battle between gods and giants became an allegory of the Attalids' victorious wars.*

63 *Hellenistic art also featured an intimistic trend, focusing on the representation of feelings—as shown by this beautiful statue of a young boy wrapped in a short cloak, found at Tralles, in Asia Minor.*

continued to enjoy the cultural prestige worthy of its splendid past. Sparta, after an attempt to impose a "popular" framework upon its institutions, was overcome by the Achaean League, with Macedonian support (227-222 BC). Greece's island cities—Kos and Rhodes in particular—experienced significant growth: from a trade standpoint they were in an excellent position, at the crossroads of east and west, and they were run by moderate mercantile oligarchies, capable of exporting local products to faraway places. (Amphorae originating from Rhodes and Kos, dated 230-220 BC, have been found in the Po valley, proof that wine was shipped to the Celts.)

In Egypt, Alexandria under the Ptolemies was unrivaled as a center of trade and culture. The city's museum and library were cultural institutions of outstanding importance, while its school of art was among the most admired of the Hellenistic world, on a par with the renowned school at Pergamum. Toward the middle of the century, the city was the point of departure for expeditions that conquered Cyrenaica, Lycia, Panfilia, and Cyprus. Egypt's power began to wane in the early years of the 2nd century BC, as a result of corruption among its rulers and the incipient expansionism of Rome, which—having gained control of Carthage—had set its sights on dominating the Mediterranean basin.

Antioch, in Syria, eventually became the capital of the vast Seleucid kingdom. The city played a fundamental part in Hellenizing the multiplicity of races and cultures that had existed for thousands of years in this region, one of the richest and most prosperous on the entire globe. The liberal policies of the kingdom's rulers remained constant throughout the century, but the Seleucid dominion was eventually split up into a series of states big and small, from India, Bactria, and Persia to Asia Minor, where the kingdoms of Armenia, Cappadocia, and Pergamum emerged.

	Macedonia	Cyprus
	Epirus	Bithynia and Pontus
	Achaea	Galatia
	Asia	Cappadocia
	Lycia and Pamphylia	Cilicia

In the second century BC the emerging power of Rome clashed with the declining power of the Macedonian rulers. Not content with the punishment meted out to Philip V for supporting Hannibal during the war of 215-205 BC, the Romans took further military action in 200-196 BC, under the pretext of freeing the old *poleis* from Macedonian dominion. At the head of the Roman armies, Titus Quinctius Flaminius defeated the enemy at the Battle of Cynoscephalae and proclaimed the liberty of all Greek cities at the Isthmian games of 196 BC.

This "liberation" was in fact the first step toward subjugation of a cradle of civilization whose importance and fascination were fully apparent to the culturally sophisticated members of Rome's senatorial elite. After a series of wars against the dynasties of Syria, Rome gained control over the Seleucid Kingdom ("demoted" in 129 BC to a mere province). The Battle of Pydna in 168 BC had brought the Third Macedonian War to a close and signaled the demise of the Macedonian monarchy; the region was divided into four republics under the protection of Rome.

In the first half of the century Rhodes supported the enemies of Rome, a strategy for which the island of the Colossus later paid dearly. In 166 BC the Romans declared Delos a "free port" and sealed the doom of Rhodes' economy. The last Macedonian revolt, supported by numerous Greek cities led by Corinth, ended with yet another Roman victory: in 146 BC Corinth was seized and razed to the ground. (Carthage was also destroyed in the same year.) Save a few "open" cities, Greece became the Roman province of Achaea. The myriad states that had risen from the ashes of the great dismembered kingdoms of the *diadochoi* were all taken over by Rome in the 2nd and 1st centuries BC, generally by force but occasionally ceded spontaneously (as in the case of Pergamum, bequeathed to Rome by the last Attalid). Egypt held on to its autonomy until the fateful year 31 BC: on the day after the Battle of Actium, in which Mark Antony was defeated by Octavian, Cleopatra VI, last queen of the Ptolemies, committed suicide, and the age-old kingdom of the pharaohs passed into the hands of the newly installed prince of Rome.

64 *The Roman period was the time of maximum growth for Delos (2nd-1st century BC), which had become an Aegean free port to the detriment of Rhodes. Here works of an excellent artistic level were produced, such as this head from a lost bronze statue (c. 100 BC). The identity of the subject is unidentifiable, but his features are realistically individualized.*

65 *The Romans' admiration for Greek art was reflected in its systematic copying of the most beautiful and famous works, despite great differences in value between one copy and another. This beautiful Hermes, for example, a copy of an original Praxitelean work of the first half of the 4th century BC, shows high quality.*

CIVILIZATION AND CULTURE IN ANCIENT GREECE

66-67 *An intimate scene from daily life is shown on this painted pottery artifact found at Capua and probably dating to 300 BC. Two cloaked girls are portrayed playing a knucklebone game— with dice obtained from large mammal vertebrae (sheep or cattle). The freedom of composition and the nice variety of gestures belong to the Hellenistic style.*

GREEK DWELLINGS

For many centuries the house played a marginal role in the everyday life of ancient Greek men. The wonderful climate meant that much of their time—whether occupied with work, politics, or leisure pursuits—was spent out of doors. Houses provided mainly nighttime shelter—not even all meals were consumed there.

For women, however, irrespective of class, the house was a prison without bars where they spent most of their existence hidden away in a section of the house called a *gynaeceum*. The sole exceptions were women who chose the morally reprehensible but socioeconomically rewarding position of *hetaera*, a cross between a highly cultured mistress of a salon, a secret lover—for reasons of genuine passion or economic advantage—and a classy courtesan.

The Archaic period saw dwellings change from their most primitive and basic structures, derived from the protohistoric *megaron*, to a variety of more articulated forms and layouts. Houses were either square or rectangular in shape, sometimes with an apse, or

68 *An exquisite family scene is conveyed in this delicate yet severe pottery* pinax *from Calabria. A goddess lifts the lid of a wicker basket inside a room equipped with furnishings of various sorts.*

projecting semicircular construction. Floor plans were organized so that the rooms were aligned in a row or in rows facing one another; in some cases they gave onto a private court, in others onto yards shared with other dwelling units.

Building techniques varied enormously. Timber with *pisé* was used widely for frameworks, as an alternative to plaster-finished unbaked bricks on stone foundations. Roofing solutions were less varied: only occasionally did single or twin sloping roofs replace the flat roof of Cycladic tradition, which also served to collect, store, and distribute rainwater.

Coinciding with the new, rational focus of urban planning that emerged in the second half of the 5th century BC, builders seem to have paid more attention to the functional and comfort-related aspects of domestic space, in what may have been an early signal of the imminent conversion to a more

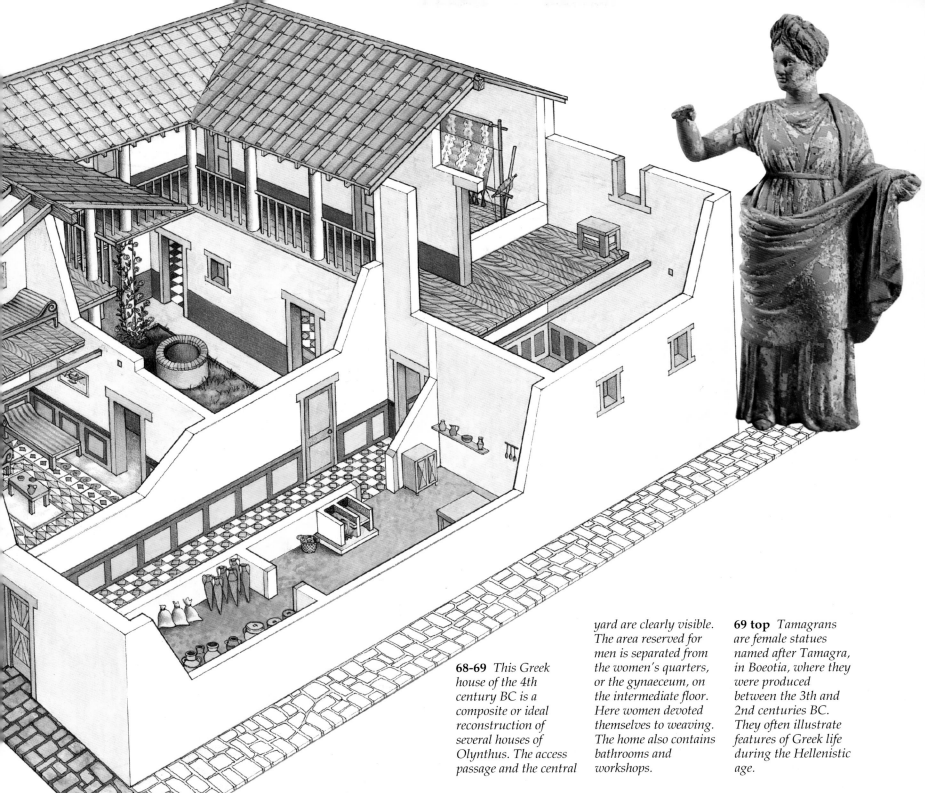

68-69 *This Greek house of the 4th century BC is a composite or ideal reconstruction of several houses of Olynthus. The access passage and the central yard are clearly visible. The area reserved for men is separated from the women's quarters, or the gynaeceum, on the intermediate floor. Here women devoted themselves to weaving. The home also contains bathrooms and workshops.*

69 top *Tamagrans are female statues named after Tamagra, in Boeotia, where they were produced between the 3th and 2nd centuries BC. They often illustrate features of Greek life during the Hellenistic age.*

individualistic approach toward life.

This impression is conveyed by the buildings of Olynthus, a town situated in the Chalcidian peninsula. Although Olynthus was located in a peripheral area of Greece, it acquired a position of prestige and bore many resemblances to the most powerful cities of the time—a position it retained until 348 BC when it was razed by Philip II of Macedonia. Today the archaeological site provides precious insights into the urban and architectural features of a town of about 20,000 inhabitants. The town's gridlike layout was based on wide north-south boulevards intersected by narrower streets at right angles. But the terrain and the need to expand led to the creation of diagonal routes as well. The original

layout of old quarters was rebuilt to incorporate the new residential quarters in the north of the town. An alley along the main axis through the quarters served for traffic and drainage and to separate two rows of five standard-plan dwelling units.

Olynthus actually marked a turning point in Greek house construction, with a definite shift toward more articulated, standardized forms—a real innovation in the history of Greek architecture. In the most common floor plan, the rooms were arranged around a courtyard with at least one arcaded side; they generally included a living room, a kitchen, and a small bathroom. Evidence has been found of buildings in which an upper floor covered at least part of the dwelling.

A considerable number of detached houses have been unearthed on the east side of Olynthus; many of them boast an unusually large number of rooms around an arcaded central court and can be

considered precursors of the aristocratic villas of the later Hellenistic and Roman periods. Floor mosaics are another typical feature of these houses: created from pebbles found in riverbeds, they depict mythological figures.

The Greek house reached the apex of its development in the Hellenistic age. Dwelling units were peristylar, with their many rooms giving onto a pillared inner court. Stone or mosaic paving was widespread, and interors were decorated with drapes, tapestries, carpets, and, more commonly, wall paintings. Attention was paid to creating scenic effects related to the surrounding landscape. Through the centuries the house was upgraded from the humble shelter of town-dwellers to the small, private "castle" of law-abiding citizens, satisfied with themselves and with the solid walls of their home, an unpretentious showcase of a lifestyle in which appearances mattered most.

Many precious materials were used by the Minoans, Mycenaeans, and Greeks to embellish their homes, for personal adornment, and as prestigious evidence of high social status and wealth. These precious materials included timbers like cypress, cedar of Lebanon, Aleppo pine, boxwood, and—more rarely—ebony; ivory; semiprecious stones such as chalcedony, carnelian, amethyst, pink-tinged, green, and smoke-gray quartz, rock crystal, lapis lazuli, and turquoise, as well as the more humble crystalline calcite, tourmaline, obsidian, and garnet; *pâté de verre*, colored by skillful Phoenician and Egyptian craftsmen; and most important of all, precious metals.

Greece never yielded much gold: mines existed only in the outlying mountainous regions of Thrace and Macedonia, and on a few Aegean islands. The many gold artifacts of Minoan Crete and the Mycenaean world were made from gold purchased in the East. In the second millennium BC the Hellenic peoples maintained flourishing commercial and diplomatic relations with Egypt, Syro-Palestine, Asia Minor, and Mesopotamia. By the 7th century BC, once the Greeks emerged from the poverty of the Dark Ages, oriental jewelry was being imported in large quantities, and before long, it was extensively copied by orientalizing workshops in Greece itself and in the colonies.

But not until the 6th century BC did awareness of gold's value give rise to a booming coinage-based economy and to more widespread use of gold for jewelry

70 *This wonderful boat-shaped earring was crafted from mixed techniques— molding, embossing, granulation, knurling, and engraving. It shows the high artistic level of the goldsmiths of Tarentum (present-day Taranto), in southeastern Italy, in* *the 4th century BC. On each side, separated by a palmette and two rosettes, is an image of Nike, the goddess of victory. Below, in a whirl of small globes and fine gold links, there are two doves and seven amphora-shaped pendants.*

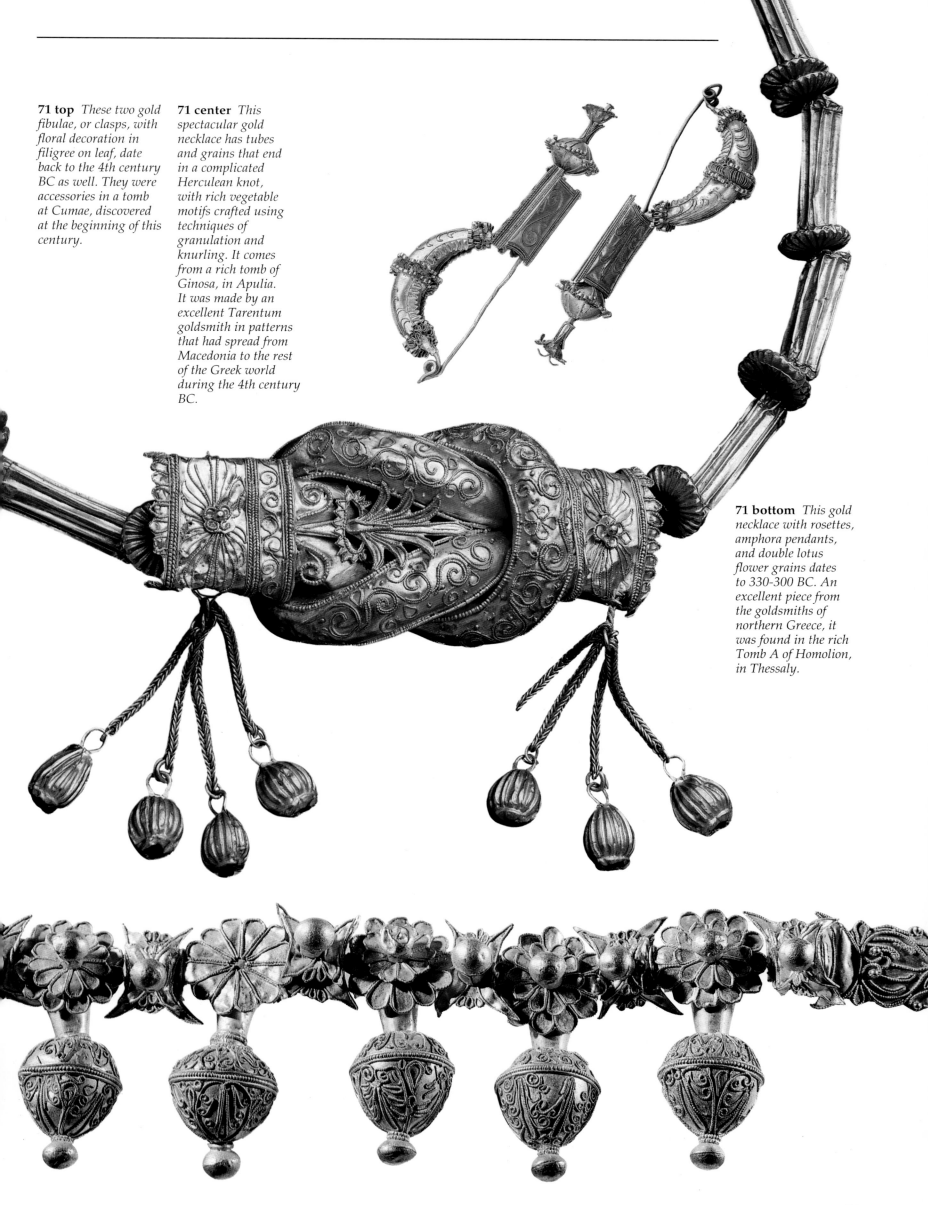

71 top *These two gold fibulae, or clasps, with floral decoration in filigree on leaf, date back to the 4th century BC as well. They were accessories in a tomb at Cumae, discovered at the beginning of this century.*

71 center *This spectacular gold necklace has tubes and grains that end in a complicated Herculean knot, with rich vegetable motifs crafted using techniques of granulation and knurling. It comes from a rich tomb of Ginosa, in Apulia. It was made by an excellent Tarentum goldsmith in patterns that had spread from Macedonia to the rest of the Greek world during the 4th century BC.*

71 bottom *This gold necklace with rosettes, amphora pendants, and double lotus flower grains dates to 330-300 BC. An excellent piece from the goldsmiths of northern Greece, it was found in the rich Tomb A of Homolion, in Thessaly.*

and other luxury artifacts. Minoan jewelry is stunningly beautiful. In its imagery, it reflects the naturalism typical of Cretan art, but technically it has more in common with Egyptian and oriental models. It is characterized by the abundant use of repoussé, engraving, inlay, and gilding, and it is associated with semiprecious stones and glazed terracotta. Peloponnesian goldsmiths transformed the more austere artistic language of the Mycenaeans in response to new ideas they picked up on an "interactive cultural network"; they used information on new techniques to experiment with all kinds of innovative formal and decorative ideas.

Finds testifying to these cultural exchanges are many: the presence, in the *tholos* tomb at Vapheio, of a Minoan cup beside a Mycenaean imitation; oriental images copied—sometimes rather clumsily—on the heads of fibulae or on seal rings; imitations of Anatolian techniques, using niello, on a splendid series of daggers with inlaid designs; highly original funeral masks; wares with plant or marine motifs; *rhyta* with animal motifs. These items have been discovered in the tombs of Mycenae, Midea-Dendra, and Tiryns, where locally made pieces are found alongside imports from Crete and the islands under Minoan influence.

72 bottom left *This magnificent earring with pendant representing the head of a woman adorned with jewels is in the Tarentum tradition; it comes from a tomb of Crispiano.*

72 bottom right *This pair of earrings with griffin heads dates to the 4th century BC. However, the iconography can be traced back to the 7th century, since it* derived from the "monstrous" animal tradition of Orientalizing art. It also shows the continuity of some decorative themes in Greek art.

72-73 *This superb gold diadem has flowers of gold and enamel. It was probably produced by goldsmiths from Tarentum and deposited in a rich tomb in present-day Apulia in the 3rd century BC.*

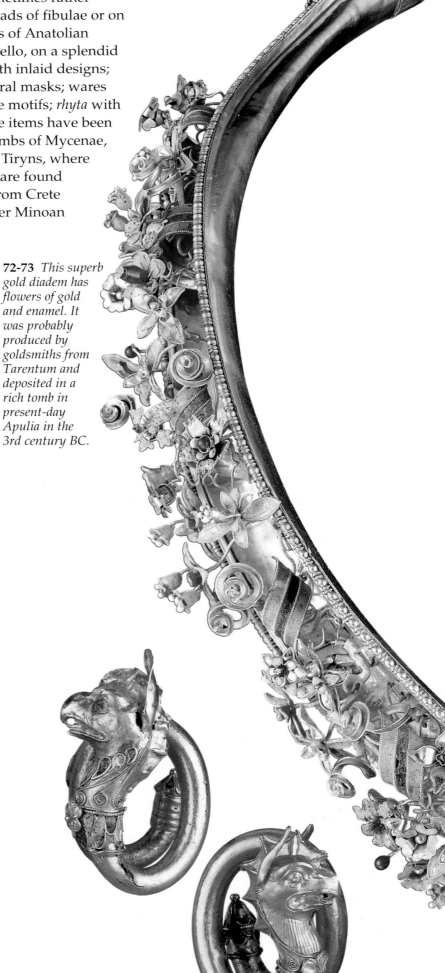

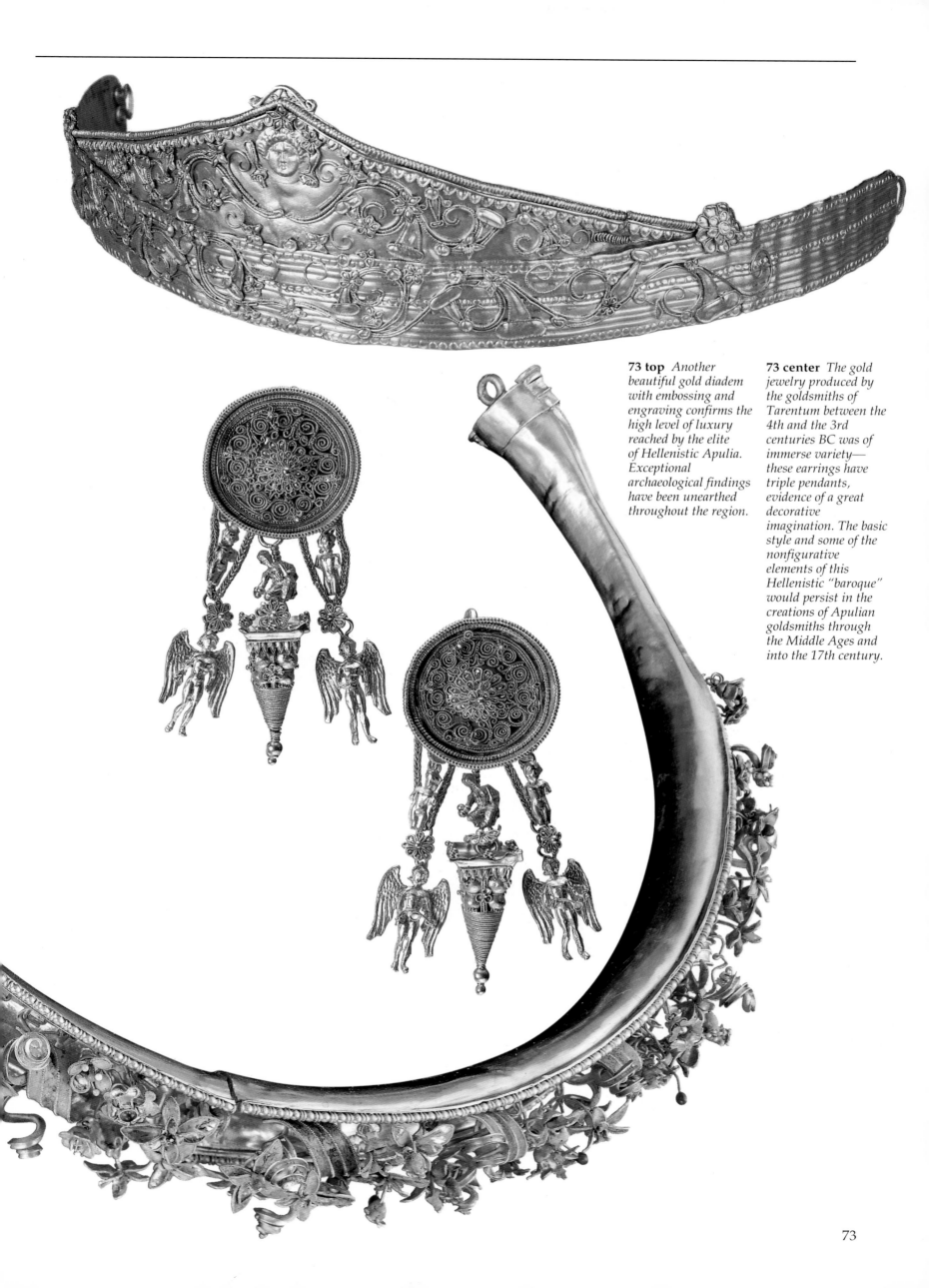

73 top *Another beautiful gold diadem with embossing and engraving confirms the high level of luxury reached by the elite of Hellenistic Apulia. Exceptional archaeological findings have been unearthed throughout the region.*

73 center *The gold jewelry produced by the goldsmiths of Tarentum between the 4th and the 3rd centuries BC was of immerse variety— these earrings have triple pendants, evidence of a great decorative imagination. The basic style and some of the nonfigurative elements of this Hellenistic "baroque" would persist in the creations of Apulian goldsmiths through the Middle Ages and into the 17th century.*

74 top *This myrtle twig in flower came from a luxurious gold crown dating to the second half of the 4th century BC, in central Macedonia.*

74 bottom *This diadem—with bronze leaves and insects and berries in clay, covered with gold leaf—shows the artistic connection between the goldsmiths of Greece and those of* Magna Graecia *in the 4th and 3rd centuries BC. The piece comes from Campania.*

74-75 *This beautiful gold crown with laurel and oak leaves is a unique creation of Thessalian goldsmithery in the Hellenistic age. It was found near Volos, a seaport of Thessaly, and may be dated between the end of the 4th and the beginning of the 3rd century BC.*

75 center *This gold diadem, contemporary with the previous one and coming from Tarentum, faithfully reproduces a wreath of oak leaves, the tree dear to Zeus.*

75 bottom *The charm and inexhaustible creativity of Greek goldsmiths are often seen even in simple objects. This small scepter is covered by a thin gold mesh that ends in a Corinthian capital, from which oak leaves emerge.*

75

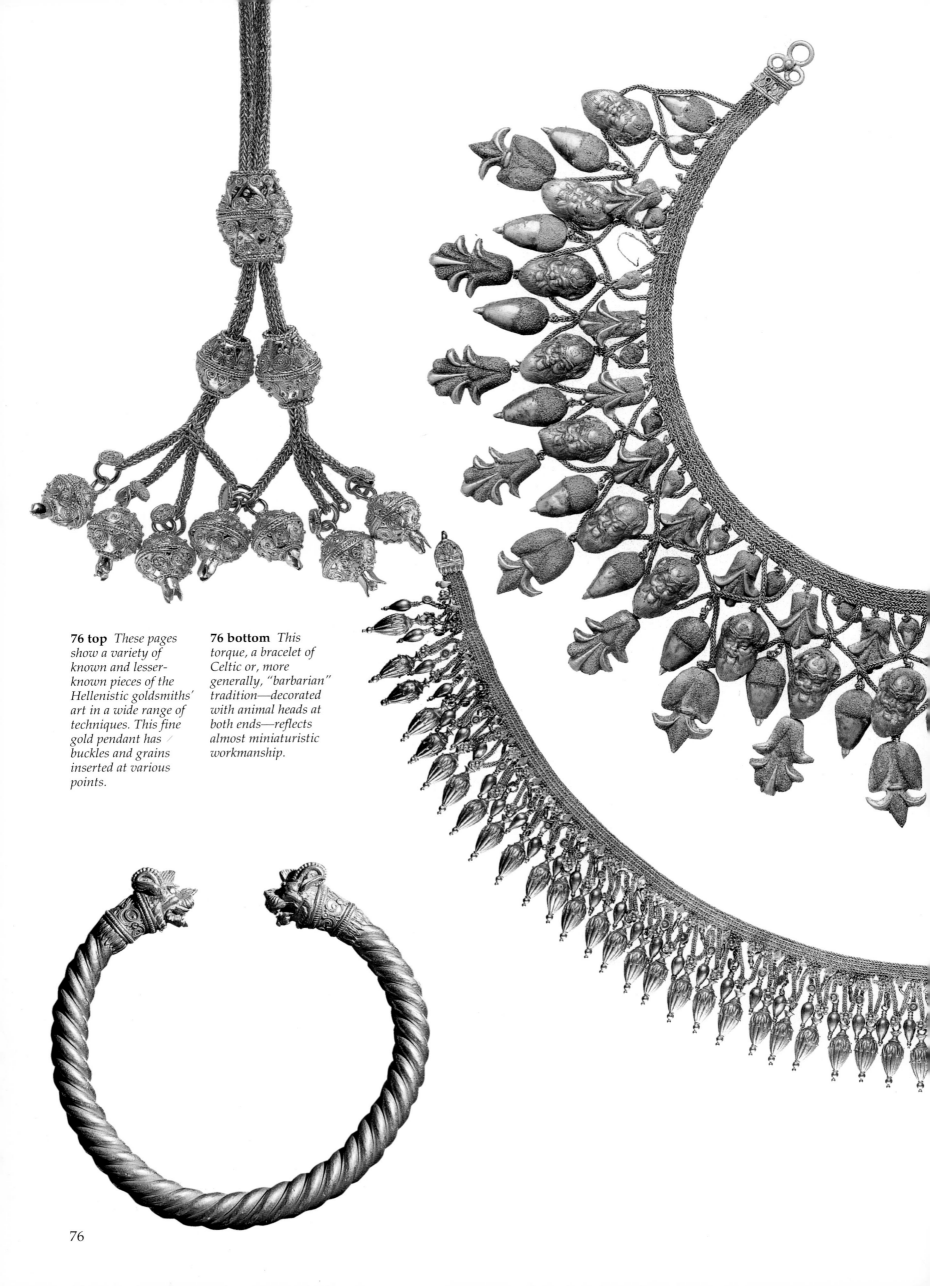

76 top *These pages show a variety of known and lesser-known pieces of the Hellenistic goldsmiths' art in a wide range of techniques. This fine gold pendant has buckles and grains inserted at various points.*

76 bottom *This torque, a bracelet of Celtic or, more generally, "barbarian" tradition—decorated with animal heads at both ends—reflects almost miniaturistic workmanship.*

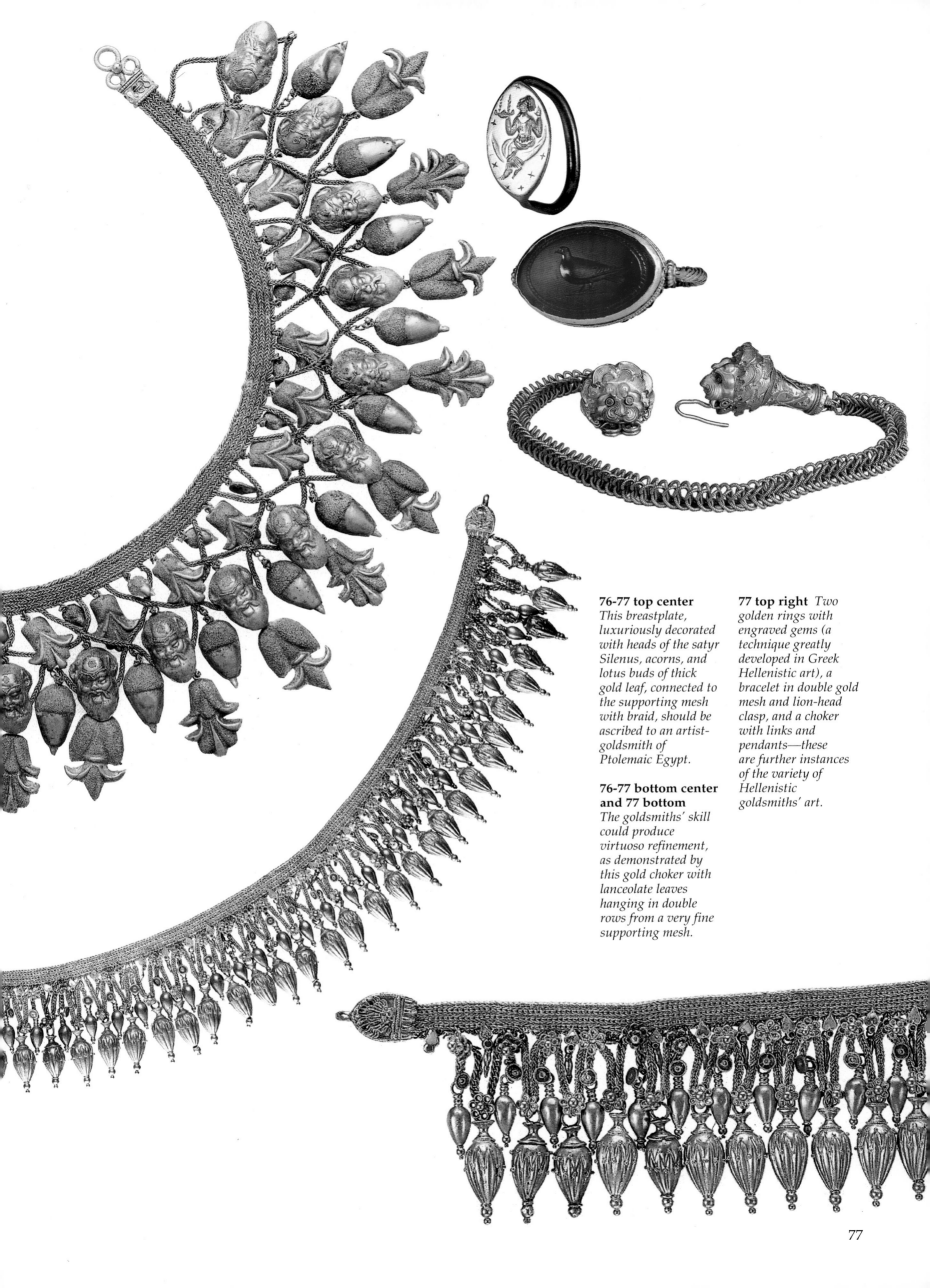

76-77 top center
This breastplate, luxuriously decorated with heads of the satyr Silenus, acorns, and lotus buds of thick gold leaf, connected to the supporting mesh with braid, should be ascribed to an artist-goldsmith of Ptolemaic Egypt.

76-77 bottom center and 77 bottom
The goldsmiths' skill could produce virtuoso refinement, as demonstrated by this gold choker with lanceolate leaves hanging in double rows from a very fine supporting mesh.

77 top right *Two golden rings with engraved gems (a technique greatly developed in Greek Hellenistic art), a bracelet in double gold mesh and lion-head clasp, and a choker with links and pendants—these are further instances of the variety of Hellenistic goldsmiths' art.*

Relatively small amounts of gold jewelry were produced in the Geometric period, but on the earrings, rings, and bracelets they made for their aristocratic clientele in 8th-century Athens, Eleusis, and Eretria, goldsmiths followed the prevailing trends for abstract designs and nonfigurative geometric motifs. This period saw the beginnings of gold-mesh and microgranular techniques, which came into vogue in the following century, when the Orientalizing style caught on. The Orientalizing style is known for its animal- and fantasy-based imagery, its elegant "baroque" gems, and its authentic masterpieces of jewelry design in enormous variety, evident in decorative applications for garments, household goods, and personal accessories.

A major role in these developments was played by the easternmost towns of

78 left *The splendor of the age of Alexander and the great inventiveness and sensibility of Macedonian artists are found in this large krater, with volutes in gold bronze, richly decorated in relief, and with figures in full relief. It was* discovered in a tomb near Salonika and dates from 330 BC. It belonged to an aristocrat, Astiounios, son of Anaxagoras of Larisa, as reads an inscription on the edge. The body depicts the wedding of Dionysus and Ariadne, with* *unrestrained dancing Maenads carried away in ecstasy and satyrs excited by the frenzied swaying of Dionysus' disciples. Everything in the vase seems made to astonish the guests at banquets where the krater undoubtedly served excellent wine—a gift within* *the gift, a hymn to the ephemeral pleasures of earthly life and to the primitive instincts that cause its miracle, as well as delight in the aristocratic world for which works such as this one were created.*

78 right and 79 left *These two fillets in embossed, chiseled, and filigree gold come from Thrace and date to the first half of the 3rd century BC. They represent two griffins, mythical animals appreciated by the "barbarians" and here employed to decorate the trappings of a horse—which certainly belonged to a Thracian prince.*

the Greek world, with their closer ties to the disseminating centers of Levant, and perhaps also due to the economic patronage of local aristocrats or tyrants. Various finds in Rhodes and the cemeteries of Crete, Milos, and Corinth have also yielded many significant items.

The affluence of the sanctuaries in the Archaic and Classical periods helps explain the quality and quantity of jewelry and artifacts unearthed at Delphi, Olympia, Metapontum, and Locri.

The ascendance of Greece over the other trading powers of the Mediterranean led to the production of precious ornamental objects on a large scale in widely scattered places, sometimes on the fringe of the Greek world, colonies included. Precious tablewares, decorative elements on household furnishings made of wood or bronze, jewelry that mirrored the current phase of Greek art—all point to the outstanding artistic skills of the craftsmen who made them.

But from the goldsmiths of the 4th century BC and the entire Hellenistic period came the most stunning of all creations, outstanding for the richness of their design, composition, and decorative quality. In these features Western Greek colonies—especially in present-day Apulia—followed the lead of towns in Macedonia and Thessaly. In the 5th century BC, in places as distant as Syracuse and Athens, renowned engravers like Evenetes were making minting dies for gold and silver coins—miniature, ultra–low relief sculptures that incorporated the genius of the most celebrated masterpieces of Greek plastic art.

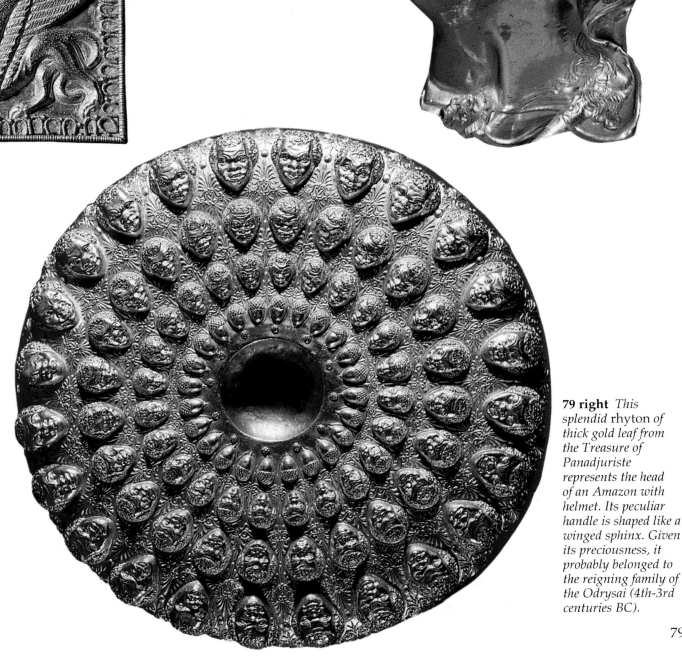

79 center *This phiale from the so-called Treasure of Panadjuriste (from Thrace, c. 310 BC) is a magnificent embossed, carved, and chiseled goblet for libations. It represents three concentric circles of African heads (delicately and realistically portrayed, despite their gradual reduction in size) and one of acorns, with vegetable motifs of lotus flowers in between—a motif that may be of Egyptian origin.*

79 right *This splendid rhyton of thick gold leaf from the Treasure of Panadjuriste represents the head of an Amazon with helmet. Its peculiar handle is shaped like a winged sphinx. Given its preciousness, it probably belonged to the reigning family of the Odrysai (4th-3rd centuries BC).*

CULTS AND RELIGIOUSNESS AMONG THE GREEKS

80 left A true masterpiece of the last stage of Peloponnesian Archaic art, this rare bronze original, the Apollo of Piraeus (500 BC), portrays the god in the act of receiving an offering.

80 top right A bronze statuette from the early 5th century BC provides a typical portrait of the father of the Olympian gods, Zeus, the powerful lord of lightning, the restless seducer of goddesses, nymphs, and—less often—mortals.

80 bottom right This beautiful statue of Athena Aphaea rose, in a divine epiphany, in the tumult of a battle between Greeks and Trojans on the western pediment of her temple in Aegina (510-500 BC).

81 This clay pinax from the early 5th century BC in Calabria preserves a scene of Dionysus offering ritual gifts (vine shoots, a kantharos, a cock) to the underworld couple, Kore and Hades.

The polytheism of Hellenic religion was shaped by a number of factors. The Olympian deities shared by all Greeks (and named after Mount Olympus, the "roof of Greece" where they were believed to live) were relatively few; they coexisted with numerous lesser gods, deified heroes, and demons of both sexes. Divine omnipotence was limited by Fate, and the gods bore a great resemblance to humans—a highly developed (and anthropocentric!) notion of superhumanity and an automatic limitation of mysticism. There was no organized clerical order, since priests and priestesses merely handled cult manifestations and did not form a class designated to impose an orthodoxy. Above all, the Greeks conceived of religiousness as respectful behavior toward the gods and toward the moral values of the community, not as a matter of personal conscience.

Their religion nonetheless had mystical elements of clear oriental derivation. There were also mystical "deviations" in the chthonian cults of Dionysus, Demeter, Kore-Persephone, and Hades; in the philosophies of Pythagoras and Plato and in the later cults—from the Hellenistic period until the days of the Roman Empire—of particular gods, such as Hermes Trismegistus, Isis, and Mithra, to name only the best known. The absence of sacred texts was compensated by the Greeks' immense mythological legacy, which writers, poets, and philosophers were able to draw on freely and interpret.

The deities were many. Foremost amongst them was Zeus—father and brother of all the gods, god of the sky and of light, ruler of the cosmos, and protector of all legally constituted power and right—and he was venerated by all Greeks. Hera, his hot-tempered sister and unhappy bride (marital fidelity was hardly a strong point of the lord of Olympus), superintended marriage and wedded life, maternity, and domestic affairs; she was worshipped particularly in Argos, Olympia, and Samos. Poseidon, daring and impetuous lord of the primordial forces of earth and water, instigator of tempests and earthquakes, was revered in the seaboard town of Isthmia, near Corinth. Athena, the warrior virgin, was protectress of the city that bore her name; she presided over craft activities and encouraged civilized behavior among men, guaranteeing law and order against barbarism; her cult was devoutly observed in Aegina and Tegea as well as in Athens.

Apollo was a handsome yet ambiguous god, bringer of health and terrible epidemics, patron of music and letters; his wishes were made known through the enigmatic responses of oracles. He was worshipped mainly in Delphi and Delos, but imposing temples dedicated to his cult were also erected in Corinth, Phigalia, Thermos, and Didyma. His sister Artemis—the hunting goddess related to two eastern deities, the "Mistress of Animals" and Isis—protected nature in the wild and monitored the dividing line between the primordial human condition and civilized society; important sanctuaries were dedicated to her at Ephesus and Corcyra (present-day Corfu), among others.

The cult of Aphrodite, beautiful goddess of love in all its manifestations, originated from the Semitic goddess Astarte-Ishtar and was centered on Paphos, on the island of Cyprus, and Cythera. Many other divine figures were also important: Hermes, the messenger god, protected merchants, heralds, and thieves, guided souls on their way to the Underworld, guaranteed borders, and was a healer. Demeter, protectress of land and agriculture, was the object of the Eleusinian mysteries; the chthonian goddess Kore-Persephone was her daughter, who married Hades.

Dionysus, god of wine and ecstasy, was the guardian of escape from the burden of everyday reality and of the acting out of life's dramas in theatrical tragedy and comedy. Hephaestus, smith of the gods, was the lame but dearly loved husband of the beautiful Aphrodite. Ares was the mysterious and divine protector of the warrior spirit. Heracles, a semidivine man, rose to immortality after performing a series of labors. Asclepius, god of medicine, was particularly venerated at Kos, Pergamum, and Epidaurus.

THE GREEK TEMPLE AND ARCHITECTURAL ORDERS

An important difference exists between the Greek temple and the Greek sanctuary. A sanctuary was built in a place that was "appropriated" by a deity after a manifestation or apparition; a temple was erected after a human being decided to consecrate the site to a god (who thus became its "owner") and construct a place of worship within the sacred precinct *(temenos).*

The earliest temples—from the 10th to 8th centuries BC—were often simple huts, but before long they were replaced by much larger and finer buildings. This evolution was made possible by gradual changes in construction techniques and materials: stone took the place of wood and unbaked brick, so that structures became more stable and longer lasting. The suggestion that this change was prompted by cultural contact with the Egyptian and Near-Eastern world is in effect unfounded since there is plentiful monumental architecture at Helladic, Minoan, and Mycenaean sites.

The first phase in the evolution of the Greek temple took place in the 8th and 7th centuries BC, as attested by excavations at Thermos, Isthmia, and Olympia, and by clay models from Argos and Perahora. The first temples were built with a stone foundation, a timber frame in post and lintel construction, and walls of plastered unbaked brick.

The roof and facings—the latter designed to protect the wooden upperworks—were of brightly painted clay, sometimes adorned with ornamental figures in relief. Great attention was paid to embellishing these and other prominent structures, such as the columns of the peristyle or inner court. The peristyle columns, which surrounded the building on at least three sides and helped support the roof, were probably finished with decorative fluting even during this earliest phase. The influence of these aesthetic canons is still seen in the stone temples of later centuries: the traditionalism implicit in

religious rituals was also maintained by architects and artists, as is evident from the early coding of the orders of classical architecture.

Another striking feature of the Greek temple was its functions, which were not limited to those of more familiar places for worship. The innermost room, cella or *naos,* contained the cult statue of the deity and was used by

priests for worship; sometimes there was an adjoining *adyton,* inaccessible to laypeople, in which an ancient cult image was venerated and the god—if he so wished—made his will manifest. Very frequently the temple building included a *pronaos,* a portico giving access to the cella, and an *opisthodomos* or rear chamber, symmetrical to the pronaos, whose functions are still not entirely clear. Perhaps as a tribute to the prehistoric tradition of performing cult rituals in the open air, the altar stood in

82-83 *In this ideal reconstruction of a typical Greek temple constructed from rows of columns of the Doric order, all the basic architectural components are visible, as are the decorative qualities often lost, such as polychromy. The inner rooms—the naos, pronaos opisthodomos, and* adyton—*are small and cramped, since the rituals were mainly practiced on a large altar situated in front of the building.*

the open, generally in front of the temple, at the foot of the stylobate, or foundation.

The orientation of Greek temples is always east-west, a clear reference to the course of the sun. Between the 6th and 2nd centuries BC, Greek architects experimented with many different kinds of structures. Some suggest that the most important intention was to

83 *In a rare artistic document of the 6th century BC, a sacrifice is depicted on a painted wooden tablet. It was miraculously found in good condition in a cave near Sicyon, in Corinth.*

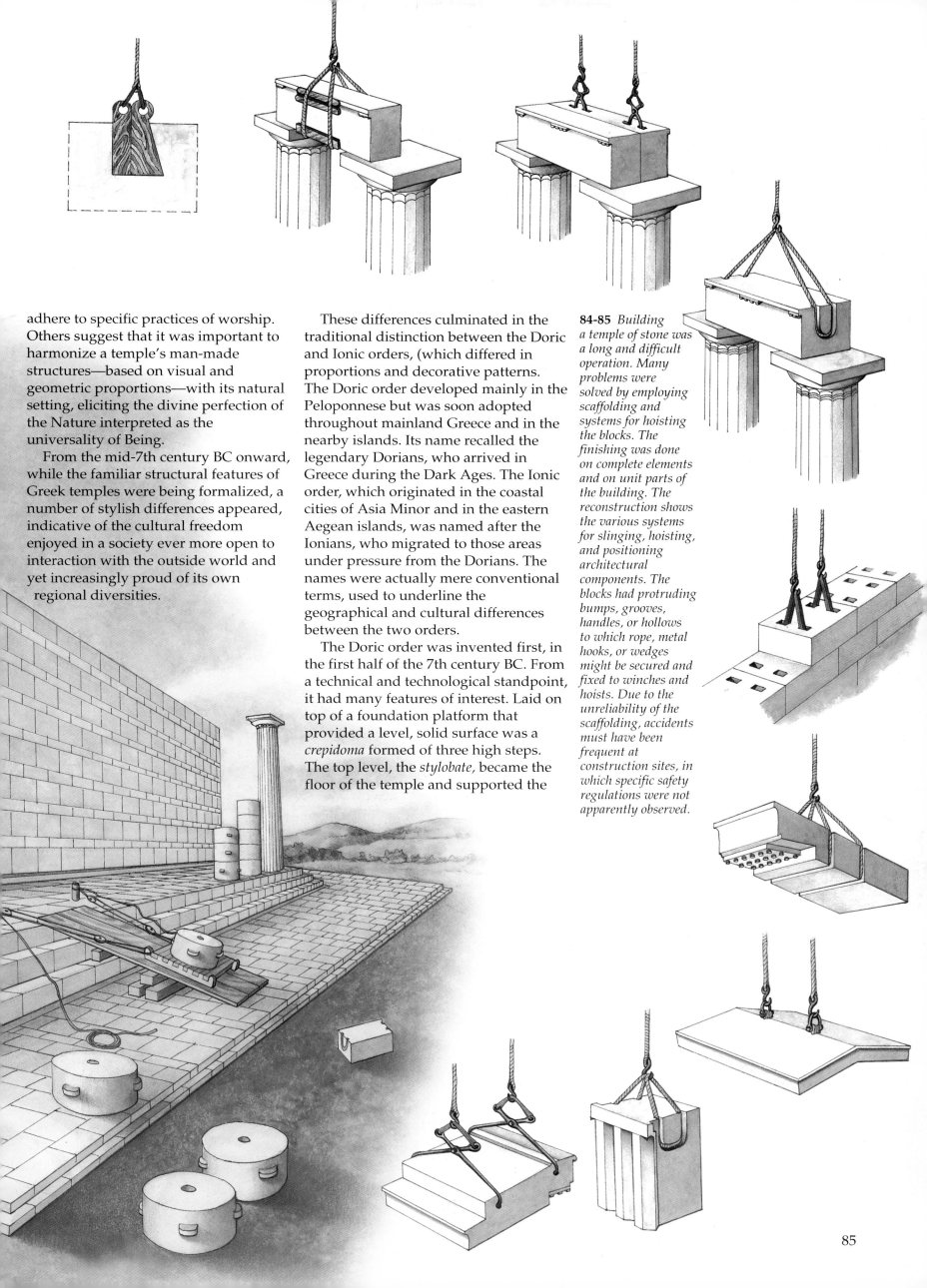

adhere to specific practices of worship. Others suggest that it was important to harmonize a temple's man-made structures—based on visual and geometric proportions—with its natural setting, eliciting the divine perfection of the Nature interpreted as the universality of Being.

From the mid-7th century BC onward, while the familiar structural features of Greek temples were being formalized, a number of stylish differences appeared, indicative of the cultural freedom enjoyed in a society ever more open to interaction with the outside world and yet increasingly proud of its own regional diversities.

These differences culminated in the traditional distinction between the Doric and Ionic orders, (which differed in proportions and decorative patterns. The Doric order developed mainly in the Peloponnese but was soon adopted throughout mainland Greece and in the nearby islands. Its name recalled the legendary Dorians, who arrived in Greece during the Dark Ages. The Ionic order, which originated in the coastal cities of Asia Minor and in the eastern Aegean islands, was named after the Ionians, who migrated to those areas under pressure from the Dorians. The names were actually mere conventional terms, used to underline the geographical and cultural differences between the two orders.

The Doric order was invented first, in the first half of the 7th century BC. From a technical and technological standpoint, it had many features of interest. Laid on top of a foundation platform that provided a level, solid surface was a *crepidoma* formed of three high steps. The top level, the *stylobate*, became the floor of the temple and supported the

84-85 *Building a temple of stone was a long and difficult operation. Many problems were solved by employing scaffolding and systems for hoisting the blocks. The finishing was done on complete elements and on unit parts of the building. The reconstruction shows the various systems for slinging, hoisting, and positioning architectural components. The blocks had protruding bumps, grooves, handles, or hollows to which rope, metal hooks, or wedges might be secured and fixed to winches and hoists. Due to the unreliability of the scaffolding, accidents must have been frequent at construction sites, in which specific safety regulations were not apparently observed.*

columns. The columns had no bases, possibly a remnant of earlier wooden temples, in which pillar supports had been set directly into the ground. The shaft of the column was fluted and robust. It bulged slightly near the middle, in an *entasis* designed to emphasize the strength of the supporting column but also to compensate for the impression of slenderness conveyed in an optical effect. The uppermost part of the column was the capital, which supported the *entablature,* or upperworks. The Doric capital consisted of an *echinus,* or curved molding, shaped like an upturned, truncated cone—initially rounded

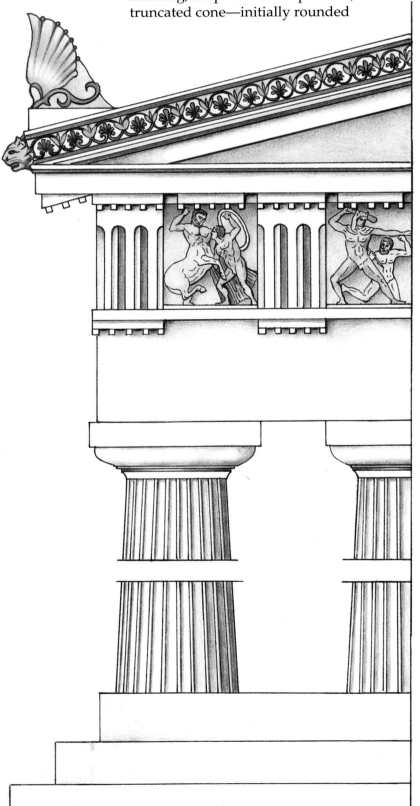

and flattened, but later increasingly streamlined—and an *abacus,* or top slab. The influence of wooden Archaic models is particularly evident in these elements.

Above the *architrave,* or lowermost part of the *entablature,* was a plain frieze decorated with alternating *metopes* and *triglyphs*—these too derived from earlier wood-carved ornamentation. On the short sides, two recessed triangular spaces were formed by the sloping roof. These spaces— called *pediments*—were filled with imposing reliefs and even sculptures. Lastly, decorative gutters and ornaments called *antefixes* were mounted along the eaves and cornices of the pediments, while small statues or *acroteria*—inspired by naturalist motifs or depicting gods or demons—had prominent places at the corners of the pediments.

Early in the 6th century BC the Ionic order of temple architecture was developed by architects from Greek colonies in the eastern Aegean and Asia Minor. The structures and building techniques evolved in much the same way as those of the Doric temple, although the changeover from wood and unbaked brick to stone was slower than in the Doric areas.

The characteristic features of the Ionic order are attributed, in part, to Asia Minor's close cultural contacts with the Near East and its architecture. The imposing forms of the Ionic order bore the stamp of the monumental building complexes of Mesopotamia and Persia. At the same time, the order's harmonious proportions and ornate ornamentation evoked the elegance typical of the palaces of great oriental kings. With the introduction of the *dipteral* plan—a double row of columns—the house of the deity seemed to be surrounded by an orderly and imposing "forest of stone." Such temples were reminiscent of the scenic effects of the vast *hypostyles*, or structures crowded with multiple rows of massive columns, in sanctuaries in Egypt and the Near East, which were designed to emphasize the huge distance between mortal and divine.

Two structural elements—column and frieze—distinguished the Ionic from the Doric order. The Ionic column did not rest directly on the stylobate. Rather, it had a molded "cushion" base that also accentuated the clean lines of the tall, fluted shaft, which had no entasis. At its top was a delicate capital, whose echinus was decorated by stylized rounded moldings set between two generously proportioned scroll-like volutes.

These features seem to have origins in the transition from wood to stone: the introduction of stone for the base of

the column made it possible to isolate the wooden shaft from the damp ground. Meanwhile, the capital appears to have originated from models skillfully carved from wood.

The Ionic frieze no longer comprised the alternating triglyphs and metopes of the Doric order. Instead it consisted of long, carved stone narrative panels, again following a taste more oriental than Greek.

Closely related to the Ionic capital was the so-called Aeolic capital, widely found in the areas where the Aeolic dialect was spoken (Boeotia, Thessaly, part of Asia Minor, and the islands of the northeastern Aegean). Its most prominent characteristic was the large stylized volutes that sprang from the shaft and had openwork carvings.

Since the time of Vitruvius' *De Architectura* (1st century AD), the Corinthian order has traditionally been included among the Greek architectural orders. Actually, this convention is chronologically and historically incorrect, since the Corinthian capital, reputedly invented by Callimachus in the last quarter of the 5th century BC, was rarely used in the Greek world and did not constitute a new architectural order. Before it became popular in Roman times, it was used sometimes as an alternative to the Ionic capital. Roman architects of Hellenistic culture subsequently developed a Corinthian "order" inspired by the Doric and Ionic orders, which by that time were less and less used. The structures and proportions they used had numerous variants and combinations that reveal the fundamental eclecticism of their artistic approach.

The Corinthian capital is characterized by a huge inverted bell—a *kalathos*—surrounded by backward-bent acanthus leaves. This miniature triumph of gently curving lines and surfaces offered skilled craftsmen an arena for creating chiaroscuro effects. The shaft of the column and its base followed the Ionic model, albeit with a number of variants.

86-87 *Shown here are the ideal reconstructions of the most famous Greek orders—Doric, Ionic, and Corinthian. The differences between the first two orders, which were more frequently used from the 7th to the 3rd century BC, are evident, both from a structural and from a decorative viewpoint. The grooves of the Doric order, for example, have a greater stiffness, while the light and shade shifts are more abrupt compared with the Ionic order, which is more decorative both in the capital and in the frieze. The Ionic frieze reflects the preference for broad narrative sequences and complex, refined compositions among Asia's Greeks. On the ends of the pediments are* acroteria, *or minor decorative elements, while along the eaves are gargoyles with lions' heads.*

GREEK THEATER

88 An Archaic relief from the Ionic school shows two dancers in action to the sound of a double flute. In Greek drama, tragedy as well as comedy, the actors' performances were accompanied by intermezzi sung and set to music, or danced and mimed. In the recent staging of ancient plays, sequences of dancing, singing, music, and miming are once again being used.

The origins of Western theater coincided with the birth of Greek civilization and, by the end of the 6th century BC, after a brief process of self-definition, it already existed in consummate form. Drama differed from all other forms of visual and performance art, since it was much more than mere description or narrative. It also transcended sterile, self-indulgent ceremonies and rituals intended as displays of personal attributes, statements of clan, caste, or religious identity, tributes to a deity, symbolism, exorcism, catharsis. In Greek theater dramatist and actor—respectively, through ideas and performance—escape from the subjective dimension to assume a new identity, destiny, and dimension.

For the audience, attending the theater is not merely an opportunity to observe. Nor is drama simply a portrayal of everyday life, current events, or myths and legends. It is action meant not to "entertain" spectators but to involve them on a level that is ethical, spiritual, political, psychological, and existential. Behind the metaphor of theatrical space, time, and action lies the real spectacle—be it tragic or comic—of the human condition and the questions it poses. In ancient Greece and particularly in democratic Athens, from Cleisthenes to Chaeronea, this was the real significance of the genres we call tragedy and comedy. These genres were not far removed from present-day theater: many of the finest Greek plays are still performed successfully.

We have no precise knowledge of how the two genres initially evolved. The few bits of information left by Herodotus, Aristotle, and others are contradictory. Only odd fragments of the work of the earliest tragic poets and comedic playwrights have survived. Yet they are examples of a clearly defined literary genre, with rigorously

established (and respected) conventions, internal structure, language, and meter. Only 33 tragedies and 18 comedies—not all of them complete—have been preserved in medieval codices and a few rare fragments of papyrus texts.

The illustrious tragic poets Aeschylus, Sophocles, and Euripides; the great comic playwrights Aristophanes and Menander; and Phrynichus and the anonymous author of *Reso,* as well as Eupolis and Cratinus, also deserve mention. Between the late 6th and the 4th centuries BC hundreds of competitions and performances of their plays took place before enthusiastic

audiences, not only in Athens but in the countless huge theaters that sprang up in cities and sanctuaries throughout the Greek world.

The theatrical performances staged in Athens were preeminent. They were mounted as part of festivals involving rituals and sporting contests, held periodically in honor of a particular deity, most often Athena and Dionysus. The festivals were organized by the state and funded by Athens' wealthier citizens. The Great Dionysia, celebrated in honor of Dionysus in the month of Elaphebolion (March/April), was undoubtedly the most important festival of all. It lasted six whole days, involved

89 *This peculiar comic mask of terracotta, dated to the 4th century BC and discovered in Taranto, documents the tradition of acting using masks, as if to emphasize the* *estrangement of man from himself in the moment of acting. It bears a peculiar similarity to comic types present on Apulian painted vases of the same period.*

the whole population (everyday activities came to a standstill), and attracted many foreigners to the city. Thousands of spectators gathered in the theater of Dionysus, on the southern slopes of the Acropolis.

The theatrical events took the form of competitions. Each year, after an initial selection procedure, three dramatists were chosen to take part. Each dramatist presented four works in the course of a day—a trilogy of tragedies and one satyr play. The satyr play, with its burlesque plot and characters and plentiful silliness and vulgarity, must have encouraged a liberating explosion of mirth and sensuality after hours of meditation and anguish during the performance of the tragedies. On the following days the works of comic playwrights occupied the stage. From morning until dusk the Athenians crowded the ampitheater, rowdily expressing their enthusiasm, displeasure, or boredom, vociferously arguing with their fellow spectators over the merits of the plays. And as the sun began to set, audience, chorus, and actors merged into one.

A panel of judges was formed, consisting of ten people picked at random, one from each of Athens' electoral constituencies. At the end of the performances, each judge would write down on a table the names of the three competing tragedies in order of their preference. Only five tablets out of the ten were picked and counted. Their votes decided the winner, who was duly acclaimed.

Ampitheaters were another invention of the Greeks. Even in the Minoan palace-settlements and in centers founded soon after the Helladic Dark Ages, public spaces were set aside for performances in the open air. From tiered seating—linear, or L- or U-shaped—spectators could not only watch performances of plays but participate in rituals that had religious connotations. Not until the 6th and 5th centuries BC did these most celebrated of Greek secular architectural structures acquire that conventional form (which probably developed from an earlier wooden version, converted into stone). The fundamental requisite was a bowl-shaped setting—enhanced from nature or created artificially—situated on high ground.

The theater was a meeting place for thousands of citizens, who gathered to watch plays created by the genius of the tragic and comic poets. It also offered a venue for leisure pursuits and for discussions and arguments on countless topics—politics, customs, fashion, behavior, historic events,

90 *This painted clay model represents the backdrop of a theater scene, from the 3rd century BC.*

myths, religion, and moral issues. The ampitheater thus became a characteristic feature of the Greek city, and by the 4th century BC its architectural form followed a precise code. Its structural components were the *orchestra,* a circular or semicircular space occupied by the chorus during the onstage action; the *skene,* the proper stage, with an architectural backdrop of three doors and spaces for the insertion of simulated panoramas and mobile sets, according to the demands of the script; and the tiered seating, or *koilon*—now better known by the Latin term *cavea*—more or less carved out of the side of a hill, semicircular in shape, with vertical tiers of steps intersected by stairways for access. The cavea was sometimes divided horizontally into two or three sectors, by corridors called *diazomata.*

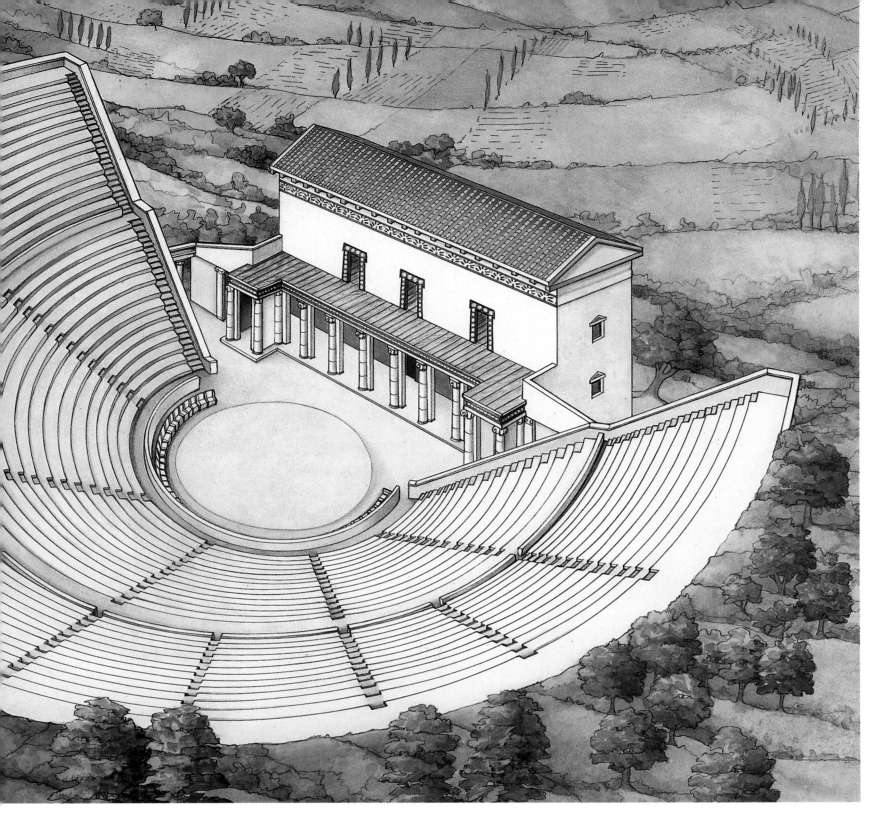

The first row of seats, right next to the orchestra, was called the *proedria*. It was reserved for priests and public magistrates, as attested by the inscriptions frequently found on it. The audience entered the amphitheater along two wide corridors, the *parodoi*, located between the cavea and the backdrop, at the sides of the orchestra.

One of the most amazing aspects of Greek amphitheaters is their perfect acoustics. Any sound can be carried from the stage to the very top row of the cavea without any variation in pitch, intensity, or length. This fact is further evidence that the ideal of *mimesis* (imitation) was innate in the Greek concept of theater. A fine amphitheater—perhaps the very finest—can be seen at Epidaurus in the Argolid, in the celebrated sanctuary of Asclepius, the god of healing. The

theater was already famous in ancient times for its imposing dimensions, harmonious proportions, and splendid acoustics. The ringing sound of a coin being dropped on the stone at the center of the orchestra can be heard perfectly at any point of the cavea, which extends far up the hillside and has seating space for no fewer than 15,000 spectators. This amphitheater was built around 350 BC by Polyclitus the Younger (the architect, so called to distinguish him from the celebrated sculptor of the same name). What strikes visitors most is the overall harmony of the theater's composition, conveying the impression of a design project that set out—for this was surely Polyclitus' intention—to bring together and fuse actors and audience, dramatists' texts and spectators' ideas, words, and thoughts.

90-91 This ideal reconstruction of a Greek amphitheater highlights a constant element of Greek theatrical architecture: the use of the surrounding panoramic landscape as a sort of huge extension of the stage set, a setting that could intimately blend the microcosm onstage with the external universe, leading spectators to enter a dimension outside daily life and totally immerse themselves in the space and time of the play's action.

SPORT

92 top *Three boys engaged in a running race decorate one side of a famous base belonging to the (now missing) funeral statue of a young Athenian man (510 BC).*

92 center *This* lekythos *with black figures, by the Painter of Edinburgh, dates to the late 6th century BC and shows young javelin throwers training in a gym.*

92 bottom *This Panathenaean amphora with black figures (dated to 525 BC) documents a sports competition generally within the reach of aristocrats only: the horse race with a quadriga, or chariot drawn by four horses.*

No people of antiquity attributed as much importance to sport as the Greeks. Gymnastics—physical exercise carried out by males only, completely naked—was an integral part of the education of every individual and one of the many distinguishing factors that the Greeks believed set them apart from barbarians. Every city invested substantial resources in the construction of a *gymnasion*, a complex very similar to a present-day college campus and including a *palaestra* for physical education. This structure normally consisted of a square court surrounded by porticos that offered welcome shade and cooling drafts, with service facilities, changing rooms, and fountains; around it were treelined avenues, frequently baths, and buildings used for educational activities.

Teaching was done on the personal initiative of elementary teachers, philosophers, and experts in various disciplines. (Pupils of the practical arts, including the fine arts, obtained hands-on experience in workshops.) Sport necessarily meant competitive sport and was part of young men's education—perhaps a remnant of age-old initiation rites designed to instill courage, virtue, and fighting skills— as well as a cultic offering. It had been the custom, among the aristocratic elites of the Mycenaean and Homeric

world, to hold sporting contests in honor of the dead.

A systematic link was thus established, very early in Greek history, between religious festivals and competitive sporting events, held in the great sanctuaries both outside and within the principal poleis.

Literature offers references to some of the great sporting events of the ancient Greek world: the celebrated Olympiads, introduced, according to myth, by Heracles in 776 BC; the Pythian games, held in Delphi in honor of Apollo; the Nemean games, celebrated at Nemea in honor of Zeus and to recall one of Heracles' labors;

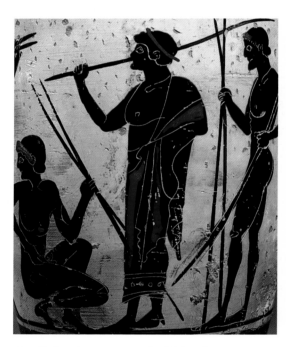

the Isthmian games, held in the sanctuary of Poseidon on the Corinthian isthmus; and the Panathenaean games, part of the great festivities organized in Athens to honor Athena. Any departure from fair play was severely punished, and the only prize besides the purely symbolic laurel wreath was the glory in which the winner basked and that reflected on his people and native city-state, thus honored in the eyes of all Greece.

The most important athletic disciplines were running, with races

92-93 and 93 top
The same funeral base with the three young men engaged in running also shows these peculiar scenes of an ancestor of hockey (top) and an intense scene of *wrestling (bottom), with the athletes' bodies in tension, in a position of engagement that emphasizes the powerful muscles, portrayed according to Attic conventions.*

over various distances and even in armour (*hoplitodromeia*), discus and javelin throwing, long jump, boxing, wrestling, and *pancration* (a contest involving both boxing and wrestling). Strictly for the well-to-do were disciplines involving horses, like chariot racing.

Musical, vocal, and poetry contests were commonly associated with athletic events, further evidence of the Greek ideal of unity in the education of young men.

Before a day of training under the watch of his coach or taking part in a contest, the athlete performed a preparatory ritual that consisted of covering his completely naked body with perfumed oil from a leather *aryballos*, or flask. Later, when his strenuous physical exertions were over, before taking a relaxing bath, he scraped his skin clean of dust, oil, and sweat with a *strigil*, a curved instrument designed specifically for this purpose.

The popularity of sport among the Greeks is amply attested by finds of athletes' equipment (strigils, *halteres*—weights used to aid jumping—bronze liners of aryballoi, javelins, and the like). It is also attested by the frequent choice of sporting events as a figurative theme on Attic vases of the 6th and 5th centuries BC. In many cases these vases were tributes to the young people of a city, to the military valor exalted by the practice of sport, and perhaps—in vases found among grave goods—to the premature death of a young man, a metaphor of life as a contest fought against death.

94 top *This fine bronze helmet of Corinthian type was found in Apulia. It is equipped with jaw and nose guards, is quite elongated, and is embellished with relief decorations on the front.*

94 center *This front leaf, anatomically molded by embossing by a skillful craftsman of Magna Graecia, comes from a bronze cuirass of the late 4th century BC.*

94 bottom *The Cavalryman of Grumentum (in southern Italy), a bronze of 550 BC, shows a warrior in fighting trim, protected by a helmet, jacket, and cuirass.*

Countless ancient literary sources referring to the "art" of warfare, as well as archaeological finds, give a clear idea of developments in ancient Greece as some of the most inhumane activity perpetrated by humankind—from the heroic deeds of Mycenaean warriors immortalized in the poems of Homer to the great military exploits of Alexander the Great and Demetrius Poliorcetes.

The clothing and armor worn by Greek foot soldiers or hoplites varied enormously, but it was always essentially practical. Helmets were generally made of bronze, lined with leather, and sometimes padded. Wherever they were made (Corinth, Illyria, Macedonia, Thrace), the objective was to afford the maximum protection against small missiles thrown into advancing rows of hoplites, as well as against blows received in man-to-man fighting. Protection for the face, nose pieces, and thick, sometimes decorated coverings were wrapped around the head and tied with laces wound through one or more holes, so as to leave only the eyes, tip of the nose, and mouth exposed.

The same features applied to corselets and breastplates, which were generally made of thick, fabric-lined leather reinforced—in less sophisticated versions—with metal strips; better-quality ones were entirely covered with shaped metal. Completing the infantryman's outfit were arm guards and greaves, as well as the ever-present shield. The cavalry, made up entirely of aristocrats and the well-to-do, paid for their advantage of greater speed and mobility with less

95 *Also coming from Apulia, this frontal (right) and breastplate (bottom left) are the trappings for a horse. Like the Corinthian helmet, they may be dated to the early 5th century BC.*

effective protection of both horse and rider.

Weapons were of many types: the most lethal were long spears designed for thrusting rather than throwing and capable of inflicting deep wounds, and even worse lacerations when they were pulled out. Also commonly used were light throwing spears, arrows with tremendous impact force, smaller missiles like lead pellets, and stones thrown with simple catapults. Weapons with sharp cutting blades, like swords, were used as well: although the wounds they caused were not always fatal, they often led to

death in any case from tetanus or blood poisoning.

Military tactics centered on the use of massed formations, of which the celebrated Macedonian phalanx was the most intelligent and flexible version prior to the advent of the Roman legions. Fighting techniques changed over the centuries and according to whether fighting was on land, aboard ship, or in a siege. For sieges, war machines were used, or defensive systems like the ones made famous in the Hellenistic period, ranging from mobile towers to catapults and burning glass.

96 top *A detail from the base of a* kouros *of 500-490 BC shows this image of a marching hoplite. The Corinthian panache helmet raised on the head, the lance, the shield, the cuirass and the shin guards are all portrayed according to the literary epic tradition.*

96 center *This fairly intact plate from the Ionic frieze of the Monument of the Nereids at Xanthos, in Lycia, dated to the early 4th century BC, shows the dramatic scene of a fight between hoplites in front of the walls of a city, with battlements with semicircular merlons.*

96 bottom *A duel between fully armed hoplites is the main scene of this* skyphos *or goblet with black figures of the Chalcidian type, dated to the mid-6th century BC.*

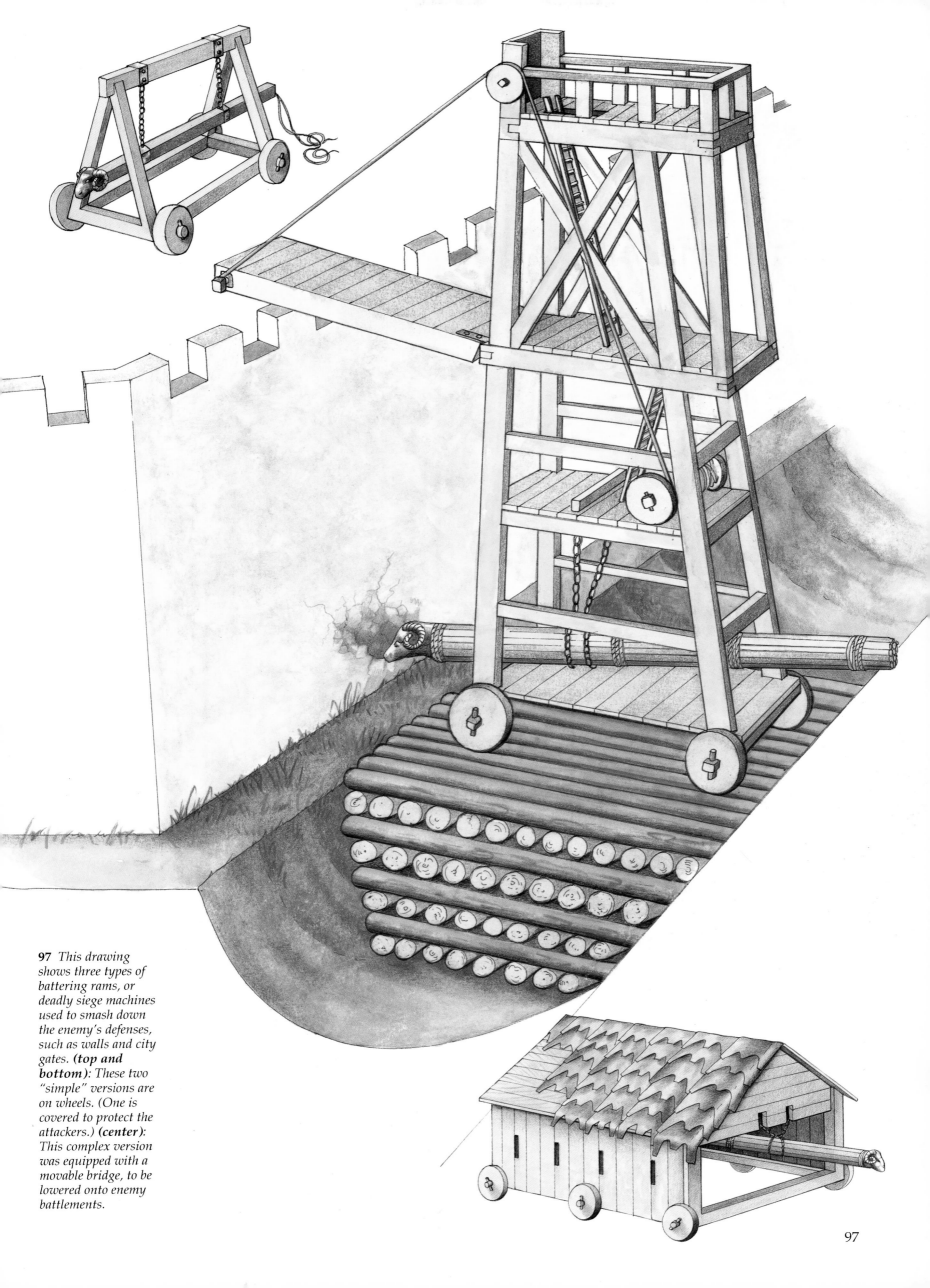

97 This drawing shows three types of battering rams, or deadly siege machines used to smash down the enemy's defenses, such as walls and city gates. **(top and bottom)**: These two "simple" versions are on wheels. (One is covered to protect the attackers.) **(center)**: This complex version was equipped with a movable bridge, to be lowered onto enemy battlements.

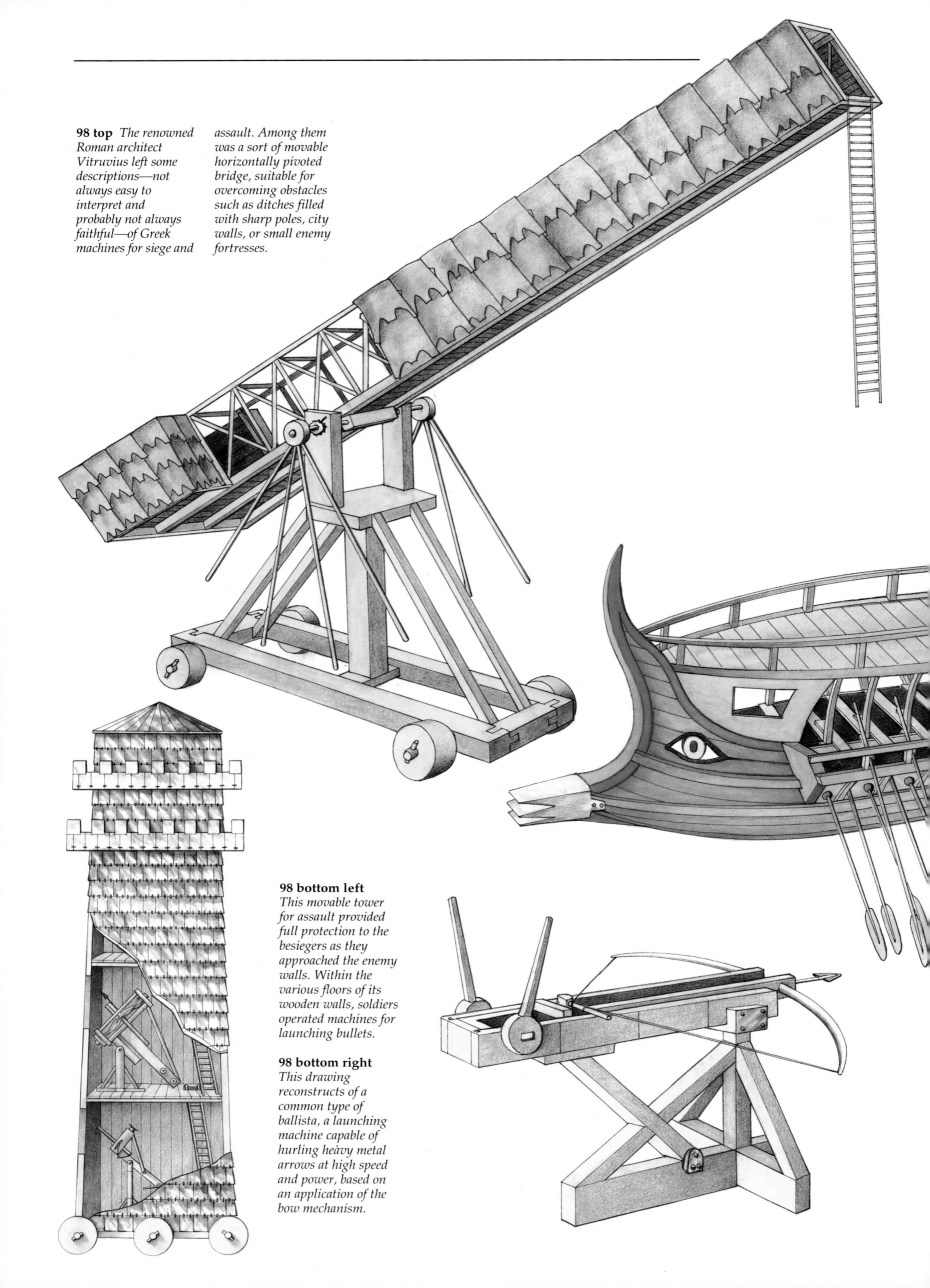

98 top *The renowned Roman architect Vitruvius left some descriptions—not always easy to interpret and probably not always faithful—of Greek machines for siege and assault. Among them was a sort of movable horizontally pivoted bridge, suitable for overcoming obstacles such as ditches filled with sharp poles, city walls, or small enemy fortresses.*

98 bottom left *This movable tower for assault provided full protection to the besiegers as they approached the enemy walls. Within the various floors of its wooden walls, soldiers operated machines for launching bullets.*

98 bottom right *This drawing reconstructs of a common type of ballista, a launching machine capable of hurling heavy metal arrows at high speed and power, based on an application of the bow mechanism.*

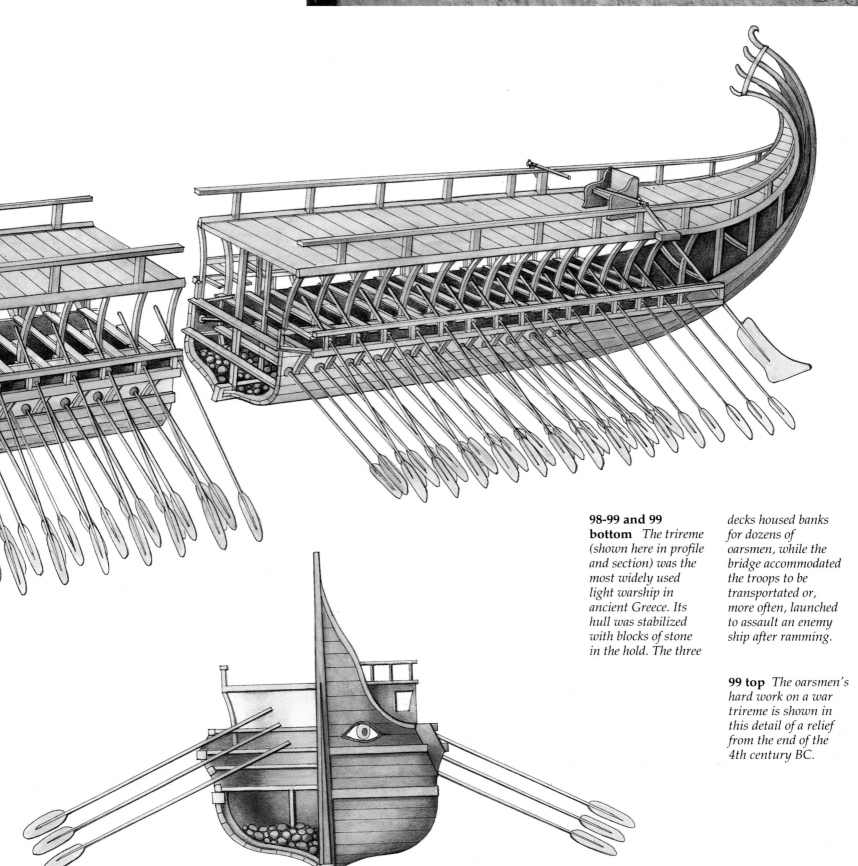

98-99 and 99 bottom *The trireme (shown here in profile and section) was the most widely used light warship in ancient Greece. Its hull was stabilized with blocks of stone in the hold. The three decks housed banks for dozens of oarsmen, while the bridge accommodated the troops to be transportated or, more often, launched to assault an enemy ship after ramming.*

99 top *The oarsmen's hard work on a war trireme is shown in this detail of a relief from the end of the 4th century BC.*

GREEK ART THROUGH THE CENTURIES

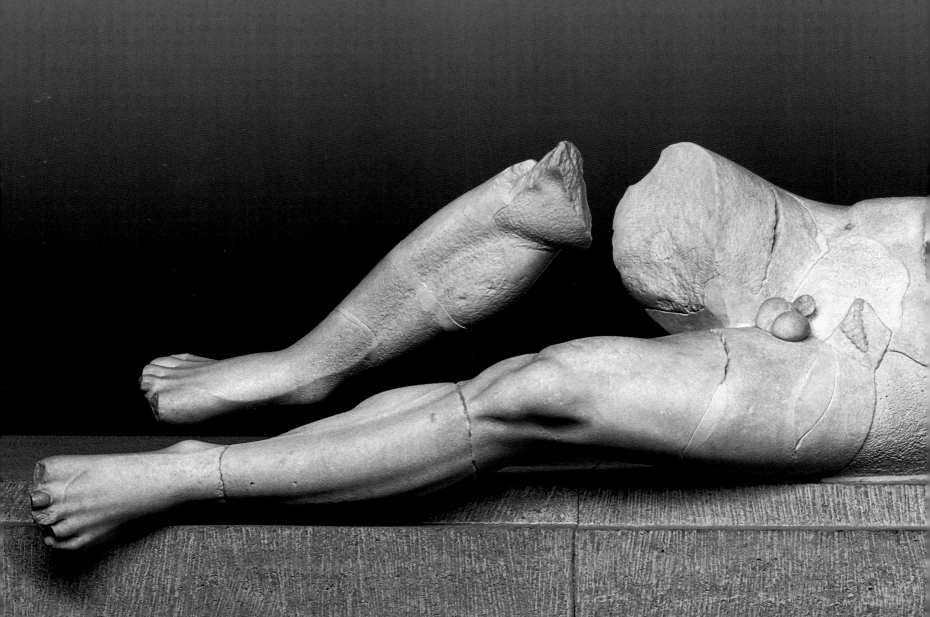

100-101 *This beautiful image comes from the western pediment of the temple of Athena Aphaia in Aegina. The statue of a dying warrior marks the end of Archaic conventions in Greek sculpture at the beginning of the 5th century BC.*

IN PURSUIT OF PERFECTION

Greek art, in the strictest sense of the term, dates from the 10th to the 1st century BC. Its course was characterized by great unity, range, and depth, and like the rest of Greek culture, it had a determining influence on the entire development of Western civilization. Its beginnings coincided with the economic, demographic, and cultural recovery that started around 1000 BC, at the end of the Helladic Dark Ages, when invasions by the Sea Peoples and the migration of the Dorians—the last Greeks of Indo-European origin—had destroyed the Mycenaean kingdoms and interrupted Mediterranean trade. From the Aegean to the shores of Asia Minor, these migrations triggered the vast diaspora of Ionians and Aeolians, peoples who were also Hellenes, as proved by their close linguistic affinities with *koine dialektos,* the language spoken by all Greeks.

As early as the 9th and 8th centuries BC, a truly innovative concept of art was advancing, within an emerging and multiform culture. Of seminal importance were the search to understand the essence of the universe and the harmoniously perfect, mathematical laws by which it is governed; the desire to represent not only the exterior form of reality but also its intricate web of underlying philosophical, ethical, and political values, without letting spirituality slip into mysticism (which was nonetheless present in certain aspects of Greek religion); the exaltation of *logos,* reason, as the ultimate dimension of the human mind, serving to mediate man's relationship with the Absolute through knowledge and love of reason— *philosophia*—and reaching beyond the limits of time and space imposed on the human condition, and beyond appearances; elaboration of an artistic language perfectly synthesized with content, since language expresses the interior rather than the exterior reality of things.

This process of exploration and discovery reached its climax in the 5th century BC, the most splendid cultural and political period in the history of Greece, as was later acknowledged by the Romans, introducing the term classical to refer to it. The art of this period—further enriched by the innovative ideologies, subject matter, and styles of the 4th to 1st centuries BC—has had an immense impact on the art of the Western world, right up to the second half of the 19th century. It has been a constant point of reference, at times inspiring imitations, revisitations, and revivals, at others total rejection of "Classical" tenets.

We too will now journey along this amazing path, but not without first considering the remarkable foundations laid in the third and second millennia BC in the Cyclades, Crete, and Mycenae, civilizations whose artistic development already differed from the dominating art forms of Egypt, Mesopotamia, and Asia Minor.

102 and 103 A masterpiece of mature classical art, the so-called Aphrodite Kaufmann is a wonderful head of the goddess of love and beauty. It emphasizes the many-sided and at the same time typical character of the artistic language that reached its highest level with the greatest artists of the 4th century BC. This work, attributed to young Praxiteles or his followers, is one of the best expressions of the quest for beauty in Greek sculpture.

THE ART OF ANCIENT GREECE
THROUGH THE AGES

Prehistory and Protohistory
(c. 45,000-1220 BC)

The Neolithic age comes early to this region (seventh millennium BC) and results in advanced settlements, like the proto-urban structures of Sesklo and Dhimini (in Thessaly). Following the diffusion of metallurgy in the fifth and fourth millennia BC, the first evidence of civilization among the Indo-European Hellenes is the Aegean culture of the Cycladic islands (third millennium BC): its art, characterized by linear elegance and harmonious geometric forms, is exemplified by numerous statues and statuettes in local marble (so-called "idols"). The highly sophisticated Minoan civilization blossoms on the island of Crete: many imposing palace-settlements are built, and a palatial brand of figurative art takes root, marked by linearity, color, and vitality of expression. The almost contemporary rise of the Mycenaeans in the Peloponnese and Aegean brings a new culture to the fore: pomp and splendor pervade its art, conceived as a celebration of its warrior aristocracy; its boldest innovations are seen in gold jewelry, pottery, and architecture (palace-settlements and *tholos* tombs, in megalithic technique).

Cycladic art
(c. 2800-2000 BC)

Minoan art
(c. 2100-1450 BC)

Mycenaean art
(c. 1700-1220 BC)

The Helladic Dark Ages
(c. 1220-900 BC)

The demise of the Mycenaean culture is followed by a troubled period in the Mediterranean, with further Indo-European (Dorian) invasions and consequent turmoil on the Greek mainland. Scattered surviving communities produce exceedingly simple forms of figurative and decorative art in late Mycenaean style; their settlements are mere shadows of the earlier palaces (Dreros, Karphi, Kavousi). A slow economic and demographic recovery in the 10th century BC brings new forms of art, reflecting man's new attitude toward the complex but orderly pattern of the universe: this art is rigorously abstract and geometric, as attested by ceramic products from all parts of Greece, with Athens in the lead. Agglomerations of settlements create urban centers, where burgeoning trade stimulates new forms of artistic language.

Sub-Mycenaean art
(c. 1220-1000 BC)

Proto-Geometric period
(c. 1000-900 BC)

The Geometric Period
(c. 900-700 BC)

Throughout Greece and particularly in Athens, the revolutionary geometric approach to artistic expression evolves in increasingly sophisticated forms, with infinitely varied decorative motifs and the eventual reintroduction of occasional figurative scenes, still essentially angular in style. The cohesive focus of 7th-century Attic vase-painters, masters of ornamental balance, is replaced by the more widespread presence of figurative themes, inspired by the epic culture of art's patrons, the ruling aristocracies. In architecture new configurations of temples and houses are seen, these too marked by geometric rigor and rationalism. Sculpture reappears, in wood, ivory, or small bronzes, again with a strong Geometric influence.

Early Geometric period
(c. 900-850 BC)

Middle Geometric period
(c. 850-750 BC)

Late Geometric period
(c. 750-700 BC)

The Orientalizing Period
(c. 700-610 BC)

With colonization now in full swing and close, enriching commercial and cultural contacts established with the Mediterranean, Anatolian, and Mesopotamian East, the abstract Geometric style declines and the figurative naturalism of oriental art comes to the fore.
Before long Greek artists abandon its age-old conventions and elaborate it into their own style, as attested by beautiful pottery (Corinth, Cyclades, Ionia, Dodecanese), the first monumental stone sculpture, and elegant gold jewelry. A certain oriental influence is seen in architecture too, most evident in the preference for imposing constructions and chiaroscuro effects, overabundant ornamentation, and the self-eulogizing largesse of patrons, the ruling tyrants and aristocrats. In *Magna Graecia* innovative urban planning schemes are introduced.

Early Orientalizing style
(c. 700-675 BC)

Middle Orientalizing style
(c. 675-640 BC)

Late Orientalizing style
(c. 640-610 BC)

The Archaic Period

(c. 610-490 BC)

The progressive abandonment of the figurative repertoire and Orientalizing style signals the total autonomy of Greek art and its first steps toward Mediterranean hegemony. Architecture codifies the orders and the form of the temple, moving toward much more frequent and imposing use of stone. Corinth and Athens inundate markets with figured ceramic products, decorated with theological, mythological, and epic scenes (often with topical references); Athens dominates the scene until the end of the 5th century BC. Throughout Greece—but especially in Athens, the islands, and Ionia—life-size or larger stone statuary makes its mark, ushering in a truly distinctive style. Already implicit in this new idiom is an awareness of art's communicative, propagandistic, and celebratory functions. A major goal is the cohesive and unitary representation of the human figure.

Early Archaic period
(c. 610-570 BC)

Middle Archaic period
(c. 570-530 BC)

Late Archaic period
(c. 530-510 BC)

Final Archaic period
(c. 510-490 BC)

The Classical Period

(c. 490-323 BC)

After a rejection of Archaic conventions and a transitional phase characterized by stylistic calm and balance, Greek art sets out to represent the dynamism of the human body in space. Its idealized beauty and interior emotions are interpreted as positive or negative manifestations of man's varyingly cohesive and unitary dialectical relationship with deities, laws, and community and with the ethical values championed by Athenian democracy. Sculpture and vase painting offer emblematic examples. Architecture attains maturity, with exceptionally harmonious forms and structures; the apex of decorative elegance and grandeur is reached, as testified by increasingly ornate and complex pedimental compositions. Philosophy is the source of the theoretical and practical vision applied by Polyclitus, Phidias, Ictinus, and Callicrates, as well as many famous painters of the period. Their teachings also influence 4th-century architectural and artistic developments, characterized by an emphasis on emotions and a relativism, which convey the crisis experienced by the Athenians between the Peloponnesian War and the death of Alexander the Great.

Severe style
(c. 490-450 BC)

High Classical period
(c. 450-400 BC)

Late Classical period
(c. 400-323 BC)

The Hellenistic Period

(323-31 BC)

The immense empire of Alexander the Great is split up into kingdoms, leagues, and minor states, but the diffusion of Greek artistic culture— even outside the Hellenic world— inspires artistic styles and trends of the very highest level. No longer dominated by Attica, the art would becomes polycentric, and the cities of Pella, Rhodes, Alexandria, Pergamum, Athens, Tarentum, and Syracuse are its new capitals. Once again under the patronage of kings and aristocrats, art and architecture are geared to emotion and narrative (acclamatory or low-key), with a magnificence designed to add prestige to power. Greece and Greek art maintain their hold even after conquest by Rome (146 BC). The language of Hellenism survives until Augustus comes to power and contributes significantly to Roman art too.

Early Hellenism
(c. 323-220 BC)

Middle Hellenism
(c. 220-100 BC)

Late Hellenism
(100-31 BC)

106 *Cycladic marble idols take different forms, evolving from a primitive violin shape, sometimes with indications of sexual characteristics (bottom left), to schematically anthropomorphized types. They are generally erect figures in extremely stiff postures, which allows for compact representation of the trunk and the limbs. (The upper limbs are sometimes folded onto the breast.)*

ART IN THE THIRD AND SECOND MILLENNIA BC: CYCLADIC, MINOAN, AND MYCENAEAN

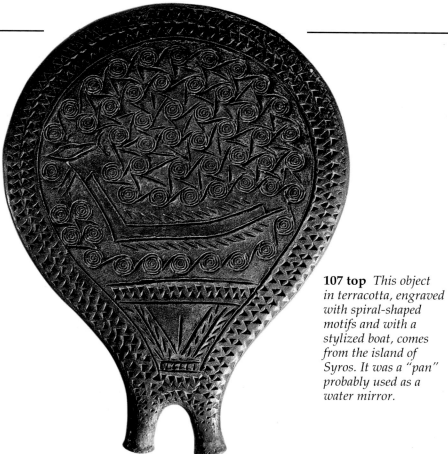

107 top *This object in terracotta, engraved with spiral-shaped motifs and with a stylized boat, comes from the island of Syros. It was a "pan" probably used as a water mirror.*

107 right *This Cycladic statuette representing a poet intent on playing the lyre comes from the beautiful island of Syros. In the heart of the Aegean sea. Syros was a very busy commercial place between the third and the second millennium BC.*

107 left *A painted ceramic support for a lamp shows the close relations between the island of Milos, where this was found at the important site of Philakopì, and Crete during the second millennium BC. Interesting is its decoration, with a few stylized figures of walking fishermen carrying fish.*

The earliest artistic representations created by Indo-European Greeks date back to the middle Bronze age (2800-2200 BC). The area of greatest interest is the archipelago of the Cyclades, where the first buildings made of stone and unbaked brick were erected in flourishing villages on Syros, Keros, Amorgos, Naxos, Milos, and tens of other islands dotting the Aegean. These buildings can be considered archetypal of Cycladic architecture, characteristically based on cubic and rectangular structures with the intricately worked fabric that present-day tourists find so fascinating.

It was in these villages that the typical Cycladic pottery was produced—burnished clay wares with close-set nonfigurative patterns in relief—as well as splendid statuary in local marble, together considered the finest and most significant examples of the artistic skills of the Aegean peoples. The human figure was schematized with a rigorous sense of form and proportion: male and female deities (a fairly frequent subject is a goddess interpreted as Great Mother) are portrayed erect, with a slight hollow to distinguish the legs, a profile reduced to the essentials, a smooth head and shoulders, the breasts and nose hardly noticeable. This extreme simplification—a far cry from banal naturalistic representations—points to a remarkable ability to capture the essence of reality and remain detached from its changing surface forms.

The celebrated Flute Player and Lyre player statuettes reveal an amazing capacity to express the complexity of the human figure in action in space, achieved through the pure geometry of harmoniously intersecting lines. But their significance goes far deeper, as an unconventionally naturalistic portrayal of an aristocratic world where banquets were accompanied by the moving notes of the flute or by bards reciting poetry set to music.

By around 2200 BC, the focal point of trade had shifted to the southern Aegean. Crete had established its great maritime hegemony, thanks to the island's exceptional resources, the business acumen of its merchants, and its position as a geographical bridge between Egypt, Asia Minor and Greece. Before long Crete was also preeminent in the Mediterranean as a center of artistic development. By 2100 BC the network of Minoan emporia extended as far as Samothrace, in the northeastern Aegean. On Crete itself, in the space of two centuries, the island's "princes" turned prehistoric village settlements into palaces; an architectural/urban model previously unseen in the Western world and, in terms of luxury and splendor, worthy of the monarchies of Egypt and the Near East. The surviving structures of the great palaces of Knossos, Festos, and Zakros and the villa of Hagia Triada—the latter was mostly rebuilt in the 17th century BC—point to outstanding skills in design and organization. Colossal complexes of more than thousand rooms, often built two or three stories high, their amenities included staircases, corridors, porticoes, and ramps suitable for vehicles, arranged around a huge rectangular central court. Among their most significant features are the absence of fortifications, the combined use of wood and stone for load-bearing structures, the logical distribution of facilities among the various wings of the palace in spite of apparent chaos, and an overabundance of rooms. The rational approach to planning is seen in the positioning of storerooms and in the grouping of the workshops used by craftsmen in service of the *minos*.

Particularly striking is the elegance of the architectural and pictorial ornamentation in the living quarters, throne rooms, reception rooms, and porticoes. Here a sense of color attests to the pleasure-loving lifestyle of the Cretans, who had no time for mysticism. During excavations in Knossos over a period of thirty years (1903-31), under the supervision of Arthur J. Evans, the palace-settlement underwent a disastrous "restoration." The result may be to the liking of tourists in search of the picturesque, but absurd and anachronistic concessions to undiscerning "lovers of ruins" have turned several pieces of the complex—uncritically reconstructed in painted reinforced concrete—into backdrops for picture postcards. Nevertheless, thanks to comparisons with the palace-settlement of Festos, which was excavated with far different scientific criteria and with far more respect by the Italian School of Archaeology in Athens, it has been possible to determine the fundamental scheme and the technical solutions used by the Cretan architects.

Naturalism was undoubtedly the unifying element of Cretan artistic representation. Color in painting and delicacy of pattern and line in metalworking and jewelry heightened the descriptive and narrative expressions of the artist's almost palpable delight in the world around him, in everyday life and in the wonderful variety of nature.

The frescoes that decorate the palace of Knossos and, to a lesser degree, other royal residences are artworks of exceptional beauty. Shattered into minute fragments by earthquakes and devastation in the second half of the second millennium BC, they have in many cases now been reconstructed and give a fairly good idea of the Minoan approach to painting. Outstanding works like the Prince of Lilies, Blue Ladies, Bull Race, the Parisienne, Dolphin Frieze, and the splendid

108 *Elegant and solemn, the Prince of Lilies is one of the most famous figures from the large painted friezes that decorated the rooms and porticoes at Knossos. The fresco emphasizes the vivid naturalism of Minoan art between 1700 and 1400 BC, going beyond the formal and chromatic conventions of ancient Egyptian painting.*

109 *The excavations led by Greek archaeologist Spiros Marinatos on the site of Akrotiri, on the island of Thera (Santorini), brought to light the splendid frescoes that decorated the houses of the Minoan center there. They were destroyed by a violent volcanic eruption, probably in the 16th century BC. This large image, found in the House B, shows a scene of boxing between two boys. The artist tried to portray the action of the two young men naturalistically and realistically through the crossing of the blows. The boy on the right, off guard, has just landed a hook, but he has exposed himself to the jab of the rival, who tries a right straight.*

110 top *The famous sarcophagus of Hagia Triada is exceptionally well preserved and documents the chromatic vividness of Cretan painting. The side picture, among stylized floral friezes, shows a scene of preparation for a* *religious rite. It ends in a sacrifice, whose purpose may be related to the funeral context to which the object itself pertains. Note the typical Cretan costumes and the commonly used objects.*

sarcophagus at Hagia Triada, with its scenes of solemn processions, are examples of the Minoan artists' lead over their Egyptian counterparts. The Minoan lines do not confine the figures to flat two-dimensional forms but provide sufficient fluidity to make them dynamic; the gestures become more vibrant; the composition breaks away from excessively rigid conventions; and the colors have a luminousness unknown in the East.

A splendid collection of Cretan paintings may be found in the palace of Akrotiri, on the island of Thera (Santorini), also known as the Pompeii of the Aegean. Here naturalism reaches its height in dynamic scenes of ships and navigation, probably celebrating the trading supremacy of the Minoan mariners, while exotic touches—for example, in the Blue Monkeys fresco—alternate with references to sporting events (exemplifed by the "Boxers"), possibly forerunners of the sacred contests of the Homeric and classical age. Jewelry, metalwork, statuary, pottery—all express the vibrant naturalism that pervades Minoan art. The examples are many: a beautiful gold pendant from Mallia, on which two wasps cling to the corolla of a flower; an exquisite steatite and gold rhyton from the Little Palace at Knossos, used for holy libations; gold cups—found at Vapheio, in Mycenaean Laconia, but the work of Minoan artists—decorated with wonderful scenes of country life (harvest, bull hunting); the famous Snake Goddess in ivory and gold, prototype of Artemis *Potnia theron* of the Greeks, with her small, slender body and large breasts, an irrepressible symbol of fertility like the bull, sacred animal of the Cretans. Potters abandoned the nonfigurative motifs of the past to experiment with naturalistic imagery: the sea and marine creatures are very much in evidence, as are flowers, as attested by finds at Gournia and Kamares.

110-111 *This outstanding fresco from Knossos shows the* taurocatapsia, *the sort of bloodless "bullfight" reserved for young Cretan men, which cannot with certainty be related to an initiation, ritual celebration, or feast.*

The fresco goes beyond the spatial two-dimensionality that reached Cretan art through Egyptian art. The fact that the bull and the jugglers are not on the same level, and the way of outlining the bodies suggest an intention to show three-dimensional figures.

111 *This splendid fresco from Akrotiri comes from the West House (16th century BC). It represents a woman, perhaps a priestess, who is burning incense in a characteristic perfume-burner with a flared shape.*

112 bottom and 113
The outstanding tholos *tomb at Vapheio (in Laconia) most probably that of a Mycenaean "prince," is famous for the rich objects found therein, including these two beautiful cups of embossed gold (15th century BC). The first is a masterpiece by a Cretan goldsmith, working in the exquisite naturalistic style typical of Minoan art. It depicts the capture of a bull, who has been lured to a luxuriant olive grove and then is quickly fettered after a brief, deceptive idyll with a cow, used by hunters as a decoy.*

112 top *In this cup, a work of lesser artistic value but still as precious as the one shown below, the figures are the work of a Mycenaean goldsmith. The more vigorous and less refined style is well suited to the subject: one bull is running away, among palm trees and olive trees; another is struggling in a hunters' net; a third is launching in a mad charge.*

Mycenaean civilization became the center of artistic initiative after the 14th century BC (although a number of important examples of Mycenaean art date from the two centuries before). By then, the aristocracies of the Peloponnese and other areas had gained political, commercial, and economic control over the Aegean and were forcefully spreading their influence over the entire Mediterranean. Centers perched on natural heights since the 17th century BC evolved toward an urban model that had much in common with the palace-settlements of Crete; in many respects they resembled medieval walled towns, huddled around the castle of a feudal lord. The plentiful examples include Mycenae, Argos, Tiryns, and countless other sites concentrated in the Argolid, Laconia, and Messenia but also found in

Attica, Boeotia, and Thessaly, where many places are celebrated in Homer's epic poems.

In time, the Mycenaean palaces increased in size and number of rooms (while still adhering to the ancient *megaron* model, with a great central hall). Courts surrounded by porticoes were added, together with entryways called propylaea and service facilities. Around the main palace, dwellings were built, probably occupied by dignitaries with political and military functions. The palaces were protected by immense walls, constructed from large roughstones, or megaliths. Along the walls were battlements, passageways, galleries, posterns, and gates. The palaces were built on two floors, with a vast, central megaron surrounded by living quarters and service facilities; the focal point was the throne room, where a huge hearth was the most prominent feature. (A fine example has been unearthed at Pylos.)

Other buildings inside the megalithic walls included cult spaces, craftsmen's workshops, and dwellings occupied by aristocratic warriors and in some cases by merchants. Ornamentation in these buildings appears to have been influenced by the Cretan palaces: wall paintings embellish the most important rooms, and there are also some of the amenities seen at Knossos (bathrooms with painted tubs, and elegant porticoed areas seemingly used for relaxing strolls in the shade).

Archaeological finds have brought to light Mycenaean art of exceptional quality: fragments of frescoes unearthed in Mycenae, Tiryns, and Pylos can give only a vague idea of the brilliant colors that embellished the palaces, even allowing for Myceanean painters' restraint compared with their Minoan counterparts. A far greater impact is made by splendid objects created from precious metals like gold and silver that have been found in the tombs of kings and aristocrats, like the celebrated burial masks (including the one erroneously attributed to Agamemnon, actually datable to the 16th century BC), damascened and niello-inlaid daggers, huge ritual vases shaped like animals *(rhyta),* and treasure troves of jewelry—not forgetting the elegant pottery, whose decoration has abandoned Minoan naturalism in favor of rationalistic stylization.

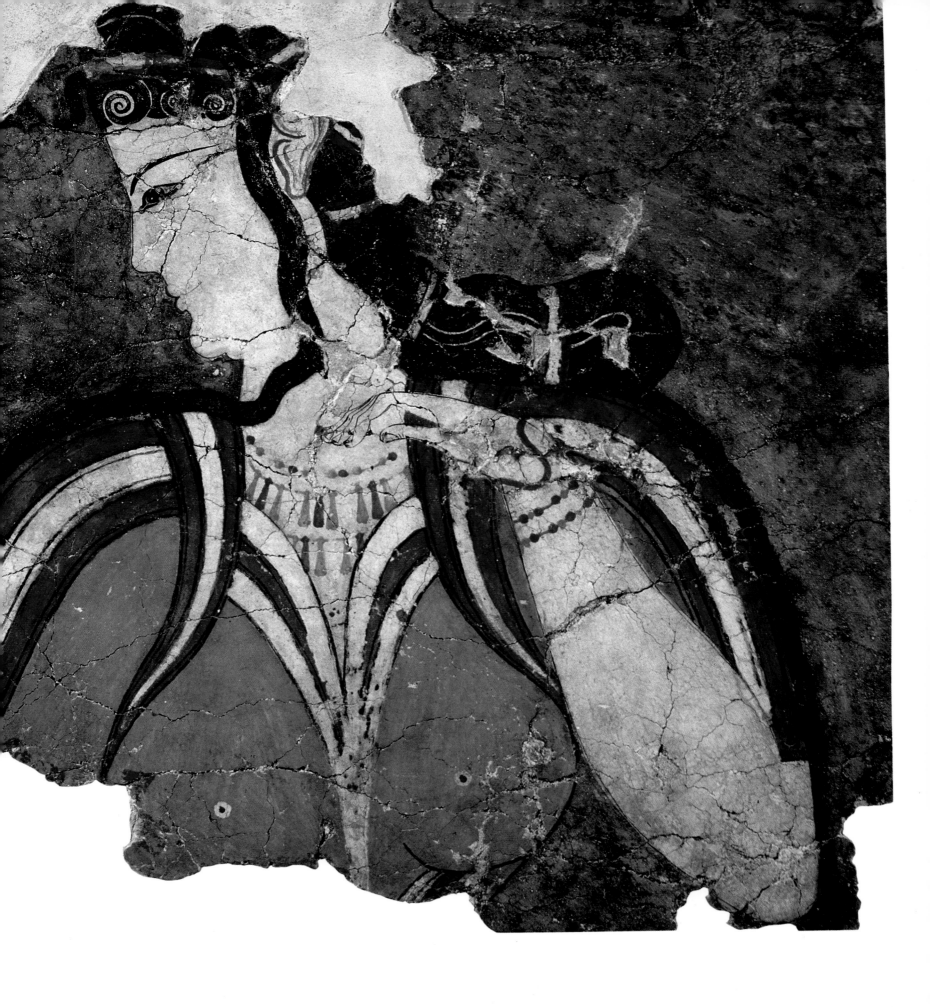

114 left *A female idol of painted terracotta from Mycenae shows the typical pattern of a praying person, with arms up and a stylized profile, reminiscent of a phi, the Hellenic "f."*

114 bottom right *A characteristic example of Mycenaean painted ceramics, this vase dates to the 13th century BC, when the typical naturalistic style of the palaces tended toward* simplification and schematization. The shape of the vase has an elegance that exceeds its functionality, limited by the small handles—not very practical—on the shoulder.

114-115 *This extraordinary fresco of the 13th century BC, from Mycenae, documents the remarkable influence that Minoan painting had on Mycenaean painting* after the Achaean conquest of Crete. This splendidly dressed young woman is admirably portrayed with smooth lines, bright colors, and fine details.

116 top *This precious diadem of gold leaf, decorated with stylized flowers, comes from Tomb III of the Funeral Circle A of Mycenae, uncovered by Schliemann. It dates to the 16th century BC.*

116 center *This outstanding casket of precious wood covered with gold leaf, embossed with naturalistic motifs, comes from Tomb V of the same Funeral Circle.*

116 bottom *Less well known than the so-called funeral mask of Agamennon, this stylized funeral mask of gold from Tomb IV of the Funeral Circle A of Mycenae dates to the 16th century BC.*

117 *The famous "funeral mask of Agamennon" actually belonged to a Mycenaean prince who lived at least three centuries before the commander celebrated by Homer's poems. It was found in a grave of Funeral Circle A of Mycenae (16th century BC). It is extraordinarily interesting from an artistic point of view because it documents the Mycenaean artitstic conception of the human figure, marked by a simplified naturalism, in which the dead person's face is characterized only briefly (the beard owing to old age, the eyes tightly shut in eternal repose).*

THE EXPLOSION OF THE GEOMETRIC STYLE

118 top *Totally decorated in Geometric style, this Attic krater may date to the end of the 9th century BC. It is quite typical from a formal viewpoint.*

With the instability and troubles of the 12th and 11th centuries BC came the slow decline and disappearance of the Mycenaean civilization and its art.

But in Attica and other areas untouched by the Dorian invasion—like Ionia, the Cyclades, and Euboea—as well as in the Dorian-populated regions of the Argolid, Laconia, and Crete, the 10th century BC saw the cautious beginnings of an economic and demographic recovery that led to the formation of proto-urban communities, an early, tentative progression from the palace-settlement model. Townships like Karphi, Dreros, and Emporion offer fairly clear instances of this trend.

In the field of art, Greek ceramic workshops were producing new and more functional types of vases,

using an innovative decorative style that, from the very start, was radically different from the naturalistic motifs favored by Minoan and Mycenaean craftsmen. Applying a remarkable sense of balance to composition, vase painters used sinuous bands, concentric circles, and semicircles. This was the beginning of the so-called Geometric period (10th-8th century BC), in which vases were decorated with increasingly delicate and ornate abstract designs, based on linear and plane-geometrical elements and figures. As well as a rigorous respect for symmetry, vase painters showed outstanding talent for creating countless variations.

Geometric art reflected a new perception of the cosmos. Nature was no longer viewed simply as a universe whose appearances were to be represented: it was rather a complex, infinite reality governed by its own laws. It was this order that the artist set out to portray, rather than nature's misleading plethora of apparent and constantly changing forms.

Economic and demographic recovery continued slowly but steadily throughout the 9th century BC. By the 8th century the Dark Ages had been long forgotten. In a given area, clusters of small communities disappeared, replaced by a single dominating center. Alternatively, villages tended to gravitate toward a single site, chosen for its preeminence or favorable topographical position: the resulting *synechiae* were the forerunners of the

118 center *The late Geometric production of Corinth (last quarter of the 8th century BC) showed a wide diffusion of* kotylai *and* skyphoi, *or drinking vases used in banquets.*

118 bottom *In the first half of the 8th century BC, especially in Athens and in Euboea, Greek ceramists introduced figurative motifs within the complex weft of geometric decorations that embellish the vases they produced. Funeral scenes are frequent, alluding to the use for which many of these vases were intended; persons of high social standing are shown ritually laid out in burial clothing. In this scene we see the exhibition of a dead body and funeral lamentations, according to a tradition widespread throughtout the whole Mediterranean area.*

poleis. Regrettably we have little evidence on which to base a reconstruction of the layout of important centers like Athens, Sparta, and Corinth. Over the centuries these famous and prosperous cities have been rebuilt time and time again, and many traces of previous cultures have been lost: today we can identify little more than the land area they occupied, their public areas and cemeteries. More plentiful remnants of the glorious past have survived in Smyrna, Eretria, and Knossos.

The architecture of this period appears to had been characterized by a certain poverty of materials and solutions. Most buildings had stone foundations, a wooden frame, and walls of unbaked brick. In type they varied from the late Mycenaean megaron structure to new building plans based on a small number of square or rectangular rooms (presumably following the same geometric criteria as applied in vase painting). Simple forms and materials were also used for temples and sanctuaries, of which there were many—evidence of the importance attached to the worship of the deities.

Significantly, religious sites are often found in places connected in some way with the earlier Mycenaean civilization or with mythical heroes celebrated in the Homeric epics or in epic poetry of local origin. Places of cult were endowed with precious votive offerings, in particular bronze tripods embellished with elegant, stylized horses or skillfully coordinated geometric patterns—clear evidence of the talent and expertise of Hellenic metalworkers.

In the pottery of the middle and late Geometric periods, rectilinear motifs combined in infinite ways were increasingly popular. A bold innovation in the first half of the 8th century BC was the introduction of *metopes* or spaces in which artists painted scenes with stylized and geometrized human figures or with tiny zoomorphic friezes.

Toward the end of the 8th century BC, Attic pottery entered a new phase, breaking away from the rigidity of geometric patterns to favor a more prominent presence of human figures and epic and mythological themes. Decorations on splendid kraters and large amphorae, often used as grave markers over the tombs of men and women respectively, convey an impression of disorder indicative of the desire to break away from abstract art.

119 *The masterpiece of Geometric ceramic painting is this large amphora of Dipylon (760-750 BC), more than one and a half meters high. It was originally placed as a tomb marker on a female grave. The organic unity of its decoration is perfect, as is the representation of the funeral mourning.*

119

THE ORIENTALIZING PERIOD

120 top left *An example of the rich figured production of Corinth in 7th century BC, this small* oinochoe, *or wine pitcher, has animal friezes and the typical* horror vacui, *or dread of empty space.*

120 top right *A masterpiece of Orientalizing style from Paros (a Cycladic island), this* oinochoe *is shaped like a griffin vulture's head—iconography of Near Eastern origin. It dates to the first half of the 7th century BC.*

120 bottom left *A small Corinthian vase for ointment, this lovely* alabastron *completely decorated with the sinuous figure of the demon Typhon, with animal figures depicted in black paint with red finishing touches, and with graffito details.*

Between c. 725 and 675 BC, oriental works of art imported to the West in huge quantities led to the widespread diffusion of a new artistic, iconographic, and in part ideological visual language.

Its impact was felt throughout the Mediterranean, both in the Levantine regions, increasingly marked by Assyrian hegemony and the decline of the Egyptian and Hittite powers, and in the West, where the scene was now dominated by Greek and Phoenician colonialism and the reemergence of trade on a vast scale. But the style's most profound influence was in Greece, which is why the 7th century BC is known as the Orientalizing period of Greek art.

It was in the 8th century BC that Greece and its oldest western colonies first discovered the artistic cultures óf the East—from the age-old but declining Egyptian empire of the pharaohs to the shorter-lived kingdoms of Mesopotamia, Syria, and Asia Minor.

The routes traveled by Phoenicians, Greeks, and Etruscans were also taken by traders carrying exquisitely crafted products from the East, exported to meet the growing demands of Mediterranean aristocracies, who were fascinated by elaborately and imaginatively decorated oriental art works. Thanks to the high quality of these products and their departures from the austere Geometric style—whether Greek, Villanovan/Etruscan, or Iberian—oriental art was soon adopted as a model.

To the West came objects of outstanding artistic quality: beautiful tablewares made from precious metals, skillfully embossed and incised; bronze caldrons from northern Syria and Urartu; jewelry, carved ivory, and other exotic items to be displayed as a sign of prestige and economic power. For many of these products undoubtedly arrived as gifts to seal trade alliances between western aristocracies, who exported raw materials (primarily metals) to the territories they controlled, and far-off oriental or Greek partners from whom they bought finished products. Less stunning but no less important were the products of local artists and craftsmen who borrowed from the vast pictorial repertoire—both figurative and naturalistic—offered by the East.

Thus oriental art and vitality had a significant general influence on the reawakening West. Greece was the first politically advanced and culturally solid civilization to be influenced by the Orient. However, it quickly assimilated the ideologies, techniques, and other stimuli offered by eastern cultures and redeveloped them in its own incisive and autonomous way. Its pottery is the most important evidence of this process.

Corinth had meanwhile gained supremacy as a trading power,

121 *This large krater with column-shaped handles is in the ancient Corinthian style. We can see both its sides. (top): the banquet of Heracles and Eurytos. (bottom): a fighting scene between hoplites.*

exporting its fine-quality pottery far and wide. The extensive distribution of its products demonstrates that the Mediterranean was by no means the exclusive trading arena of the Phoenicians but was divided into freely accessible areas of influence. The craftsmen of the Mediterranean frequently adopted or copied one another's designs: the Carthaginians, for example, frequently copied the designs and decorative motifs of Greek pottery from imported originals. During this period Greek vases were characterized by a mix of forms and iconographic motifs, as were the oriental products that inspired them.

By the early 7th century BC, the new iconography and subject matter had been fully absorbed, although fundamental differences existed from region to region. In areas like Attica, where the old aristocracies clung to tradition as well as to their privileges, there was greater reluctance to abandon the old Geometric style and adopt the freer and more fanciful oriental patterns.

The Orientalizing style advanced everywhere, although without eliminating the fundamentally rationalist spirit and coherent approach to design of Geometric art. The diverse motifs—exotic creatures and monsters, royal hunts and processions, symbols and purely ornamental patterning—

were soon reelaborated as Greek artists searched for an inner equilibrium, a synthesis between form and content not evident in the products of the East. For example, the shapes of vessels retained their functional and practical characteristics and were even enhanced, but the themes and decorative elements changed. Imaginative design was made to adhere more closely to orderly composition; the repetitive flatness or "unrealistic naturalism" in oriental art was replaced by more coherent forms

122 left
Dating to the first half of the 7th century BC, this bronze leaf, embossed and engraved with the murder of Cassandra by Clytemnestra, comes from Heraion of Argos.

122 right *This fine, terrible head of a griffin vulture decorated a bronze tripod that was imported to Delphi from Urartu in the first half of the 7th century BC and offered to Apollo.*

and greater narrative expression. Slightly less importance was attributed to symbols and more to ideas—this was, after all, the century that saw the birth of philosophy in the the Ionian colonies of Asia Minor. The effects of this reelaboration are clearly seen in the remarkable pottery production of Corinth, as well as in proto-Attic and Graeco-Oriental pottery.

The work of western craftsmen is easily distinguished from its oriental equivalents in caldrons and tripods. Until the 9th century BC, these large semispherical vessels, made of bronze or precious metal lamina, were used mainly at sumptuous banquets of the aristocracy, in keeping with traditional Mycenaean practice. From the 8th century BC onward, they were increasingly placed in places of cult as votive offerings for gods or heroes. Their widespread distribution points to the progress made by western metalworkers; in the 8th and 7th centuries BC, their methods were notably influenced by Near Eastern technology, primarily from the Syro-Hittite area and from Urartu (eastern Turkey).

The earliest major statuary in Greece was also directly influenced by the East, as is evident in the imposing, stiff figures represented in the conventional frontal pose.

But the Greeks very quickly broke away from

the models offered by Egypt and Mesopotamia, both for figure representation and for small bronzes (and their "poor" version in terracotta). They did not consider frontality an expression of human subjection in divine presence; it was simply a convenient solution that they soon modified to achieve greater realism. Their notable efforts in this regard are seen in the greater attention to proportion that characterizes Greek statues.

Unlike sculptors, painters, and metalworkers, Greek architects were independent of outside influence, as testified by temple architecture. Still, even here there are occasional references to the East: for example, the decoration of wooden structures with polychrome terracotta added a vibrant eastern note to monumental buildings. This is the period that saw the emergence of the whole concept and structure of the Greek temple, together with the Doric and Ionic orders; sanctuaries also developed a richer and more elaborate monumental dimension.

123 left
This appliqué *shaped like a winged mermaid came from an Orientalizing caldron produced in Greece and offered* ex voto *at the sanctuary of Olympia in the mid-17th century BC.*

123 top right *This masterpiece of the Rhodian Orientalizing style is the famous Oinochoe Lévy, which may date to c. 640 BC. It is decorated with a sequence of fine friezes with lines of wild goats and is completed by a series of extremely imaginative animal and geometric decorations.*

123 bottom right
The delicacy of Orientalizing art is shown in this gold leaf decorated with metopes, showing a few examples of the rich, imaginative oriental repertory. It was found in the sanctuary of Apollo at Delphi.

THE ARCHAIC STYLE

In the 6th century BC the East was in the hands of great empires—first the Assyrian, later the Persian—but their cultural and artistic supremacy was by now a thing of the past: it became fossilized on the models that had made its distinctive style and ushered in the Orientalizing style in Greece.

Greece occupied the dominating place in the cultural scenario. In the 6th century BC the Greeks were competing for trade with their Phoenician rivals and no longer bowed to the artistic preeminence of the Orient. The shift in the artistic style of Greek art did not merely stem from a change in taste. The Greeks had consolidated their own cultural characteristics, first in politics and literature at the end of the 7th century BC. Soon after came a renaissance of artistic expression, and its products quickly invaded Mediterranean markets. From then on Greek culture was the frame of reference for Western civilization. Its success derived from its ability to constantly reshape forms of expression, in a dialogue conducted both at home and with the non-Greek world, in theory and in practice, in abstract concepts of design and in the practical, creative aspects of everyday life.

Developments in Greek city building were early signs of divergence from oriental models. In the 9th and 8th centuries BC a number of poleis were applying rational criteria to the distribution of urban spaces and their functions. By the end of the 7th century, while the problem of urban planning was totally ignored in the East, colonial settlements like Metapontum, Megara Hyblaea, Poseidonia (Paestum), and Selinus were prime examples of

124-125 *The northern frieze of the Siphnian Treasury at Delphi (c. 525 BC) is decorated with a masterpiece by a late Archaic Ionian artist. The balance between light and shade in the mad battle between the gods and the giants, who rebelled against their power and the perfect order of things, should be appreciated. The bodies face each other dramatically. The gods can be recognized by their typical feature (the lion skin on Heracles' shoulders, the cuirass with the head of Medusa for Athena). The giants, so standardized as to be unrecognizable, are hidden under heavy armor and helmets, shapeless amalgams of Evil. Finally, the attempt to express movement and spatial depth through the division of planes and gradations of thickness reveals an effort to portray the third dimension.*

systematic planning of the urban fabric and its outlying territory based on a grid layout. Land areas were organized according to function, but without disregarding aesthetic considerations. This is borne out, for example, by the search for particularly suitable sites on which to erect temples. In Greece proper the tumultuous growth of large city-states between the 9th and 7th centuries BC delayed the emergence of urban planning schemes. A plan of limited scope was implemented in Athens during the rule of tyrants (c. 560-510 BC). For the benefit of worshippers and the community at large, the tyrants spent lavishly on numerous buildings and works of art in the most important Panhellenic sanctuaries, on occasions instigating the construction of cult centers of monumental dimensions. This phenomenon was particularly evident in Greek settlements in the eastern Aegean and Asia Minor, with the perfection of the Ionic order and its use in grandiose forms, as in the third temple of Hera on Samos and in the temple of Artemis at Ephesus.

Meanwhile, the Doric order was being developed by architects in western colonies. It first appeared in several variants, generally sharing the same imposing forms and simple harmony of proportions, and often incorporating elements of the Ionic style and local

tradition. Sanctuaries are of particular interest in this period, on account of the "ritualized disorder" that characterized their layout.

Delphi and its celebrated sanctuary, with the oracle of Pythian Apollo, is a case in point. No urban planning was followed for the creation of this holy place, and whatever buildings occupied the space inside the *temenos*—the sacred precinct—remained untouchable. Here there was greater scope than elsewhere for innovation and experimentation, and architectural and artistic ideas from all over Greece were put into practice. This

fact is attested by the splendid Siphnian Treasury, whose frieze decoration is considered the culminating point of Archaic Ionic sculpture.

The term *Archaic* is used to designate Greek art of the 6th century BC and refers to its "old" look *(archaios)* compared with artworks of the following century, which the ancients themselves saw as the climax of their search for perfection. The value of the term becomes clear when sculpture from this period is examined and its radical break from Orientalizing models becomes fully apparent. Artists eager to

125 top *The oldest equestrian statue is the famous Rampin Horseman, perhaps representing a son of Pisistratus, the Athenian tyrant (550 BC). It is a splendid example of Archaic Ionic sculpture in Cycladic marble. The delicate plasticity of the limbs, the relaxed face in the "Archaic smile," and the horse's neck are literally soaked in light.*

125 bottom *The splendid* kouros moschophoros *(570-560 BC), the oldest large statue found in the Acropolis of Athens, was dedicated to the goddess protectress of the city by a certain Rhombos. It represents a man carrying a calf on his shoulders as a sacrificial offer. This work breaks the rigid*

convention of frontality of the Archaic kouroi *and aims at a higher level of definition of anatomical representation. The eyes were originally of shining material. The transparent effect of the light ritual garment worn by the young man should also be appreciated.*

experiment with style and form often chose holy sites, consecrated to a particular god or goddess, as their testing grounds: possibly an acropolis or sanctuary, sometimes burial places, where monumental tombs of nobles and notables left evidence of their existence for posterity. Pediments with figures executed in relief were a further important element of Archaic temple architecture.

The dominating subject of these sculptures was mythology—religion's figurative account of the universe, to which philosophers were then devoting much more rational inquiries. Life-size statues of the human body first appeared on the Greek art scene in the 7th century BC.

126 top *This fragmentary statue, from the Acropolis of Athens, portrays a sphinx with the typical features of winged lioness and a woman's head. It dates to the third quarter of the 6th century BC. The Archaic characters are mostly evident in the face, streaked by the "smile," in the somewhat hard cutting of the eyes, and in the hair loose on the shoulders, in repetitive flat waves.*

126 center *A most interesting series of polychrome clay antefixes, or eave ornaments, comes from the important Archaic temple of Thermòs, in Aetolia. This one dates to the mid-6th century BC and represents the sneering head of a satyr, one of the semiferal creatures of Dionysus' retinue. It is a grotesque image of great expressive intensity.*

126 bottom
This masterpiece of Archaic Attic ceramic painting is the famous François Vase, made by the great ceramist Ergotimos and by the Greek painter Cleitias in about 570 BC. A large krater with volutes found in a tomb of Chiusi (in Etruria), it is decorated with six registers depicting scenes from epics and mythology, totaling 270 figures and 121 inscriptions.

127 *This* kore *from the Acropolis of Athens, one of the last examples of Archaic Attic sculpture (530-520 BC), shines in her white insular marble, enriched with a multi-colored dress and jewels (a diadem, earrings with floral motifs, an armilla). The shapes, whether exposed flesh or veiled by rather natural drapery, absorb light thanks to the many soft shifts of plane.*

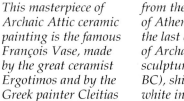

Throughout the following century the initially static and rigid forms of young women *(korai)* and young men *(kouroi)* moved toward representations that were idealized in terms of naturalism, coherence, harmony, and beauty. Archaic statues do not portray personal features or emotions; nothing about the subject's age, socioeconomic condition, or personal history is revealed by its facial expression or posture. What's more, while the *korai* wear traditional elegant garments, the *kouroi* are completely naked: in keeping with convention, male nudity is intended to highlight the perfection of the human form, regarded by philosophers as indissolubly combining the visible and the invisible, the material and the abstract.

The statues often depicted young or not-so-young aristocrats, entrepreneurs, warriors, athletes, physicians, politicians, priests, and priestesses. But their individuality was of no interest to the sculptors, their patrons, or the public. The intention was simply to offer the gods and posterity an image of the splendor of youth, a supreme expression of the Being materialized in man.

In votive and funerary statuary, the first *kouroi* had a stiff and heavy look; the *korai* were like cylinders, with practically no resemblance to any natural form. Around 560 BC attempts to reproduce a type of beauty that was both ideal and real were intensified: anatomy was studied in greater depth, plasticity improved, drapery became softer, and there were suggestions

128 top left *A work from 540-530 BC, this famous* kylix *showing Dionysus on a ship is one of the last masterpieces of black-figure ceramic painting by the great Exekias. It alludes to a myth of the abduction of the god by pirates and their transformation into dolphins.*

128 top right *This krater with volutes, from the end of the 6th century BC, shows on the neck a long red-figured band depicting a fight between Hector and Achilles.*

128-129 *This panel, from the base of a* kouros *from Piraeus (510 BC), shows two young men inciting a fight between a dog and a cat.*

of movement, however slight. Only the faces continued to have the fixed expressionlessness characteristic of the period, the so-called "Archaic smile."

By the end of the 6th century *kouroi* and *korai* had reached their highest point of refinement; the new century ushered in changes that rejected existing conventions, as in the pedimental sculptures of the Doric temple of Athena Aphaea at Aegina. These new developments were extensively influenced by regional styles, while critics now attribute greater importance to their interaction and reciprocity: Doric-Peloponnesian, characterized by solid shapes, skillful disposition of masses, and powerful use of chiaroscuro; Ionic (from both the islands and Asia Minor), gloriously successful in its sensitive treatment of light and delicate use of relief, accentuating the natural slimness of the male figures and the grace of the beautiful *korai;* Attic, reaching boldly toward a synthesis of the two previous styles, toning down their excesses and magnifying their finer points to eventually create the masterpieces of the early 5th century BC.

By the middle of the 5th century, Corinthian pottery had passed its peak and Mediterranean markets were flooded with vases from numerous other centers of production. Exports of figured Attic pottery to the entire ancient world—especially to Etruria—soared: workshops in the *kerameikos* quarter of Athens, where potters and vase painters worked practically in symbiosis, moved on from the animal-frieze motifs of the Orientalizing tradition to draw on an inexhaustible mine of Greek myths and epic tales. The great painters of black-figure pottery were Cleitias (whose signature appears with that of the potter Ergotimos on the celebrated François Vase), Lydos, the Amasis Painter, and Exekias.

Within a half-century a new red-figure technique had been invented, allowing even greater freedom of expression; among its most successful painters was Euphronius. As well as vases created by famous potters and painters (and the fact that they left their signature shows they were aware of their prestige), medium- and low-quality pottery was produced in huge quantities, along semi-industrial lines, for the mass market. Many of these products echo the fashionable styles of the day and even the creative heights reached by the "big names." Whether they are products of art or craft is hard to say. But the economic importance of this production activity, in response to huge demand, is undeniable.

THE SEVERE STYLE
(500-450 BC)

130 *Aegina was home of an important sculptors' school. This beautiful woman's head with a helmet (possibly Athena) comes from the island and may date to the first half of the 5th century BC.*

The evolution of Greek art in the first half of the 5th century BC coincided with changes in philosophical thinking and drew inspiration from them and other areas of cultural expression.

Intensive research into the nature of reality had been conducted—since the mid-6th century BC—by the philosophical schools that had sprung up throughout the Hellenic world, from Ionia to *Magna Graecia.* In the visual arts, the sense of the "oneness" of reality that they engendered was reflected in the rejection of schemes and conventions for the representation of reality. Greek artists searched determinedly for the ideal, perfect expression of the nature of Being: they tried to develop an artistic form in which reality was portrayed in all its significance and expressed coherently, above and beyond the limitations of time and space imposed by everyday life and sensory perception.

In the first half of the 5th century BC a new prominence was attributed to the concept of Beauty as an expression of inner beauty, implying that high spiritual and moral values result in an equally lovely external appearance. As maintained by the greatest philosophers of that period, Parmenides of Elea and Heracleitus of Ephesus, the perfect harmony of forms and values was a demonstration—to one and all—of the unity of Being: an indivisible, eternal, dynamic, and multiform reality.

Writers of antiquity used the word *severe* to describe the first half of this transitional phase in Greek art, corresponding to the first half of the 5th century BC. Their intention, with this term, was to underline the moderation and equilibrium of an artistic style that made harmony and perfection its goal. During the same period, architectural production advanced at an almost feverish pace throughout the Greek world. From Sicily to Campania, from

131 *A wonderful torso of a human image of the river Kladeos, from the eastern pediment of the temple of Zeus at Olympia. As if awakening from a deep sleep, he turns to the center of the scene, where a chariot race between the cruel king of Pisa, Oenomaus, and the young Lycian prince Pelops (after whom Peloponnesus would be named) is about to begin. The strong torsion of the trunk represents the liquid nature of the river spirit, which mixes its waters with those of the Alpheus in the green plain of Olympia.*

132 left *The famous Charioteer of Delphi, a masterpiece of Severe sculpture, was among the votive offers to the tyrant Polyzelus of Gela, winner of the chariot race in the Pythian games of 478 BC.*

132 right *The fine bronze head of Apollo Chatsworth, discovered in Cyprus, is datable to c. 460 BC, when the island was under Athenian rule. It expresses a severe protoclassical dignity, a look enlivened by the eyes, which were of* pâté de verre.

133 *The proud head of the famous bronze Zeus (or Poseidon) is absorbed as he throws a lightning bolt (or trident) (470-460 BC). The statue was found in the sea off Cape Artemision (in Euboea), so its original context and function (votive, cultural, or other) cannot be known. The unstable dynamic of the body, developed in a harmonic and powerful whole, was based on a chiasmas structure, which Polyclitus often used in his own works. It consists of the opposition between the limbs under stress and those relaxed. The position of the body in space denotes the intention of definitively going beyond the single frontal view, typical of the statuary of the previous century and already under attack by the subtle dynamic restlessness that animated the Ephebos of Critius and the Auriga of Delphi. The statue's significance lies in this innovation and in the outstanding quality of its anatomical definition.*

Attica to the Cyclades, fast-growing cities acquired a new monumental face. Still, there were no significant changes in the models consolidated after the intense experimentation of the previous century.

The only real evidence of innovation comes from the mighty temple of Zeus at the Panhellenic sanctuary of Olympia. The games held here every four years in the god's honor became an enormously important event and an opportunity for political dialogue: while the games were under way, a sacred truce was proclaimed, with the intention of encouraging the peaceful settlement of conflicts, inspired by Zeus himself. The temple in some ways echoes the gigantism of Ionic temples, already experimented with by Sicilian architects using the more restrained Doric order, between 530 and 480 BC.

The more important developments were seen in a sector hitherto neglected in Greece proper: urban planning. Hippodamus of Miletus originated a rational regulatory code for the layout of towns, which by now had ever-larger populations and consequently more complex functions and needs. Cities were laid out following a rectangular grid system, with land distributed according to function and use. Streets, defensive works, and the positioning of sacred, administrative, and commercial areas were adapted to the site and terrain. The system, known

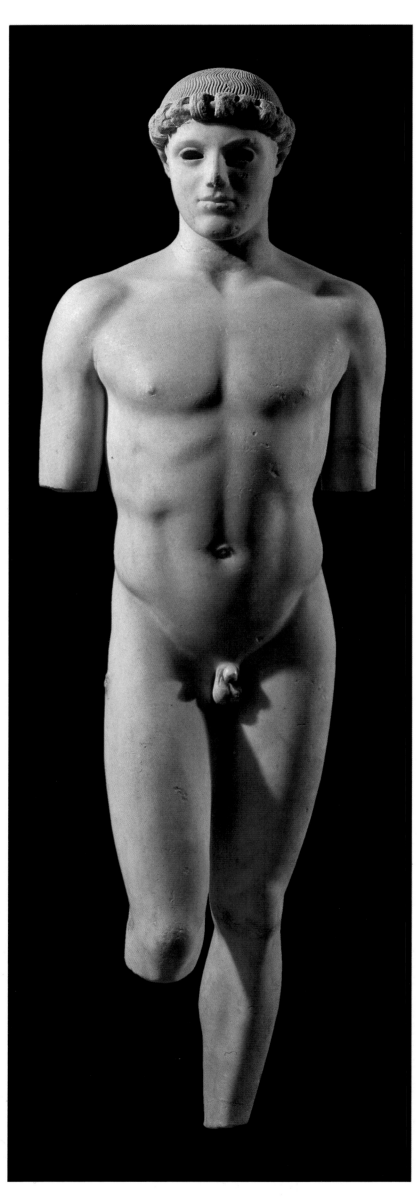

134 *This superb marble from the atelier of Critius and Nesiotes in Athens, from about 480 BC is the famous Ephobos of Critius, the first statue of a young man to go beyond the rigid scheme of archaic* kouroi, *breaking the rules of artificial symmetry in favor of the expression of a hidden movement, a restless instability, a subtle interior tension.*

135 *The germ of the Severe revolution in sculpture is recognizable in this fine head of the great dying warrior on the eastern pediment of the temple of Athena Aphaea in Aegina, identified by some with Laomedonte. Here there is no more psychological detachment: the lips open in panting, the cheekbones are raised in a grimace, and the face wrinkles up with fatigue. The dying godlike hero here appears in his more authentic, painful mortal condition.*

as Hippodamian, owed much to experiments during the two previous centuries in the colonies of *Magna Graecia.* It was most successfully used in the layout of Miletus, Piraeus, and the colony of Thourioi in present Apulia.

Much more significant and complex developments took place in figurative art. The east pediment of the temple of Athena Aphaea at Aegina marks the emergence of a new kind of formal expression, far removed from the conventional formulae of the 6th century BC. It was not long (480-470 BC) before masterpieces like the celebrated Ephobus and the Tyrannicides group were created in the Athenian workshop of Critius and Nesiotes. Contemporary bronze sculpture reached exceptional heights in the Peloponnese, where schools flourished in Argos and Sicyon, as well as in *Magna Graecia* (especially Tarentum). The tyrants of Hellenized Italy became major patrons of the arts, competing with the most prosperous cities of Greece proper to embellish the great Panhellenic sanctuaries with splendid artworks of enormous value. One such offering was the famous Charioteer group, donated to Delphi by the tyrant Polyzelus of Gela.

The intended use of a work of art often helps explain its style, as in the case of certain kinds of products from the artists and craftsmen of *Magna Graecia.* An example is the *pinakes* (pictures), or clay metopes used in Locri as votive offerings to Demeter and Persephone (Kore). Still prominent here—as in the contemporary pottery of many Western Greek colonies—were Ionian forms of the late Archaic period.

As always, however, it was major statuary that signaled the most important developments in sculpture. The bronze Zeus (or Poseidon) found off Cape Artemision, depicted in the act of hurling a thunderbolt (or trident), marks the discovery of movement and the abandonment of frontality to

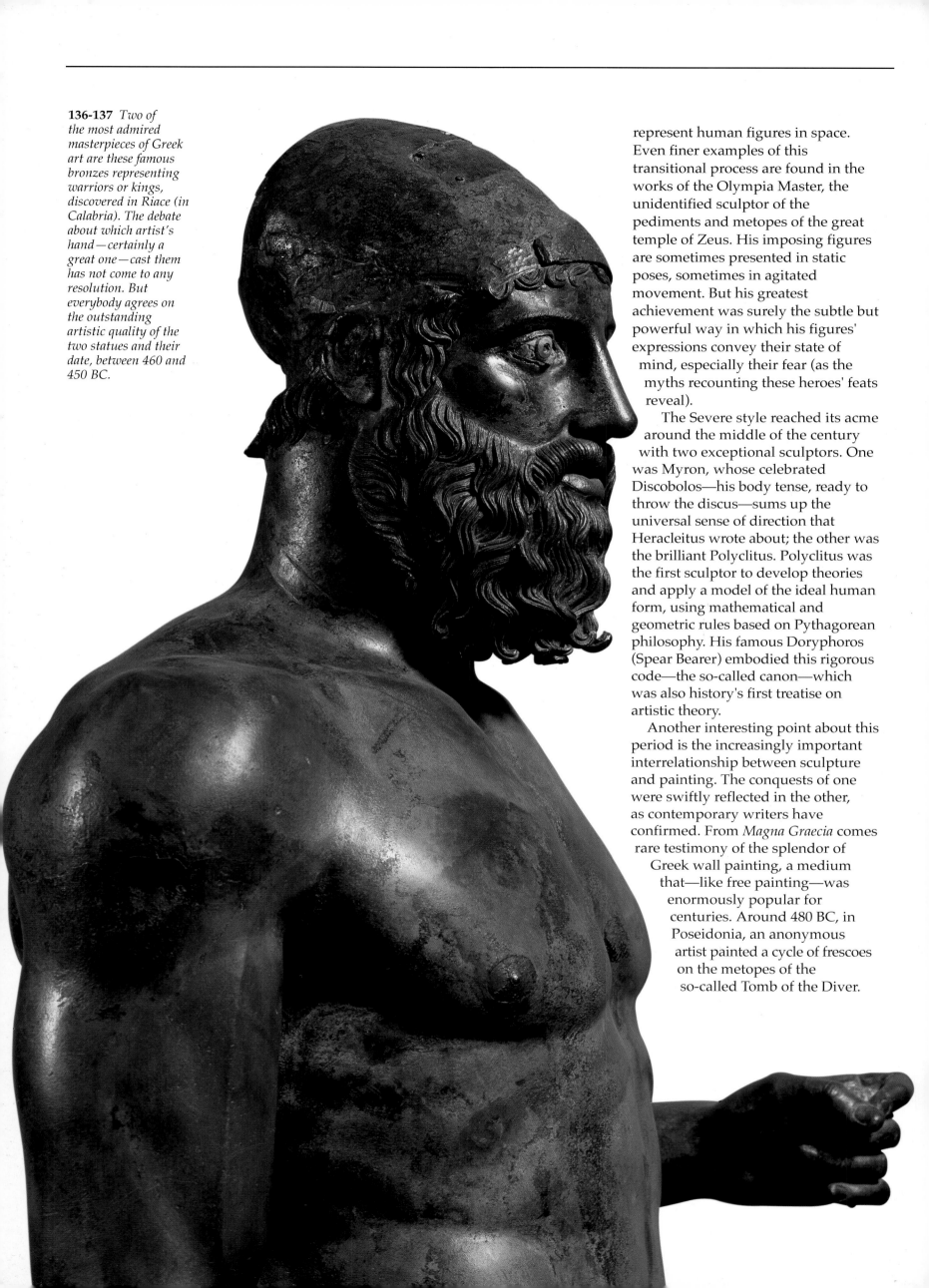

136-137 *Two of the most admired masterpieces of Greek art are these famous bronzes representing warriors or kings, discovered in Riace (in Calabria). The debate about which artist's hand—certainly a great one—cast them has not come to any resolution. But everybody agrees on the outstanding artistic quality of the two statues and their date, between 460 and 450 BC.*

represent human figures in space. Even finer examples of this transitional process are found in the works of the Olympia Master, the unidentified sculptor of the pediments and metopes of the great temple of Zeus. His imposing figures are sometimes presented in static poses, sometimes in agitated movement. But his greatest achievement was surely the subtle but powerful way in which his figures' expressions convey their state of mind, especially their fear (as the myths recounting these heroes' feats reveal).

The Severe style reached its acme around the middle of the century with two exceptional sculptors. One was Myron, whose celebrated Discobolos—his body tense, ready to throw the discus—sums up the universal sense of direction that Heracleitus wrote about; the other was the brilliant Polyclitus. Polyclitus was the first sculptor to develop theories and apply a model of the ideal human form, using mathematical and geometric rules based on Pythagorean philosophy. His famous Doryphoros (Spear Bearer) embodied this rigorous code—the so-called canon—which was also history's first treatise on artistic theory.

Another interesting point about this period is the increasingly important interrelationship between sculpture and painting. The conquests of one were swiftly reflected in the other, as contemporary writers have confirmed. From *Magna Graecia* comes rare testimony of the splendor of Greek wall painting, a medium that—like free painting—was enormously popular for centuries. Around 480 BC, in Poseidonia, an anonymous artist painted a cycle of frescoes on the metopes of the so-called Tomb of the Diver.

138 *The splendid anatomical representation of the Bronze of Riace A, the younger of the two, is emphasized in this three-quarter rear view, in which the coordination of the chiasma rhythm of the limbs and of the powerful muscles seems perfect.*

139 *In full frontal view, the stylistic refinement and the touches of true realism of the Riace Bronzes can be better observed and appreciated. The faces, framed by rich beards and thick hair, seem lifelike as their eyes are made of ivory and* pâté de verre, *their teeth of silver, their lips and nipples of copper, and their weapons—originally gripped—also of silver.*

THE CLASSICAL PERIOD
(450-400 BC)

In the second half of the 5th century BC, Athens established its definitive cultural leadership of the Greek world. Regional artistic expression merged with innovative theoretical and formal developments by Attic architects, sculptors, artists, and vase painters, as the Greeks' vision of the universe was made manifest in their art. Major roles in this process were played by Pericles and by an outstanding architect and artist, Phidias: together, in Athens, they achieved "the experiment in perfection."

This was the beginning of the so-called Classical period, to make broad use of the term applied by the ancient Romans to exceptional literature of the 5th and 4th centuries BC. But the term *classical* has long been used improperly—with no real scientific grounds—for a mythic "golden age" of culture and art. Fifteenth-century humanism and the 16th-century Renaissance generated Classicist movements inspired by the enormous artistic and architectural legacy of Rome, heir to the civilization of ancient Greece. In the mid-1700s the rationalist spirit of the Enlightenment sparked off a new appreciation for Greek art, interpreted in more scientific terms (in intention, at least). This appreciation became enthusiastic in response to 18th-century archaeological finds, by fashionable travel to the archaeological and artistic sites of Italy, Greece, and Asia Minor, and by antique collecting.

Neoclassicism, for its part, set out to

140 left *The famous Doryphoros (Spear Bearer) by Polyclitus, the work that is said to incarnate the very idea of the canon elaborated by this great Peloponnesian artist in c. 450 BC, comes to us only through Roman copies.*

140 right *Another copy from the Roman age, this one found in Delos, illustrates the grace and gesture of Diadoumenos, a young athlete recognized when he ties the* tainia *of the winner around his head; this is one of Polyclitus' most fascinating works (c. 420 BC).*

141 *A calm, almost detached energy is released in the perfect movement captured in the Discobolos (Discus Thrower) by Myron (c. 450 BC), shown here in the most famous Roman copy. It is a superb example of representing the dynamic harmony of the human body in a single plane.*

counter the irrationality of 17th-century Baroque. Its image of Classicism was conditioned by a distortedly "evolutionistic" view of art, which saw the art of antiquity as having followed a course marked by birth, blossoming, and "death" (a theory also adopted by the Romans). In the 18th century Classicism was placed on a pedestal as the absolute model for Western art and culture. The writings of the foremost exponent of artistic Neoclassicism, the Prussian J. J. Winckelmann, influenced artists awed by the grandeur of the ancient world: Piranesi, for instance, as well as young enthusiasts like Mengs, Thorvaldsen, and Canova. Winckelmann's ideas were long held in high esteem and eventually created a myth that even today sometimes influences the taste of moderately cultured art lovers.

Only in the twentieth century has the art of antiquity gradually come to be viewed in its proper historical and critical light. At last stripped of its apothesization the term *Classical*—like *Archaic* and *Severe*—can be used simply to refer to the conceptual and formal language of Greek art between the mid-5th and the last third of the 4th century BC.

On account of Athens' hegemonic role in Greek culture at large, in philosophy, the humanities, and science as well as art, the closing stages of the process of artistic experimentation came to fruition in this city. Under Pericles and his successors, Athens became the cultural capital of "Greekness." Great figures left their home towns and converged on Athens in search of recognition and success, eager to compete in a kind of perennial Olympics of great minds and to gain from experiences otherwise

possible only with years of wandering. The spirit underlying the art of this period, more than any other in Greek art, cannot be fully understood without taking into account developments in philosophical thought, especially the application of scientific inquiry, an area in which Anaxagoras and Democritus are points of reference. At the same time Zeno, successor to Parmenides, kept alive interest in the indivisible unity of Being, his vision still attracting attention in the 4th century BC. Lastly the Sophists, the first "practitioners of knowledge," appeared on the scene: with persuasive and refined dialectic, they emphasized man's central role in the sensible universe and his educatability. Their arguments were soon refuted by the controversial Socrates himself—paradoxically the greatest Sophist. Socrates' ideas were

142-143 *Art from the Classical period revolves almost entirely around Phidias. This splendid figure personifies a river of Attica, the Kephisos or the Ilyssos, on the west pediment of the Parthenon in Athens (c. 435 BC). Absolute Beauty, in its ideal form, is expressed in complete spatial freedom and the naturalness of the pose. It is what makes man similiar to a god, thus constituting the principal, the model, and the end of the universe.*

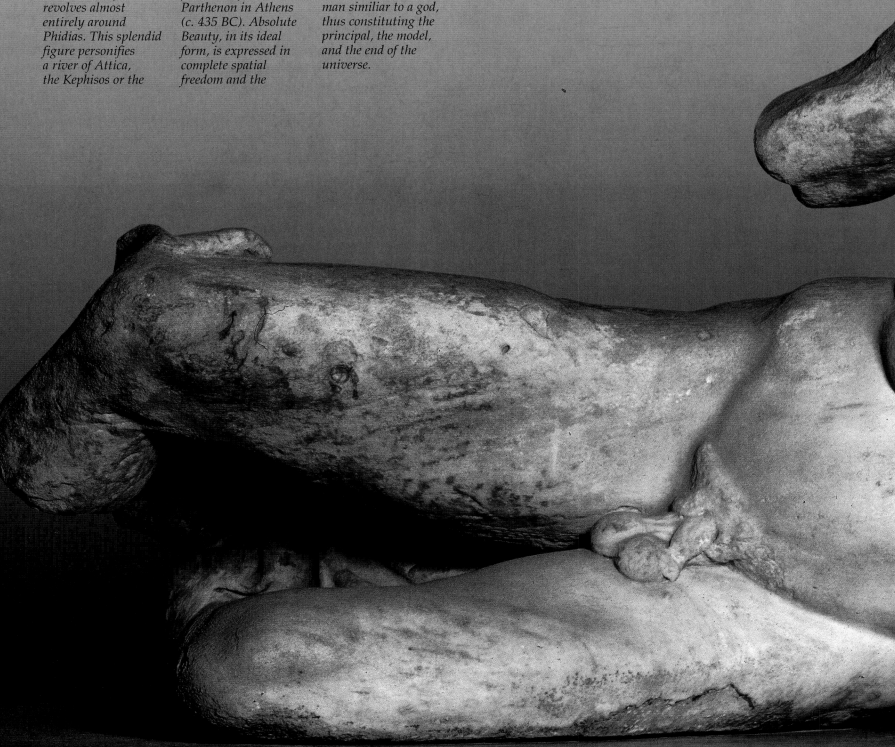

taken up and enlarged upon by his disciple Plato, with results of seminal importance for the whole development of Western thinking.

The engine of Athens' vibrant cultural life was the economic resources provided by the state and by the citizens whose political vision it embodied. As their wealth increased, so did their intelligence, taste, and awareness of participating in an extraordinary period of history. In Athens the *ante litteram* bourgeoisie thus became patrons of artistic production on a vast scale, much like the European bourgeoisie in the 13th and 14th centuries, or from the 19th century onward.

The Persian sack of Athens in 480 BC had done extensive damage to the appearance of the Archaic city, and the characteristic disarray of the urban landscape was only partly changed by improvements under the Pisistratids. Reconstruction proper made headway only under Cimon and Pericles. Under Cimon, work commenced on the monumental reorganization of the Agora, and plans were laid for the construction of a huge temple dedicated to Athena Parthenos (Athena the Virgin) on the Acropolis, to replace the Archaic one that had been restored somewhat haphazardly after the Persian wars.

Pericles, however, was the prime mover in the architectural renovation of Athens: thanks to this man of outstanding culture and broad political views—Athens' "first citizen" is how Thucydides defined him—the Acropolis and the city at large were reorganized and raised to monumental standing, in the first large-scale urban improvement scheme in Western history. Pericles wanted the identity and the political, ethical, religious, and cultural values of the free Athenian people to be reflected in suitably grand architecture and art. He would create an ensemble of buildings of unprecedented and unrivaled splendor that would be the envy of the rest of the world. Apart from a vociferous minority, his intentions seem to have echoed sentiments shared by all Athenians, who conceived of society as a harmonious equilibrium between individual and community, public and private.

The scheme got under way in 449 BC, the year a lasting peace was reached with the Persians. A series of major innovations and improvements was made in the Agora, in the city's residential districts and at Piraeus (a planning project developed by Hippodamus of Miletus), with useful enhancements to the general road

system. But it was upon the Acropolis that Pericles lavished his attention. Athens was now a flourishing city, able to stand up to any enemy, and infused with values both complex and profound: what it lacked was a monumental site that would be the tangible symbol of its civic pride. Work was started on the construction of a series of buildings, under the personal supervision of Pericles and coordinated by a project leader of exceptional technical ability and creative talent, Phidias. Working under him was a team of the very finest architects and a feverishly active workshop of artists.

The hilltop was gradually encompassed by elegant marble structures. The temple of Athena Parthenos, later known as the Parthenon, which had been left unfinished around 460 BC, was redesigned on a larger and grander scale by Ictinus and Callicrates, who applied sophisticated mathematical calculations and based the whole complex on harmony of proportions. Callicrates also designed the small Ionic temple of Athena Nike, while the new Propylaea, the imposing gateway to the sacred precinct of the goddess, was built by Mnesicles. Before long the Erechtheum—the original temple of Poseidon, a project by Philocles—and a complex of small temples housing several cults were built on the site.

Construction of the monuments on the Acropolis proceeded quickly but not quickly enough that Pericles could see their completion. By the time of his death, only the Parthenon and the Propylaea had been finished.

The great Classical art of Attica originated in the ambitious projects directed by Pericles and coordinated by Phidias, with ideas and practical contributions from a group of exceptionally talented sculptors, artists, and masons. Their art was an attempt to express the perfect unity and supreme beauty of the visible and invisible; to capture the dynamic and ever-changing equilibrium of reality, both seen and sensed; and to successfully represent ideas using forms rich in meaning.

The Parthenon is the consummate example of creative genius fused with rational planning and execution, but all the spatial and visual relationships between the great temple and nearby buildings on the Acropolis contribute to the overall impression of a studied and yet natural harmony. Elsewhere in Athens and in other parts of Attica too, monumental building projects multiplied: most notable among them were the temple of Hephaestus in the Agora, the temple of Poseidon at Cape Sounion, and the temple of Nemesis at Rhamnus, as well as embellishments to the sanctuary of Artemis Brauronia. The fame of the architects of the Acropolis quickly spread across regional boundaries. Ictinus, for example, after completing his project for the great sanctuary dedicated to the cult of the mysteries at Eleusis, was called to the Peloponnese with Callicrates to modernize the temple of Apollo Epicurius at Bassae, in Arcadia. Having finished work on the

144 left *Glimpses of the Phidian tradition can be seen in the works of the father of Praxiteles, Cephisodotus: Eirene and Ploutos are personifications of peace and richness as mother and son (374 BC); shown here, a Roman copy.*

144 right *This beautiful Roman copy of Polyclitus' statue of the wounded Amazon was executed by the artist c. 440 BC for the competition as Ephesus. It illustrates the chiastic rhythm of a supple feminine figure sensually draped.*

huge statue of Athena Parthenos, made of ivory and gold, for the cella of the Parthenon, Phidias went on to make an equally enormous cult image of Olympian Zeus for the cella of the temple of Zeus at Olympia. Phidias dominated sculpture in those years. In his work the rigorous proportions introduced by Polyclitus were enhanced by an extraordinary variety of lines and rhythms of great realistic effect.

Contending with Phidias in Athens were big names like Myron, Polyclitus, and Cresilas. Also important was the school of sculptors that developed around the construction of the Parthenon. Here the spirit and style of Phidias were continued and enlarged upon, especially his distinctive sensibility toward the human figure. Among its most prominent exponents were Alcamenes, Agoracritus, and Callimachus, whose works show different developments of the Phidian model.

A competition held at Ephesus around 440 BC is a valuable testimony to the stimulating artistic rivalry among the great sculptors and allows us to compare statues of the wounded amazon by Cresilas, Polyclitus, and Phidias (admittedly only in Roman copies). The lasting contribution of Phidias and his work also emerges from the fine funerary *stelai* made in Attica between the mid-5th and the end of the 4th century BC.

Once again the close link between trends in sculpture and painting points to the unity of Greek artistic production. In Athens the reciprocal influence of sculpture and painting became more apparent in the second half of the 5th century BC, a sign of changing relationships between artists and of keener attention paid to the experiments of others in their respective fields of competence. Artists of various kinds had plenty of opportunities to keep pace with developments: sculptors, potters, vase painters,

metalworkers, wood carvers, goldsmiths, and the like often all worked together on the same major projects; they frequently came into contact while in the employ of their ever more sophisticated and demanding patrons. The second half of the century was also marked by great achievements in painting, although all that survives is Attica's red-figure vases. Realistic portrayal of subjects was given increasing importance; Anaxagoras and Democritus wrote treatises on perspective no less than eighteen centuries before Brunelleschi. Phidias himself (with Agatarchus) was indebted to Anaxagoras: a successful painter as well as a sculptor, his approach to the Parthenon metopes reveals a pictorial vision of the space enclosed in a frame. Apollodorus, Zeuxis, and Parrhasius, for their part, were all influenced by Democritus.

At the same time, the use of perspective, foreshortening, shading, and other touches that gave figures volume and dynamism is found in a number of masterpieces that bear the signatures of contemporary Attic vase painters. Just as vase painting acquired greater plasticity and perspective, so sculpture was enriched by pictorial elements. Line gained fundamental importance as a decorative element, especially in drapery. Veillike waves of cloth, seemingly detached from the essential structural lines of the figure, are an element of statuary much favored by Callimachus, although introduced by Phidias and also adopted by Agoracritus. This use of line is also seen in the subtle grace of the Nike by Paeonius, in the sanctuary of Olympia, a votive offering made by Messenians and Naupactians as a permanent memorial to the victory over the Spartans at Sphacteria (425 BC).

145 *Around 440 BC the Ionian city of Ephesus held a competition for the best bronze statue of a wounded Amazon. Cresilas (as seen in this not-quite faithful copy from the Roman age), Phidias, Polyclitus, and the almost unknown Phradmon all entered* *their works. Cresilas' interpretation presents a beautiful woman whose traditional warrior aspect is summed up by her exposed breasts and her short hair, divided into long curly locks. The girl, weakened by her wound, raises her right arm with difficulty,* *while her face betrays her suffering. The rich, wetdrapery and the pose of her splendid body indicate, according to some critics, an attempt to overcome the "divine" balance of Phidias' art. The competition, for the record, was won by Polyclitus.*

THE TURBULENT YEARS
(400-338 BC)

The thirty-year Peloponnesian War caused thousands of deaths, famine, epidemics, social disruption, and economic crisis; it was also the historical backdrop for a change in the existential vision of the Greeks. People were no longer able to perceive—in *logos*—the unity of the universe, refuted as it was by violence and the absence of reason. For this reason, in culture and art, the 4th century BC can be described as the century of individualism and irrationalism.

Pathos—the term most commonly used to refer to the interior, existential universe to which man is drawn, attracted by its complexities and contradictions—implies something more than simple emotions: its derivation from *pascho* ("I suffer") indicates a condition of passiveness, of man's inevitable subjection to the mystery of his irrational feelings, be they positive or negative. This flight toward things irrational, abstract, metaphysical, and absolute was also seen in the evolution of philosophy. The rhetoric of the Sophists, educational in intent, was infused with optimism but was tendentially paternalistic, and it mirrored the mounting egotistical individualism in the Greek spirit. The Sophists were a kind of guru who sold their knowledge. Plato, in his voluminous works, perceived a rift between the human and the divine and postulated an absolute truth free from error; he was fiercely critical of human imperfection and propounded—in political theory, for example—an impossible model that mixed Spartan "nationalism and communism," Pythagorean mystical numerology, and the disquieting figure of the demiurge who reveals "the way" and "the truth" to the disoriented mass of humanity, thereby imposing his guiding presence and nullifying free will.

Later it was Aristotle who offered feasible ethical, political, and scientific models. By then, however, philosophy

146 *The true symbol of Olympia is this marble statue of Hermes intent on attracting, with a bunch of grapes, the attention of a small, chubby, and lively infant Dionysus, seated on his left arm.*

This work, indisputably masterful, has been attributed, not without controversy, to Praxiteles on the basis of a passage from Pausanius, but Blumel has raised doubts on the basis of style.

147 right *From an original by the young Praxiteles is an equally beautiful Roman copy, shown here, of a seminude Aphrodite, the so-called Venus of Arles.*

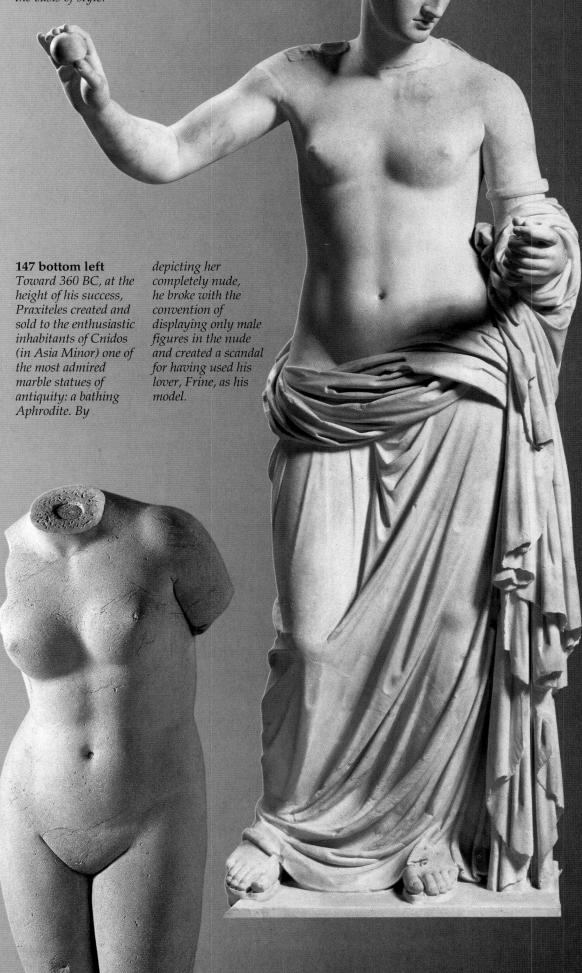

appeared to have banished for good all reflection on Being as a whole of which every aspect of the universe is part.

On the religious front, the dramatic events experienced while the "optimism of reason" was at its height had left man face-to-face with his own solitude. The gods no longer appeared as reassuring, logical, superhuman projections of the perfection of Being; instead, mirroring the fragility of all things when confronted with Destiny, they became objects of ritual homage and superstition, or disbelieving terror. In the world of literature—and theatrical poetry, in particular— Menander was the writer who most effectively represented this involution.

The 4th century *polis* reflected philosophers', politicians', and urban planners' concern with creating a city that was able to interact harmoniously with both the environment and with communities and individuals with different economic, social, and cultural needs. Universally valid models based on "scientific" theories were pursued: Hippocrates wrote about the importance of healthy surroundings, while Plato put forward arguments on what we would nowadays call environmental impact. Aristotle used his detailed knowledge of Greek cities to formulate his own theories: his ideal urban model combined the Hippodamean blueprint with the sensible, empirical approach of the colonies, with functional attributes that would still be worth following today. An interesting example of the evolving *forma urbis* is provided by Olynthus: in the main, the colonists who rebuilt the city adhered to the Hippodamean grid but introduced variants to adapt the plan to the site and terrain. Kassope, in Epirus, initially an agglomeration of rural communities in a fast-growing region, also had some original and striking features in its urban layout and architectural solutions; Priene, in Ionia, situated in a spectacular position overlooking the valley of the Maeander

147 bottom left *Toward 360 BC, at the height of his success, Praxiteles created and sold to the enthusiastic inhabitants of Cnidos (in Asia Minor) one of the most admired marble statues of antiquity: a bathing Aphrodite. By depicting her completely nude, he broke with the convention of displaying only male figures in the nude and created a scandal for having used his lover, Frine, as his model.*

River, was the first example of scenic urban planning, highly popular in later centuries.

In architecture there were also improvements and innovations. For housing, a standard format was introduced, based on rational and functional criteria by which houses were built in modular blocks, or *insulae.* This change was not only geared to rationalizing housing developments in line with new urban planning schemes; it also reflected the Greeks' shift toward the new individualistic way of thinking described earlier.

Amphitheaters, by contrast, belonged to a still public and collective dimension. More and more frequently built of stone, their structural design now followed a conventional form, of which Epidaurus offered a splendid example. Theaters become a constant feature of Greek cities, as attested by 4th-century and later examples in Dodona, Oiniadas, Priene, and Pergamum, to name but a few. The difference was that they now performed works to which the spectator could relate more as an individual and less as part of a community.

Architecture continued to be dominated by tendencies seen in the last three decades of the 5th century: elegant design, graceful harmonies, intricate proportional relationships, and stylistic

mixes verging on eclecticism, all in pursuit of lightness and pictorialism, a visual form that moved in the opposite direction from Platonic theories aimed at Beauty and what was vaguely defined as "truth."

Interesting examples—also showing the close relationship between monumental and ornamental sculpture—are offered by the *tholos* tombs in Epidaurus and Delphi, the Mausoleum of Halicarnassus, and the temple of Athena Alea in Tegea. The *tholos* tomb at Delphi in particular has such grandiose monumental characteristics that celebration of the individual practically becomes a cult, echoing earlier oriental structures as well as the most splendid temples in the Greek world.

Effects of existential disorientation among the Greeks can also be observed in the figurative languages of sculpture and painting. In the early part of the 4th century, Greek sculptors began to

portray aspects of subjective experience, with representations of moods, sensations, and emotions that stemmed from the irrational inner being: a testimony to the widening divide between human and divine. *Pathos* dominated the splendid creations of Cephisodotus, Praxiteles, Scopas, Timotheus, and the craftsmen connected with them; moving Attic funerary *stelai* are fine examples. Progressing from solid Phidean and Polyclitan traditions as well as post-Phidian developments, these artists tried to depict the volatile side of the human temperament. They set out to capture fleeting moments, symbolizing the ephemeral nature of things; they gave form to rapture and pain, tenderness and anger, in a world now devoid of ideals and faith. Light-years away from Plato's scorn for the art of his age as deceptive and based on appearances, they surveyed reality and embraced the void populated by illusions, lights, shadows, and colors.

148 *To the genius of Scopas is attributed, toward 335-330 BC, the original of this dancing maenad, a reduced-size Roman copy. Scopas' style has been recognized in the depiction of this devotee of Bacchus: in the unbridled rapture of the orgy, in the feverish frenzy of her winding and sensual motion.*

149 *From the temple of Athena Alea in Tegea (350 BC), Scopas' architectonic and sculptural masterpiece, comes this beautiful head of the goddess Hygieia, whose expressive face is typical of the sentimentalism in the visual arts of the 4th century BC, and more specifically of Scopas, perhaps the true innovator of* pathos *in art.*

MACEDONIAN HEGEMONY: FROM PHILIP II TO ALEXANDER THE GREAT (359-323 BC)

The central role played by Macedonia in Greek history during the second half of the 4th century BC had major repercussions for the evolution of Greek art. Macedonia, dominated by the Argead dynasty, had been producing significant works of art since the 6th century BC, when its contacts with central and southern Greece were still few. But closer links with the now-thriving city-states in the following century had a positive influence on the already notable creative output of Macedonian artists. Aegae and Pella, the two capitals, welcomed men of letters of the caliber of Euripides, last of a series of eminent guests at the court of King Archelaus: here he wrote *The Bacchae,* which was also performed here for the first time, and two other tragedies.

Greek contributions to Macedonian culture were most noticeable, however, from Philip II onward. The king's admiration for the culture of the poleis motivated his decision to have Alexander, heir to the throne, tutored by the greatest contemporary philosopher and disciple of Plato, Aristotle. It is nonetheless significant—and indicative of the kingdom of Macedon's important contribution to Greek culture—that on the basis of this experience, Aristotle laid the foundations for two thousand years of Western philosophy and science: human knowledge was based on "scientific" insight into reality and the intrinsic dialectic between form and matter. Looking far beyond the abstractions and impossible theorems of Plato, Aristotle applied his thoughts on empirical science to every discipline.

Since as far back as the 10th century BC, Macedonian art—unlike literature and philosophy—had many links with the great Greek *koine,* the language of culture. Its distinctive characteristics stemmed from local interpretations of common or imported models, from both southern Greece and the Aegean, with occasional oriental contributions, and from contacts—since protohistoric days—with the southern Balkans and

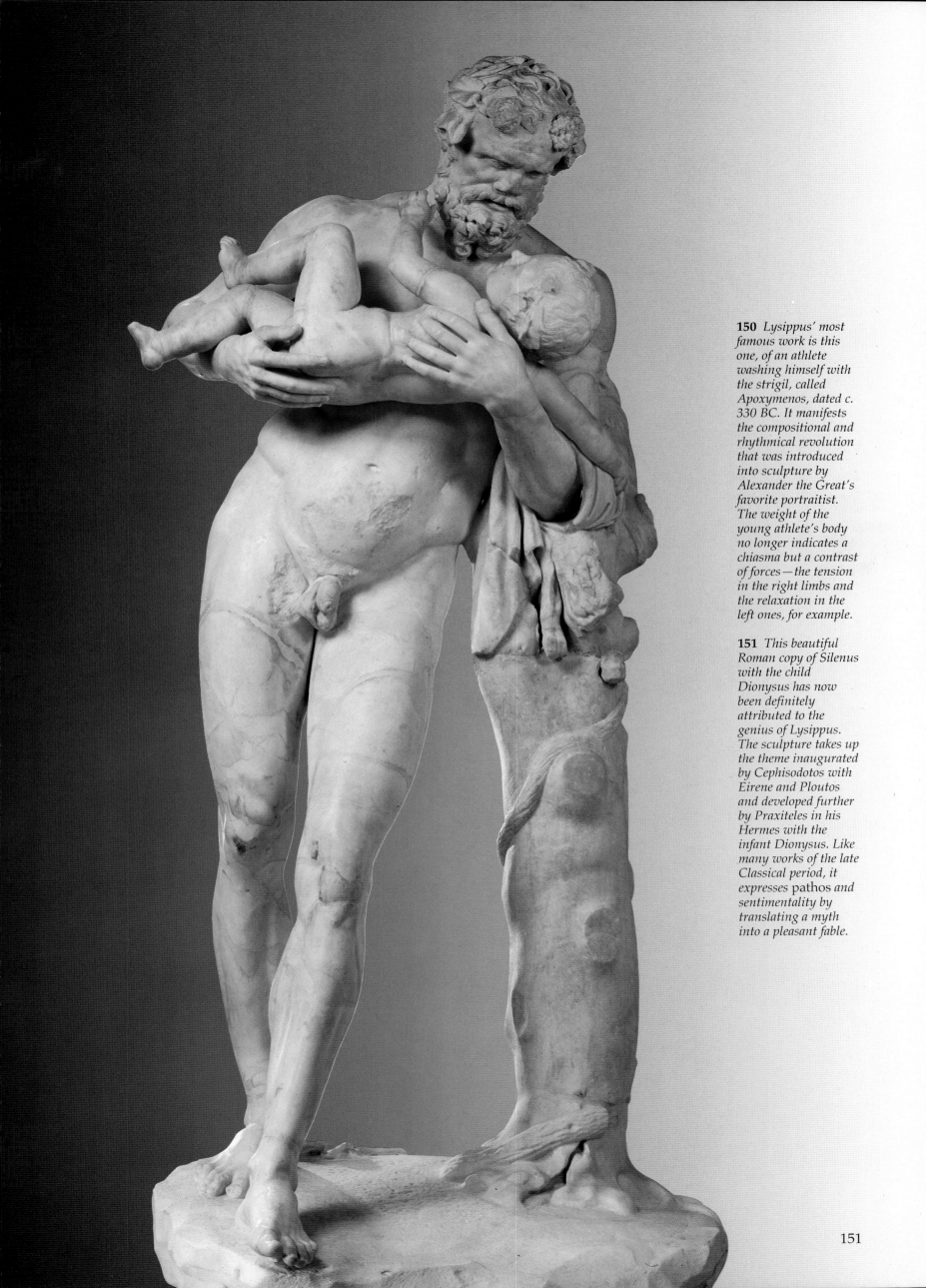

150 *Lysippus' most famous work is this one, of an athlete washing himself with the strigil, called Apoxymenos, dated c. 330 BC. It manifests the compositional and rhythmical revolution that was introduced into sculpture by Alexander the Great's favorite portraitist. The weight of the young athlete's body no longer indicates a chiasma but a contrast of forces—the tension in the right limbs and the relaxation in the left ones, for example.*

151 *This beautiful Roman copy of Silenus with the child Dionysus has now been definitely attributed to the genius of Lysippus. The sculpture takes up the theme inaugurated by Cephisodotos with Eirene and Ploutos and developed further by Praxiteles in his Hermes with the infant Dionysus. Like many works of the late Classical period, it expresses pathos and sentimentality by translating a myth into a pleasant fable.*

152 *This celebrated bronze statue is also attributed to Lysippus; shown here is an excellent Roman copy. Hermes, protector of merchants and thieves, is shown in a very human pose of resting between adventures—looking not very different from a handsome young mortal, were it not for those winged shoes on his feet.*

Thrace. Among the highlights of the 6th and 5th centuries BC are pieces of fine gold jewelry, the most typical local artistic medium, unearthed in the cemeteries of Hagia Paraskevi and Sindos, not far from Salonika. Olynthus, as we have seen, was the site of innovative urban planning experiments, in which the Greek house acquired its definitive configuration. Under Philip II and Alexander the Great, Macedonia vied with the leading artistic centers to the south. City plans throughout the region offer evidence of application of Hippodamean principles.

But other local architects, encouraged by the reigning dynasty, contributed to a revival of the palace-settlement—the seat of monarchical power, an architectural model forgotten by the civilization of the poleis. The palace of Aegae displays all the grandeur typically associated with power and prestige; but even here there are also signs of the rational and methodical design scheme that left its mark on public and private urban structures of the period.

Recently unearthed near present-day Vergina is the royal burial site of Aegae, containing the splendid sepulcher of Philip II. It is the consummate expression of a type of funerary architecture that is exemplified by no fewer than seventy similar tombs in the Edessa/Salonika/Katerini triangle. Among the totally innovative architectural features of these single- or double-"chamber" structures are their barrel-vaulted ceilings and external wall paintings.

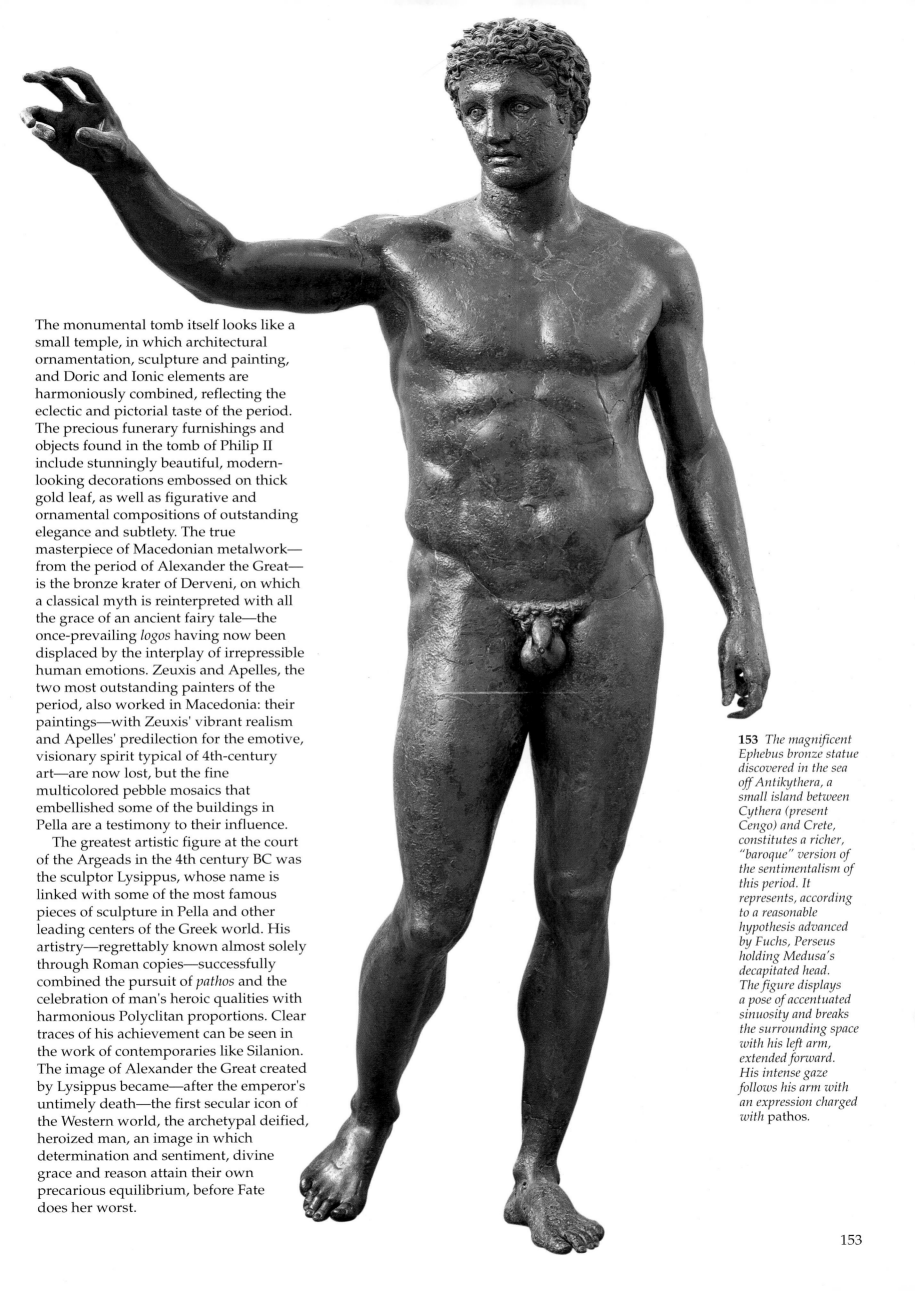

The monumental tomb itself looks like a small temple, in which architectural ornamentation, sculpture and painting, and Doric and Ionic elements are harmoniously combined, reflecting the eclectic and pictorial taste of the period. The precious funerary furnishings and objects found in the tomb of Philip II include stunningly beautiful, modern-looking decorations embossed on thick gold leaf, as well as figurative and ornamental compositions of outstanding elegance and subtlety. The true masterpiece of Macedonian metalwork—from the period of Alexander the Great—is the bronze krater of Derveni, on which a classical myth is reinterpreted with all the grace of an ancient fairy tale—the once-prevailing *logos* having now been displaced by the interplay of irrepressible human emotions. Zeuxis and Apelles, the two most outstanding painters of the period, also worked in Macedonia: their paintings—with Zeuxis' vibrant realism and Apelles' predilection for the emotive, visionary spirit typical of 4th-century art—are now lost, but the fine multicolored pebble mosaics that embellished some of the buildings in Pella are a testimony to their influence.

The greatest artistic figure at the court of the Argeads in the 4th century BC was the sculptor Lysippus, whose name is linked with some of the most famous pieces of sculpture in Pella and other leading centers of the Greek world. His artistry—regrettably known almost solely through Roman copies—successfully combined the pursuit of *pathos* and the celebration of man's heroic qualities with harmonious Polyclitan proportions. Clear traces of his achievement can be seen in the work of contemporaries like Silanion. The image of Alexander the Great created by Lysippus became—after the emperor's untimely death—the first secular icon of the Western world, the archetypal deified, heroized man, an image in which determination and sentiment, divine grace and reason attain their own precarious equilibrium, before Fate does her worst.

153 *The magnificent Ephebus bronze statue discovered in the sea off Antikythera, a small island between Cythera (present Cengo) and Crete, constitutes a richer, "baroque" version of the sentimentalism of this period. It represents, according to a reasonable hypothesis advanced by Fuchs, Perseus holding Medusa's decapitated head. The figure displays a pose of accentuated sinuosity and breaks the surrounding space with his left arm, extended forward. His intense gaze follows his arm with an expression charged with* pathos.

HELLENISTIC ART

The term *Hellenistic* refers to the historical and cultural period between the death of Alexander the Great (323 BC) and the Roman conquest of Egypt (31 BC), the oldest of the kingdoms created from the dismembered Macedonian empire. It also sums up the expansion of Greek influence into the vast territories that the son of Philip II conquered in Africa and the Orient.

The term was first used in the second quarter of the 19th century by the German historian J.G. Droysen, who saw this period as the time when Greek language, religion, political models, customs, culture, and art spread to and were assimilated by all the regions encompassed by the Macedonian conquest. In art history the term indicates the formal artistic language of this period, which had a far longer-lasting impact—at least until the 2nd century AD—on account of the enormous influence of Hellenistic culture on the art and architecture of ancient Rome.

After the death of Alexander the Great, Greeks and non-Greeks alike were common protagonists of the same historical processes and part of a universal culture that made Greekness its theoretical, logical, and material focal point. A *koine dialektos* or "common language" developed, bringing different traditions into interactive contact, enhancing their respective contributions, and fusing their cultural developments without destroying their original "regional" characteristics. As in economics, society, and politics, the foundations of culture were no longer identified with ethnic origin, religion, or political geography. Gone was the prejudiced belief that one model had to be superior to others or that diffusion of culture was necessarily a one-way process, with a misconceived distinction between winners and losers, between

154 and 155 right
Famous to the point of itself being an honest-to-goodness artistic myth, the Venus de Milo, in the Louvre, was sculpted in the second half of the 2nd century BC by a great artist, probably a mainland Greek familiar with the best stylistic and composition schemes of Lysippus. Composed by assembling six pieces of marble, each sculpted separately, today it is missing its arms, which probably shielded the beautiful nude torso. The head, miraculously intact, and the body reveal stylistic traits in the manner of Praxiteles and Lysippus, but the rhythm and movement are more complex, as if a quiver coming from the raising of the left foot had given a ripple of restlessness to the whole figure, which has a suggestive natural asymmetry.

155 bottom left *The beautiful squatting Aphrodite (c. 100 BC) takes up, but in a rather flattened form, a famous model of Doidalsas, adding the lively detail of the hands wringing the hair to help it dry, accentuating the chiaroscuro effect surrounding the face.*

dominating and dominated civilizations. Gaining prominence instead was the idea of a universal dimension of mankind that offered structured space for regional idiosyncrasies, a culture both unitary—in keeping with Aristotelian doctrine—and multiform.

In city planning, once Hippodamean standards and their functional variants had been fully accepted, attention turned to monumental qualities, spectacle, and scenic effects—expressions of the new political order embodied by the monarchies that were the legacy of the Macedonian empire. Sufficiently enlightened to understand the importance of popular approval, these rulers exploited their bond with their subjects demagogically. Citizens on the receiving end of so much benevolent attention were impressed to the point of bedazzlement by the largess that transformed provincial cities into capitals of art and culture. Hellenistic cities are an immense and ostentatious show of architecture, with often oversized defensive walls, a profusion of public spaces, and monumental and artistic structures that became Wonders of the world: the Pharos of Alexandria (cradle of the Universal Library dreamed of by Borges), the bronze Colossus of Rhodes, the great altar of Zeus in Pergamum, the votive Nike of Samothrace. In private dwellings, too, the "no frills" approach that for centuries had been typical of the homes of the poleis was replaced by more appealing designs, rooms to suit both spiritual and material needs, embellished by mosaic flooring—magical carpets of stone—wall paintings, and accessories, some elegant, others all too obviously mass produced.

Craftsmen were experimenting with the very first "factory" processes, while certain minor arts—especially gold jewelry production—reached technical and stylistic levels never seen before. Centrally planned houses, built around a court with or without a peristyle, became popular throughout the Hellenized world.

In sculpture and painting, the schools tied to the main centers of Alexander's now-dismembered empire—Pella, Athens, Pergamum, Alexandria, Antioch, Seleucia, Rhodes—merged their traditions with the polymorphous tastes of a public and patrons to whom artists submitted without having to share their ideas. Technical virtuosity was given greater importance. All attention was focused on portraying reality, frozen instants in the drama or tragicomedy of existence, or else on portraying the intangible realm of dreams: a magical smile, the swift flight of a goddess or dancer, a goddess made mortal. This is the key not only to the revival of the myth but to the development of a regal, colorful literature in Macedonia, works of an unemotional composure produced in Athens, the entertaining "penmanship" of the artists of Alexandria, the dramatic and sensual "baroque" of the masters of Pergamum, the rousing sense of color and movement typical of the school of Rhodes, the products of Tarentine goldsmiths, the terracottas of a hundred cities. It is also the key to seemingly very different works, like the supremely grotesque, "Drunken Old Woman," and the Nike of Samothrace. And it helps us understand the artistic revolution among peoples of the non-Greek world in the 3rd and 2nd centuries BC: from the Romans to the Etruscans, from the Dauni, whose painted tombs were found in central Italy, to the Sannites and Lucanians of the southern Apennines; from the Iberians of Numantia and Sagunto to the shores of the river Indus.

156 *This beautiful Roman copy, from an original by Eubulides, shows the Stoic philosopher Chrysippus seated and engrossed in thought, clothed with a humble cape (in line with the austerity preached by the Stoics). It was executed at the end of the 3rd century BC. The intense expression on a face marked by time, the closed rhythm of the composition, and the search for a calm and sentimental naturalism recall a tendency widely present in Attic Hellenistic sculpture of the 3rd century BC.*

157 *An artist from the late Hellenistic period in Rhodes seems to have been the author of this portrait (reconstructed completely out of his imagination) of Homer, which has reached us through Roman copies. The old blind poet, himself a myth and a model of Greek culture, is rendered according to formal stereotypes that make him into a sort of icon, emptied of authentic interior tension. These qualities are the deteriorating remnants of that "baroquism" that afflicted some schools of Hellenistic sculpture.*

ARCHAEOLOGICAL ITINERARIES IN GREECE AND ASIA MINOR

158-159 The northwestern corner of the Parthenon in a beautiful close-up. On the pediment was depicted the scene of the battle between Athena and Poseidon for possession of Attica: the goddess of wisdom met the horse given by the god of the seas with an olive tree, symbol of lasting peace and prosperity. This pediment was executed by the great Phidias between 438 and 432 BC, the period in which most of the construction on the Acropolis of Athens were commissioned by the democratic government of Pericles.

AMONG ANCIENT STONES,
IN THE BLUE OF
THE SKY AND THE SEA

160 left
The covered gallery of the Mycenaean palace of Tirinto (13th century BC) is an example of the megalithic technique of the "false arch," which allowed for rapid movement in case of siege.

160-161 *A beautiful view of the Minoan palace of Knossos draws attention to the ruins, abundantly restored in a "ruinlike" arrangement, from the north entrance, and to the different levels of the immense complex (17th-15th centuries BC).*

161 top left *Another important Minoan building, contemporary to the palace in Knossos, has been buried in Phaistos, toward the southern coast of Crete: in the photo can be seen the vast flight of steps to the southwestern sector.*

161 top right *This flight of steps found between the remains of the houses and the palace of Mycenae was discovered by Heinrich Schliemann and is now a popular tourist sight.*

The time has come to journey to some of the finest archaeological sites of ancient Greece. Many no less deserving sites have not been included in this chapter for reasons of space. In many cases, neglect over the generations has left them sorry testimonies, more or less abandoned ruins awaiting restoration. Still, we urge readers to seek out these sites, even with their blighted charm, as they visit the more splendid, evocative scenes from this ancient world.

Visitors to Attica, the ancient heart of Greece, have much more to see than the splendors of Athens: they can explore the ruins of the sanctuary of the Mysteries at Eleusis, or go walking in the Hymettos, Pentelicus, Parnis, and Kytheronas mountains, where they will find quarries that supplied marble for great masterpieces, meadows humming with bees that inspired writers of antiquity, and paths and grottoes associated with deities and muses; or any can wait for the sun to set behind the spectacular remains of the temple of Poseidon at Cape Sounion. They can visit the sanctuaries of Brauron, Rhamnus, Oropos, or listen for sounds of battle carried on the wind across the plain of Marathon, or climb up to the impregnable fortresses of Eleutherai and Phyle.

On the way to Corinth a few precious moments must be spent gazing at the delightful bay of Perahora, with the barely identifiable remains of two sanctuaries of Hera nearby. On the other side of the canal, close to the Aegean, is the sanctuary of Poseidon at Isthmia, site of the biennial Isthmian games, second only to the Olympiad. We shall follow the *diolkos*, the paved road along which, for over a thousand years, huge carts carried boats from the Aegean to the Ionian. Corinth itself will not disappoint us, or at least not Acrocorinth, high up on the acropolis, overlooking the gulf. The lower town is also rich in testimonies of antiquity: dominating the scene are the imposing remains of the Doric temple of Apollo, and the agora, which became a monumental forum in Roman times. Close by, water still flows from the fountain of Peirene, with its vast courtyard and elegant facade.

Farther south, at Nemea, are the ruins of the great Panhellenic sanctuary of Zeus, where further biennial games were held. Beyond Nemea a scenic mountain road leads to the enormous, lush-green depression of the storied Stymphalian Lake, ringed by the wooded peaks of Mount Cyllene and high, grassy slopes of Mount Oligyrtos. From here our route goes down toward the coast, through a wine-growing area, until we reach Sicyon, with its terraces, imposing Hellenistic agora, and well-preserved theater. In the dramatic, barren landscape of the Argolid we find not only Mycenae and Epidaurus but a hundred or more tiny acropolis settlements of the early Greeks—Lerna, Assine, Midea—as well as the palace-settlement of Tiryns, with its massive walls. In the sanctuary of Hera Argiva we listen as Herodotus narrates the legend of Cleobis and Biton. The chaos of present-day Argos, by contrast, offers an unimpressive backdrop to the city's imposing theater: a fan-shaped auditorium with tens of seating tiers hewn from the rock of the steeply sloping hillside.

In mountainous Arcadia, where

162-163
This beautiful view of the Sacred Way at Delphi was taken near the Ionic-style Stoa of the Athenians (478 BC), seen on the right. In the background can be seen the Athenian Treasury, a small gracious Doric-style temple, decorated with metopes now conserved in the local museum.

162 bottom
The small theater (322 BC) of Oropos, in coastal Attica, across from Euboea, was part of the sanctuary complex sacred to Amphiaraos, a deified hero. It was probably home to festivals and performances in his honor, along the lines of the Athenian Dionysian festivals.

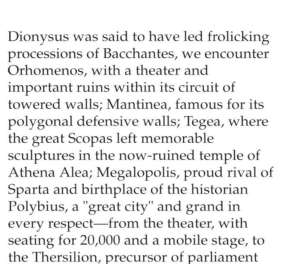

Dionysus was said to have led frolicking processions of Bacchantes, we encounter Orhomenos, with a theater and important ruins within its circuit of towered walls; Mantinea, famous for its polygonal defensive walls; Tegea, where the great Scopas left memorable sculptures in the now-ruined temple of Athena Alea; Megalopolis, proud rival of Sparta and birthplace of the historian Polybius, a "great city" and grand in every respect—from the theater, with seating for 20,000 and a mobile stage, to the Thersilion, precursor of parliament buildings.

Isolated by the high mountain chains of Taygetus and Parnon, Laconia centers on Sparta, the humble city of Menelaus, Lycurgus, and Leonidas, left devoid of ornamentation by the Spartans' indifference to art. On and around the acropolis, only a few hardly discernible ruins have survived destruction late in antiquity and at the hands of modern property developers. Messenia offers a variety of beautiful landscapes, traces of oriental navigators in the splendid Bay of the Phoenicians, Phinikounta. One place not to be missed after Messene is the palatial farmstead of Pylos, possibly the *anaktoron* of Nestor described by Homer.

In Elis expanses of fertile plain alternate with gently rolling hills, except in the south, where there are high mountains and narrow valleys. The low sandy shores fringing the Ionian Sea have wide bays interspersed with lagoons and marshes as far as the mouth of the Nedas. Here we shall find the sparse ruins of Elis, which gave the region its name, and along the coast, near Hagios Andreas, the submerged remains of Feia; farther south is the grotto of Kaiafas, with the sulfur-rich waters in which Nessus the Centaur bathed his mortal wounds.

Leaving Olympia behind, we journey to the mountains of Andhritsena to admire the spectacular temple of Apollo Epicurius at Bassae, built by the same architects as the Parthenon (and now beneath a tent-structure rather than the blue of the sky). We turn northward to

Achaea, with its low rocky cliffs interspersed with white pebble beaches, and rugged mountains crossed by deep valleys where coniferous forests and Mediterranean maquis are never far from citrus groves, oleander, and eucalyptus.

Leaving Patras, with its Roman *odeion*, we cross the strait to Acarnania-Aetolia. Here, close to the meandering course of the mythical Achelous River, the traveler may chance upon the picturesque theater of Oiniadai, a well-equipped port fringed by a long circuit of walls. Amid vast fields of tobacco are scattered ruins of the temple of Zeus and the imposing fortifications of Stratus, ancient capital of the region; at the foot of Mount Arakynthos, patient searching will bring us to the interesting sites of Pleuron and Nea Pleuron.

Along the road to Delphi it is worth making a stop at the splendid acropolis of Calydon, to look for traces of the legends

163 top *The sanctuary of Nemesis at Rhamnus, in Attica, was the object of embellishments by the best architects and artists of the second half of the 5th century BC. Besides the temple dedicated to the goddess of vengeance, Rhamnus also hosted that of Themis, but of a much smaller size.*

163 center *The sanctuary of Asclepius on the island of Kos, in the Dodecanese, was developed along a series of monumentalized terraces between the 4th and 2nd centuries BC.*

163 bottom *Rising in the sanctuary of Artemis Bravronia is the Portico of the Bears (as the priestesses of the goddess were called), created in the 5th century BC.*

164 top left
The remains of the powerful peristasis *of the Archaic temple of Apollo at Corinth (550-540 BC) still stand out against the modest hill that dominates the low-lying city, reconstructed in the Roman period.*

164 top right
The Terrace of Lions on Delos is one of the most striking places on the whole island. On a series of pedestals are the well-preserved, disquieting forms of lions, sculpted in the 7th century BC in the Orientalizing style.

of Meleager and the town's long period of glory. In the heart of Aetolia, along the shores of Lake Trikhonis, Thermum offers surprises, not least an Archaic temple. Boeotia, noble land of the tragic myths of Dionysus and the muses, is a place of vast sun-filled plains and occasional low hills. The ancient capital, Thebes, only briefly predominant among Greek city-states, has practically nothing spectacular to show of its ancient past.

Far more interesting sites await us: the "Ptoion" sanctuary of Apollo; Gla, possibly the Mycenaean settlement of Arne, scenically located on a former island of Lake Kopais; Thespies; Orhomenos, with its magnificent *tholos* tomb; Chaerona, where the independence of the poleis came to an end. A tribute, at Thermopylae, to the 300 Spartans led by Leonidas, and we arrive in Thessaly, with its broad plains stretching from the Aegean to the Pindhos range. The fascinating sights offered by the celebrated fortified Neolithic settlements of Sesklo and Dhimini and the many-towered walls of Alos will prepare us for our visit to Volos, ancient Iolkos. And not far distant are the ruins of Demetrias.

The verdant Tempe Valley brings us into Macedonia, at the very foot of Mount Olympus, fabled abode of the gods, permanently wrapped in cloud. Continuously changing landscapes provide the backdrop for observing its exceptional archaeological heritage. As at Pella and Vergina-Aegae, there are many memorable sites here: the ruins of Dion and those of Lefkadia, surrounded by luxuriant vineyards that reveal splendid

164-165 *Found on ground consecrated in ancient times are the remains of a fortified sanctuary dedicated to Poseidon on Cape Sounion. After its destruction at the hands of the Persians in 490 BC, the temple was rebuilt in 444 BC, most probably the work of the same architect as that of the Theseion of Athens and the temple of Nemesis at Rhamnus. We are not exaggerating when we state that from this most striking spot, some of the most beautiful sunsets in the world can be beheld.*

165 top
This fragment of a Severe style Attican votive stele depicts a nude youth, perhaps an athlete, depositing a crown on his own head. It dates to c. 470 BC and comes from Cape Sounion.

165 bottom *Another beautiful view of the airy and slender* peristasis *of the temple of Poseidon at Cape Sounion shows the probable Ionic-island origin of its creator, careful to measure the effects of light and shadow.*

royal burial chambers like the so-called Great Tomb. Other noteworthy archaeological sites in northern Greece—Edhessa, Olinthus, Filippi, Thassos, Abdera—are all certainly of interest but of varying appeal.

The archaeological assets of Epirus are not limited to Dodona: an unexpectedly fascinating site is the Nekromanteion, below which the Phlegethon, Cocytus, and Acheron, mythical rivers of the underworld, are said to converge. From this ancient oracle, pilgrims obtained replies to their queries from the souls of the dead. A little farther south we come to Kassope, a fine but underrated example of the application of Hippodamus' theories in a relatively limited space, on uneven terrain, and with an early predilection for proto-Hellenistic scenic architecture.

It would take an endless cruise to visit all the archaeological and scenic treasures in the beautiful Greek islands of the Ionian and Aegean. The main Ionian islands—Corfu, Paxi, Lefkadha, Kalamos, Meganissi, Ithaca, Kefallonia, and Zante—are strung out on a north-south axis from ancient Bouthroton, in Albania, down as far as Elis. Along the coasts of craggy white limestone cliffs, interrupted now and then by tiny pebble beaches fringed with luxuriant olive groves, unkempt Mediterranean maquis, or steep slopes, and inland, where the countryside is dotted with tranquil villages, bleak stony patches, wooded ravines—in every corner we discover

traces of the remote past: from the Mycenaean Bronze age, to the flourishing Archaic period of colonialism and trade, to later serene days as thriving provinces under Roman rule. In Corfu, among the archaeological museum's exhibits, is the famous Archaic pediment from the temple of Artemis. Lefkadha's most evocative site is Cape Doukato, a spectacular white limestone cliff from which—according to legend—the poetess Sappho threw herself into the sea.

Hidden away among natural beauty spots, Kefallonia has several sites of archaeological interest, regrettably often difficult to reach: the fine Mycenaean rock-built cemetery of Mazarakata is in an isolated rural location, while the massive walls that encircled Krane are high up a steep hillside. In Ithaca, homeland of Homer's Odysseus, excavations have unearthed evidence of the island's importance in the Mycenaean and Geometric periods.

Scattered across the Aegean are hundreds of islands. Some are described individually in this book, but many others deserve mention: Euboea, with the important excavations of Eretria; Chios, with the archaeological zone of Emborios; Samothrace, where the celebrated Nike—now in the Louvre—was unearthed (its base is still standing in a splendid sanctuary); Syros, stupendous island of the Aegeans; Milos, with the excavated site of Phylakopi.

In the eastern Aegean the island of Kos has close associations with Asclepius, god of medicine, reflected in its archaeological sites. Here there is no space to describe the fascinating remains of its Roman city, among the very finest in Greece, or the Hellenistic structures now mingled, in the harbor area, with Roman and early Christian remains. The island's most remarkable site—the sanctuary of Asclepius, built between the 4th and 2nd centuries B.C.—must suffice. After an ascent accompanied by a stirring crescendo of Roman baths, Hellenistic porticoes, stairways,

fountains, altars, small temples, and a Corinthian temple of Roman origin, the visitor at last reaches the summit of the hill and the ruins of the great Asclepion, a temple scenically set in splendid isolation on four terraces leveled from the hillside. Beyond the Greece we see today is the Greece of yesterday, the Greece of Asia, of Smyrna and Miletus, of Didyma and Ephesus, and a hundred more cities: scattered heirs of the Greek civilization that, from Agamemnon to Alexander, spread eastward and onward.

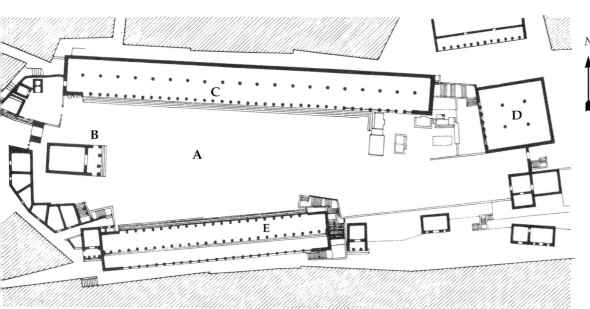

A Agora
B Temple of Dionysus
C Great Stoa
D Bouleuterion
E Thermal Building

N

168-169 *This wonderful view of the Athenian Acropolis from nearby Philopappos Hill highlights the harmonious form of the Parthenon.*

168 bottom left *Phidias' gods and heroes seem to appear everywhere among the ruins of the Athenian Acropolis.*

ATHENS, THE CITY OF THE GODDESS

A Dipylon
B Sacred Gate
C Temple of Hephaestus
D Agora
E Stoa of Attalus
F Areopagus
G Pnyx
H Acropolis
I Theater of Dionysus
J Monument of
   Lysicrates

Travelers drawn to Athens by a keen interest in the history of the ancient world's cultural capital have difficult choices to make. But the Acropolis is certainly the focal point of any visit, and every archaeological tour inevitably starts from the Parthenon, the temple that symbolizes Greek architecture and, in its structure and ornamentation, represents the very essence of the spirit of Greek civilization.

Built in 448-438 BC by Phidias, Ictinus, and Callicrates, the temple is a classic example of the Doric order, with a single eight-column colonnade in front. All its structural and decorative elements were designed according to complex mathematical calculations, in a totally successful attempt to express the harmony of proportions already experimented with by Polyclitus in his sculptures, and codified. The principles underlying this research are very probably to be found in the philosophical arguments of the

Pythagoreans and Anaxagoras on universal harmony. (They were further echoed, about half a century after the temple was built, in Plato's *Timaeus* and *Theaetetus,* with significant evidence of mathematical correspondence.) The peristyle, comprised of 8 by 17 columns and still practically intact, stands on an imposing stylobate approximately 70 meters long and 31 meters wide.

Inside, the depth of the pronaos and opisthodomos seems to be reduced to the minimum, to the advantage of the cella, on the east side, and the smaller "Chamber of the Virgins"—the Parthenon proper—on the west. In the cella is a double row of Doric columns framing in a π-shape the cult statue of Athena Parthenos, Phidias' colossal (12 meters high) gold and ivory masterpiece; in the other chamber, where the ancient wooden *xoanon* of the goddess was kept, were four Ionic columns. This was the first use of Doric and Ionic orders in the same building—a practice subsequently repeated frequently.

All parts of the temple use a measurement unit of 10 Attic dactyls (19.24 centimeters), repeated in infinite multiples, applied to the geometrical proportions for both the plan and the elevation—rather like a chessboard based on Pythagorean rules, which considered proportions expressed by the irrational number j (1.618033...) to be ideal. The colonnade is unusually close to the walls of the cella (and its columns are also closer to one another). The ratio between the lower diameter of the columns and the interaxis of the space intervals between the columns is 4:9, the same as for the dimensions of the stylobate and the cella.

Ictinus introduced a series of architectural refinements to ensure that the metric and harmonious perfection of the Parthenon—in a slightly higher position on the right—was instantly evident to anyone entering from the Propylaea. In general, depending on perspective, light, chiaroscuro effects, dimensions, relationships between

168 bottom right
The sequence of the Parthenon's peristyle appears fluid and close, thanks to the several optical corrections effected by Ictinus and Callicrates in its layout and elevation. This image of the southern side highlights the damage caused by Venetian cannon shots in 1687.

169 bottom *The so-called stele of the pensive Athena is a votive relief allegedly related to a sports competition. The goddess seems to be waiting for her protégé at the finish line. The stone dates from around 460 BC and is considered a fairly good Severe-style work.*

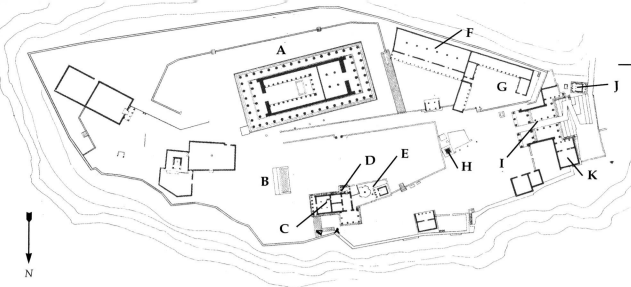

A Parthenon
B Altar of Athena Polias
C Erechtheum
D Porch of the Caryatids
E Precinct of Athena's olive tree
F Khalkotheke
  (depository for weapons)
G Sanctuary of Artemis Brauronia
H Statue of Athena Promachos
I Propylaea
J Temple of Athena Nike
K Pinakotheke

170-171 *The Parthenon, seen here from the northeastern side of Athens, had already been designed and construction had already started around 460 BC under Callicrates' lead, but it was discontinued due to the domestic political situation during the period between the Persian wars and the Peace of Callia. Pericles then undertook a new project, whose outcome is what we may see today, the result of a valuable cooperation between the architects Ictinus and Callicrates and Phidias, the great genius who coordinated all operations on the Athenian Acropolis.*

170 bottom *The Doric frieze of the Parthenon was probably the first decoration started by Phidias. Some think that the master only provided his pupils with guidelines, while others notice persistent signs of his more sober expression.*

171 *This heavy small-size Roman copy is the only evidence of the sumptuous appearance of the gold and ivory Athena Parthenos made by Phidias for the Parthenon's cella. It is the Athena of Varvakion and dates to the time of Emperor Hadrian (2nd century AD).*

solids and voids, and so on, the human eye tends to perceive a slightly deformed picture of reality. And so Ictinus made some astounding "optical corrections": for instance, an upward curvature—by as much as 6 centimeters—of the stylobate, and the practically imperceptible convexity (*entasis*) of the columns, which (especially the corner ones) were also very slightly bowed toward the cella. For today's visitors too, the traditional heaviness of the Doric order is transformed by the austere elegance and the essential harmony of the forms and proportions, while the white Pentelic marble enhances the interplay of light and shadow on the temple's lofty structures.

The ornamental features of the Parthenon, completed in 432 BC, abound in political, civic, and religious significance. The sculptures were entirely designed and in the main also executed by Phidias, with the assistance of some of Attica's finest artistic talents. Works that survived the ravages of the centuries—by Christian fundamentalists after Edict of Theodosius I (395 AD), Muslim iconoclasm after the Turkish conquest of 1456, and Venetian cannonfire in 1687—can be seen *in situ*, in the Acropolis Museum, in the British Museum in London, and in the Louvre in Paris. The pediment groups (over 4 meters high) showed, on the east, the birth of Athena from Zeus' skull, in the presence of all the gods of Olympus; and on the west, the mythical contest between Athena and Poseidon for domination of Attica, observed by Cecrops.

The 92 metopes of the Doric frieze—on which only the very faintest traces of once-vibrant colors now remain—represented four versions of the struggle between good and evil, justice and injustice, civilization and barbarism, using mythological and epic imagery very close to Greek emotions. On the east, was the battle between gods and giants; on the south, Greeks and centaurs; on the west, Greeks and Amazons; on the north, Greeks and Trojans—an evident reference to the recent victory over the Persians. Represented on the Ionic frieze along the wall of the cella were sporting events and the important four-times-yearly Panathenaic procession in honor of the goddess, part of the festivities symbolizing the Athenians' faith and their devotion to their patroness.

For the first time contemporary events joined myths and epic literature in images and in their religious, ethical and political messages. Depicted alongside gods and heroes were men and their city, glorified as mortal manifestations of the values of eternal deities and immortal heroes: the Homeric adjective *isotheos* (meaning "godlike") could not have been better applied than to this particular vision of the human dimension.

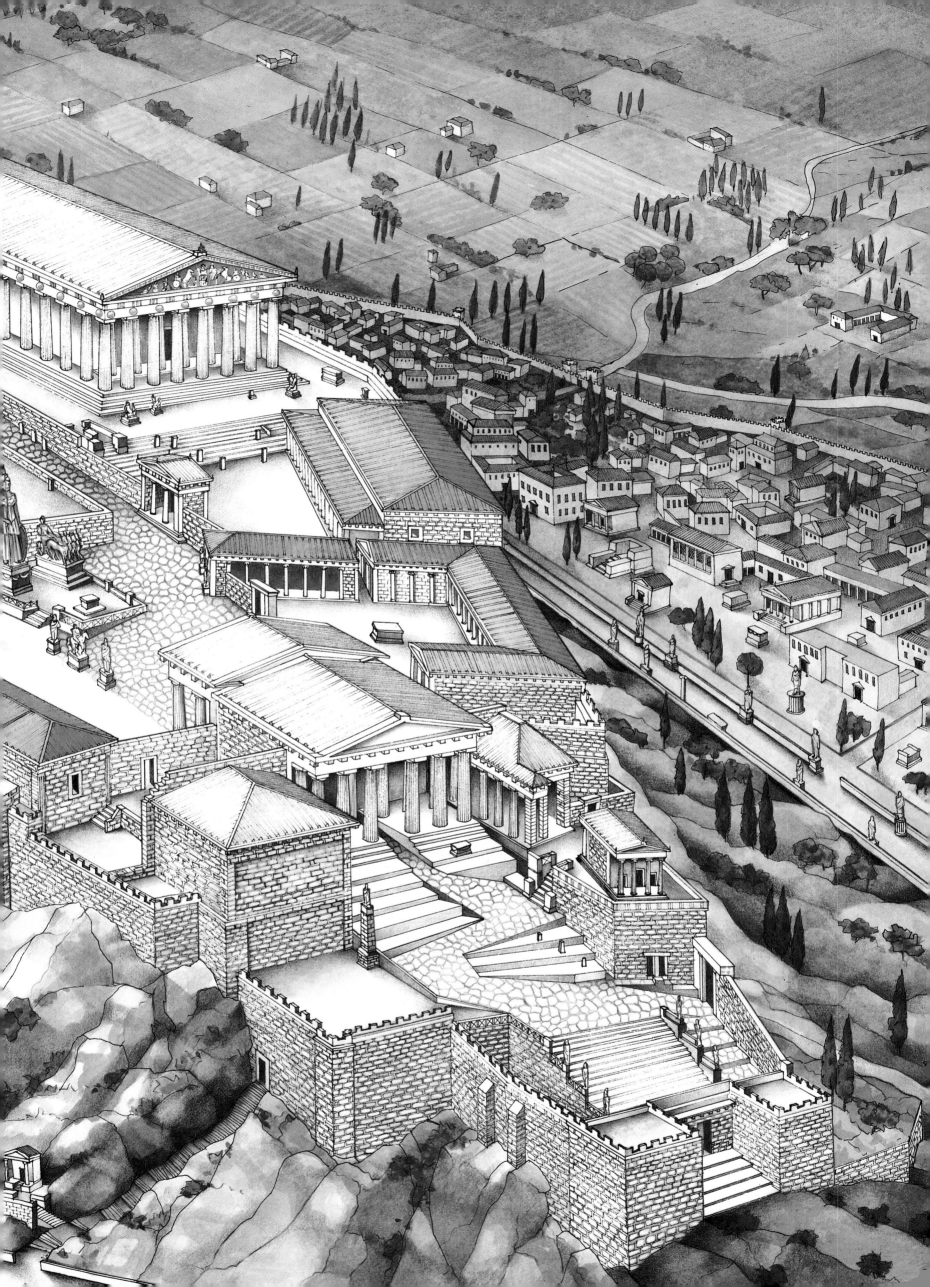

174 top *This slab from the Ionic frieze that decorated the Parthenon's cella shows a few young Athenians in a procession, carrying* hydriai *filled with water as an offering to the goddess during the quadrennial celebration in her honor. This unquestioned masterpiece undoubtedly is the work of Phidias, with his unique narrative and stylistic skill.*

174 bottom
In this slab from the Parthenon's Ionic frieze, decorated with the horsemen's departure, Phidias shows his extreme compositional skill: the uncertainty and confusion caused by the event are reproduced with great mastery. Naturalism reaches its peak in the characters' bodies and faces.

175 *The terror of heifers doomed to be solemnly sacrificed to the goddess, led by a few young cult acolytes, is one of the best demonstrations of Phidias' fine naturalism. A particularly strong contrast is made between the animals' restless motion and the peaceful youths wearing cloaks.*

In 437 BC the architect Mnesicles started his project for the Propylaea, the monumental new gateway to the sanctuary of the Acropolis, on the site of a much more modest one built under Pisistratus. After five years' work, almost certainly entrusted to the same craftsmen who had not long before completed the Parthenon, the Propylaea became the perfectly well-suited ending point for the last, winding ramps of the Sacred Way and the equally appropriate entrance to the marble "treasure chest" that the hill dedicated to Athena was fast becoming.

Providing the superb Parthenon with an entrance of fitting proportions, elegance, and dignity was no easy task. The space was asymmetrical and limited, the terrain was uneven, and the existing monuments and sacred precincts had to be taken into account. Mnesicles very cleverly designed a marble structure that, at the top of steeply rising steps, sat astride a rocky ridge, adapting to and hiding the rugged lie of the land. The proportions and dimensions of each element of the building were carefully calculated, to take full advantage of the building's spectacular position.

A Doric pronaos with six frontal columns thus formed the imposing entrance to the sanctuary of Athena. The vestibule was divided into three naves by a double row of three slender Ionic columns. In the surrounding walls were five doors, at the top of a flight of five steps, interrupted in the center by a passageway for processional chariots and animals. The steps follow the slope of the hill—an ingenious solution to the gradient problem. Beyond the doors another Doric pronaos—identical to the first—overlooked the sacred enclosure and provided a splendid frame for Phidias' huge bronze statue of Athena Promachos and a view of the Parthenon. At the sides of the Propylaea were two

colonnaded wings. The northern one comprised a further rectangular chamber, the Pinakotheke, or picture gallery, which was used to house famous paintings.

The handsome Ionic four-columned temple of Athena Nike stood beside the Propylaea on the southwestern tower, which had been faced in Pentelic marble in previous decades. It was built between 430 and 410 BC—though wars caused frequent interruptions—following a plan developed thirty years earlier by Callicrates and then used for a temple of Demeter and Kore on the banks of the Ilisos River (of which only a few 18th-century sketches remain). The truly innovative feature of the building was the original amphiprostyle plan with its beautifully harmonious proportions. Constructed in Pentelic marble, the temple was enhanced by slender Ionic columns solely at the front and rear, surmounted by a running frieze with scenes of the war between Greeks and Trojans.

Around the temple, to protect worshippers who crowded the terrace high on the slopes of the Acropolis, was an elegant marble balustrade, decorated with low-relief sculptures portraying a procession of figures personifying Victory. The exceptional quality of execution bears clear evidence of Phidias' influence. But it also shows an even more refined ability to convey the subtle interplay of light and shadow on the drapery and in the dynamic poses of the figures, and Callimachus—one of the Athenian master's most talented pupils—has been suggested as the sculptor.

An interesting note is a change in the building's political and propagandistic message: designed in 460-450 BC to celebrate Athens' definitive victory over the Persians, the temple was actually built much later, when the

176 bottom *The elegant shape of the small temple of Athena Nike, optimistically built at a favorable moment during the Peloponnesian War, stands out on the southwestern tower next to the Propylaea, fully coated with white Greek marble.*

176-177 *The Propylaea, a work by Mnesicles (437-433 BC), constituted the architectural boundary between the city and its sanctuary, a sumptuous entrance to the Acropolis. The structure was combined with the Pinakotheke, where paintings by the great masters of the time were preserved.*

177 bottom *The eastern side of the Propylaea, on the inside of the sanctuary, is well preserved. It shows the Doric style developing toward more elegant forms, while preserving its typical and traditional features— simplicity and severity.*

178 top *On eastern side of the Erechtheum, a high, six-column Ionic pronaos preceded the cella, where the ancient wooden cult statue of Athena Polias, the protector of the polis, was* *preserved and worshipped. Solemn airiness is also to be found in the northern arcade, where the mark left by Poseidon's trident during the dispute with Athena for Attica was kept.*

178-179
*The Erechtheum—
here viewed from the
southwest—was the
last building
constructed on the
Acropolis before the
end of the 5th century
BC. It replaced a temple
of Athena Polias from
ancient times, which*

*had originally stood
between the present
building and the
esplanade where the
Parthenon stood before
being destroyed during
the Persian wars. It was
built between 421 and
405 BC, based on a
project by Filocles or
Callicrates.*

179 top *The famous
Caryatids' Lodge
marked the legendary
tomb of Cecrops. The
six beautiful statues
of young women
wearing Ionic
costumes could be
the work of one of
the best disciples of
Phidias, Alcamenes.*

179 bottom *The layout
of the Erechtheum is
undoubtedly unusual,
a place where very
ancient religions
gathered, including
that of Poseidon
Erechtheus. The picture
shows the legendary
holy olive tree, a gift
of Athena.*

Peloponnesian War was in full swing, so it became essentially a tribute to the Athenians' successes over their new enemies, the Spartans.

The last addition to the Acropolis before the end of the 5th century BC was the new temple of Athena Polias, known throughout history as the Erechtheum ("Shaker"), after the Attic name for Poseidon. It was built north of the Parthenon, between 421 and 405 BC, a project by Philocles or—according to some—Callicrates or Mnesicles. Its unusual layout stemmed from the need to respect ritual tradition and the archaic sacredness of the site and house several different, age-old cults under one roof. The Ionic six-column pronaos on the east gives access to the cella, where the ancient wooden cult icon of Athena Polias was kept; on the west side, on different floor levels, were spaces consecrated to the cults of Poseidon Erechtheum, Hephaestus, the hero Bute, and the serpent-boy Erichthonius, who was particularly dear to Athena. Outside the building on this side grew the sacred olive tree, traditionally the mythical gift of Athena in her quarrel with Poseidon.

On the north side a high Ionic six-column portico protected the mark left by the trident thrown by Poseidon, to make a sea-water spring come gushing from the rock. The only decorative feature of the entire temple was a long running frieze in Eleusinian black rock, on which were mounted high-relief figures in Pentelic marble portraying scenes from Attic ceremonies and episodes involving Erichthonius.

As the architect clearly intended, the beholder's gaze is immediately drawn to the south side and the splendid porch, which protected the tomb of the mythical king Cecrops. Supporting the porch in place of columns are the celebrated Caryatids, six splendid statues of young women in Ionian dress, an architectural device that succeeds in merging refined Ionic elegance with the formal perfection of Phidian artistic expression. It seems likely that the designer of the Caryatids—who, despite their forced immobility, have an intrinsic vitality—was Alcamenes, another pupil of Phidias.

Above and beyond the fascination of the porch, the interest in all the buildings lies in their layered configuration, constructed on different levels to follow the rising, rocky terrain of the Acropolis. There is evidence of near-obsessive precision in the way the buildings respect sacred sites of antiquity, held to be scenes of supernatural manifestations. The conceptual asymmetry achieved by applying the graceful, decorative Ionic order to an unconventional structure—particularly one that provides shelter for ancient cults and cult objects—is yet another example of the capacity for synthesis characteristic of Greek culture.

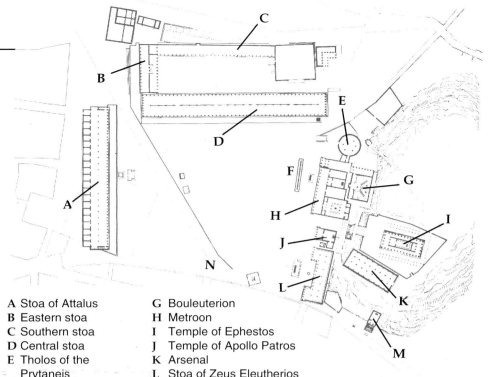

Near the north wall, close to the Erechtheum, are poorly preserved remains of the House of the Arreforoi (5th century BC), with an enclosure intended for leisure pursuits for the young women who wove Athena's *peplos*. The famous theater of Dionysus stands on the south slope of the Acropolis, in the sanctuary precinct dedicated to the god who protected the drama contests held during the great Dionysian festival: the visible structures date back to 330 BC, with many Roman additions. Around it are the remains of a Hellenistic portico that was used as a public walkway, numerous choragic monuments, and the *odeion* of Pericles (445 BC), a large

A	Stoa of Attalus	G	Bouleuterion
B	Eastern stoa	H	Metroon
C	Southern stoa	I	Temple of Ephestos
D	Central stoa	J	Temple of Apollo Patros
E	Tholos of the	K	Arsenal
	Prytaneis	L	Stoa of Zeus Eleutherios
F	Peribolos (precinct) of	M	Temple of Aphrodite Urania
	the Eponymous Heroes	N	Panathenaic Way

auditorium rebuilt in Roman times.

The Agora, with the nearby hill of the Areopagus, is the other main area of archaeological interest in Athens. Its most prominent structures today are the modern reconstruction of the great stoa built by Attalus II of Pergamum in the 2nd century BC, now housing the Agora Museum, with its displays of local archaeological finds from the Archaic, Classical, and Hellenistic periods, and the Doric temple of Hephaestus, still miraculously intact.

The temple stands on the Kolonos Agoraios, a hillock to the west of the Agora, once crowded with metal workshops. Built in Pentelic marble during the same period as the Parthenon, it is an important landmark in the lower part of Athens. The building is about 32 meters long by 14 meters wide, surrounded by columns, in rows of 6 by 13. It follows the conventional plan of the Doric temple with deep pronaos and opisthodomos,

although its cella bears greater resemblance to the larger one in the Parthenon. The structural elements of the temple, and especially its proportions, were clearly inspired by the Parthenon, whereas the ornamentation fluctuates between pre-Phidian models and the innovations seen on the Acropolis. The few surviving fragments of the pediments and acroteria have much in common with the work of Alcamenes. The reliefs in the metopes—only eighteen in number—are tendentially Archaic in style, while the Ionic frieze of the pronaos and opisthodomos reveals the very definite influence of the Parthenon.

What is interesting about the building is its cultic connection with an area of the city where metallurgical activities had long been concentrated. Although there were many cases of generous donations from guilds and private individuals eager to contribute to the embellishment of Athens and to benefit from the ensuing prestige, it is not actually clear whether this temple was built under the patronage of metalworkers. What is certain is that the whole area, never previously linked with any cult, was laid out as a garden. Perhaps the intention was to transform an old "industrial" area—hardly the pleasantest of places, what with the smoke, noise, and smells from the smiths' forges—into a space to be enjoyed by the public at large, visually linked with the nearby Acropolis and its incandescent marble.

Other places of interest are the nearby Keramikos quarter, with the Dipylon cemetery and remains of potters' workshops. Finally, a fine overview of the Athens of antiquity is offered by the National Archaeological Museum.

180 left The temple of Hephaestus stands close to the Agora of Athens, its elegant proportions derived from the Parthenon.

181 top The Dionyian theater, where tragic and comic poetry festivals took place, was reconstructed during the Roman age.

180-181 This view of the Athenian Agora as it probably looked during the Hellenistic age highlights how the irregular terrain and the preexisting arrangements limited a more rational development, in spite of improvements.

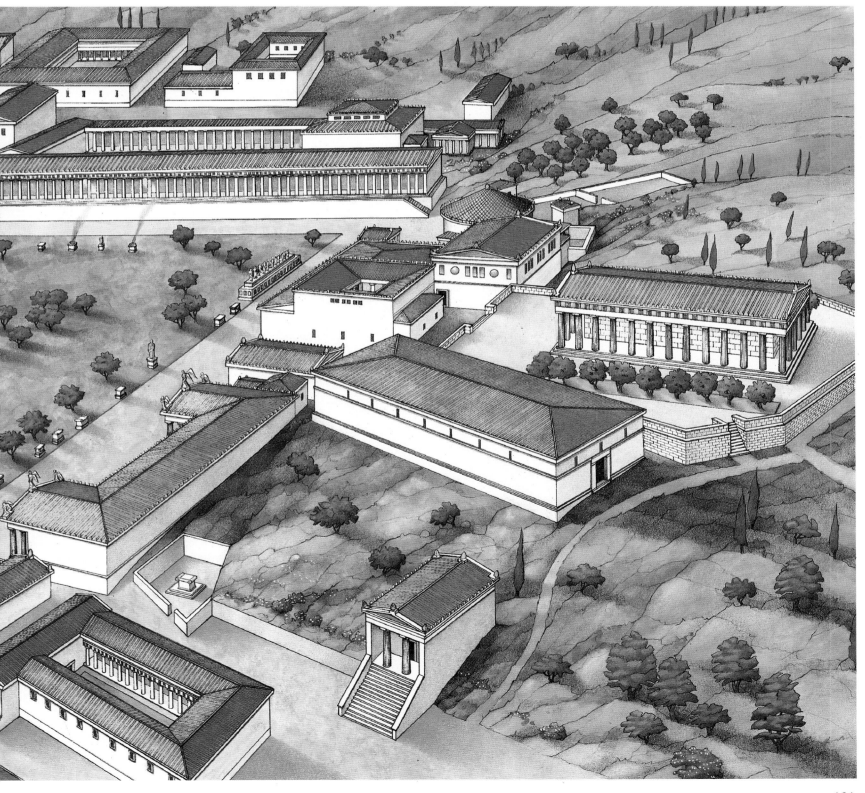

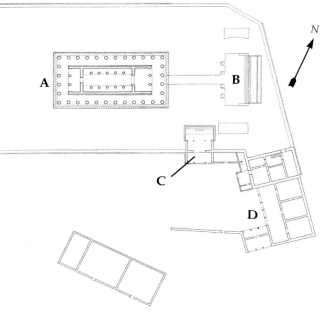

AEGINA, THE TEMPLE OF THE ISLAND

A Temple
  of Aphaea
B Altar
C Propylaea
D Dwellings
  of the priests

Throughout the Archaic period Aegina, in the Saronic gulf, challenged the commercial supremacy of its rivals, Athens and Corinth. Around 500 BC it celebrated its own power and prestige by building a magnificent temple in honor of Aphaea, a goddess likened to Athena. This Doric building is still in an excellent state of preservation. In terms of structure and proportions, it represents the first determined step toward the equilibrium characteristic of Classical architecture: the temple's slender columns convey an unprecedented airiness and brightness. Another original feature is seen in the configuration of the cella: the small naves are divided by two rows of Doric columns in two orders, supporting a ridged roof topped with acroteria and other architectural ornamentation.

But the temple owes its important place in the history of Greek art to its

splendid pediments—now conserved in the Glyptothek in Munich—which mark the transition from the Archaic to the Severe style. Carved in late Archaic style by an unknown sculptor, the life-size figures portrayed the divine appearance of Athena in the midst of a battle between Greeks and Trojans—an allegorical reference to the conflict between Greeks and Persians. The pediments suffered varying degrees of damage in an earthquake that rocked the island early in the 5th century BC: the west pediment remained virtually intact, while the east one, shattered by the tremors, was redone with the same theme around 490 BC by another sculptor.

During that short interval, however, artists had begun to break away from Archaic conventions. In both pediments the goddess is shown dressed and armed with lance and shield, and a breastplate decorated with a terrifying gorgon's head with serpent hair; she is standing prominently among groups of warriors taking aim before shooting an arrow, or grappling in a duel, or lying on the ground mortally wounded. Many of the statues were colored—and have regrettably been much damaged by overzealous and inappropriate restoration by the Danish sculptor Bertel Thorvaldsen in the early 19th century. Other details (arms, ornaments, etc.) were added in gilt bronze, as is evident from the fastening holes visible on the statues. The stylistic distinctions between the two pediments emerge on a general level and in many particulars: Not only does the composition set apart, but the artistic language in the east pediment points clearly to the new Severe style.

If we look, for instance, at Athena, the face from the late Archaic west pediment still has a solid look and essentially frontal features, fixed in the smile that conveys the impossible detachment of the gods from human and earthly things.

The east pediment Athena, by

contrast, has no smile; her face bears a serene expression conveying her superiority to the human events around her (rather than her detachment from them). Delicate relief work—sometimes shallow, sometimes deep—affords form to the face of Zeus' wise daughter; it reflects the search for a new artistic language, more receptive to the prompting of the spirit—the psychological state in which the life force, rational awareness, and the subconscious are merged.

182 *These two views of the Doric temple of Athena Aphaea at Aegina show the harmonic colonnade and the structurally innovative double order of columns within the cella, which allowed the inclusion of a ridged roof.*

182-183 *This is a spectacular view of Athena Aphaea's temple. On top were the pediments made a few years apart by two artists: their reliefs—now at the Glyptothek of Munich—show the transition from the Archaic to the Severe style.*

183 bottom *This view of the Aegina temple emphasizes the fine proportions of the building, a real artistic attraction for this largest of the islands of the Saronic gulf, today the destination of many tourists.*

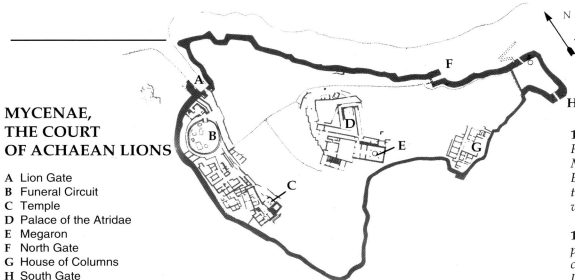

MYCENAE, THE COURT OF ACHAEAN LIONS

A Lion Gate
B Funeral Circuit
C Temple
D Palace of the Atridae
E Megaron
F North Gate
G House of Columns
H South Gate

184 top left *The Funeral Circuit A of Mycenae (16th century BC) was built within the newer enclosing wall.*

184 bottom left *This picture shows the ramp climbing toward the Lion Gate.*

184 top right *The northern postern, a secret gate well concealed among the huge blocks of Mycenae's walls, is an excellent example of "false arch" structure in the polygonal megalithic technique.*

The Argolid occupies the northeastern part of the Peloponnese. An interminable series of limestone hills and mountains, rounded by erosion and made barren by thousands of years of overgrazing and deforestation, extends as far as the region's beautiful coast, with countless sheltered inlets and bays. Water is in short supply, but wherever the terrain permits cultivation, the land produces citrus and other fruits, olives, and grapes, as well as cereals.

The region also has abundant archaeological treasures: the first evidence for the presence of humans in the peninsula was found here (in the grotto of Franchthi, dated to the Upper Palaeolithic), as was evidence of extensive human settlement from the

Neolithic through the end of the Bronze age, and early signs of recovery after the Helladic Dark Ages.

Mycenae is the region's most famous archaeological site, linked with some of the most memorable myths of Greek epic poetry and tragedy. Its rapid decline and abandonment, at the end of the second millennium BC, allowed its fundamental and most distinctive features to be passed down to posterity.

Of particular significance is its location. It stands on a steep hill within sight of the fertile plain of Argos and the Gulf of Nauplia, well protected at the rear by two mountains and deep valleys: a typical choice for the settlement site by a warfaring community. Encircling its acropolis are two rings of walls, the first built in the mid-13th century BC, using large, rough, irregular blocks; the second, larger ring in the 12th century used smoother, more regular, and equal-sized blocks. In the later wall—which incorporated the circular enclosure wall (designated A) of the celebrated shaft graves unearthed by Heinrich Schliemann in 1876—there were only two entry points: the first was the superb Lion Gate (on which two

185 top *The two lionesses decorating the famous Lion Gate lay their paws on two altars surmounted by a column very similar to those of the Cretan palaces.*

184-185 *This aerial view of Mycenae's ruins shows the dominating position of the royal palace over the other structures and highlights the absence of any town planning.*

186-187 *Mycenae's appearance at the time of its greatest wealth (14th-13th centuries BC) was much like this reconstruction, which helps us view Mycenaean architecture as less rural although it seems to have provided many solutions to problems raised by the the style of Cretan palaces.*

lionesses were in fact depicted); the second, of the "Scaean" type, was the North Gate. Posterns providing access along the northeast stretch of the walls, toward the mountain, were clearly visible to the inhabitants but practically imperceptible to anyone approaching from outside.

Not far from the North Gate is Mycenae's most amazing feat of engineering: a gallery over 90 meters long, with steps hewn from the rock, descends to a huge subterranean tank that guaranteed a constant supply of water, to which access could be made without being spotted in the event of a siege.

The Lion Gate is now practically a symbol of Mycenae and its past, but it is only one of many examples of the prowess of Mycenaean architects. This monumental entrance was built with the ancient trilithic technique—its two colossal door jambs support a massive lintel, slightly convex at the center. Instead of casting their whole weight on the lintel the huge blocks above are

shaped and positioned in successively projecting courses, so the superincumbent weight is discharged on the ends of the lintel and hence on the uprights; the resulting "relieving triangle" is blocked with relief decorations. The gate also attests to the notable figurative skills of Mycenaean sculptors: the vibrant colors and soft chiaroscuro effects of the Cretans are replaced by an expressionism more profoundly influenced by symbolic and ideological values.

Visitors to the site climb a ramp leading across the cemetery, where huge mounds conceal *tholos* tombs (many of them visitable), attributed—with great flights of the imagination—to figures from Homer's epics (Atreus, Clytemnestra, Aegisthus). Awaiting them is the stunning Lion Gate and its adjoining bastions, constructed on the Scaean model: the relief decorations above the huge monolithic lintel clearly attest to the stylistic influence of the Near East and exemplify the symbolic force of the art of this warrior monocracy.

The most notable sites inside the walls are Funeral Circle A, with its solid enclosure wall, the royal sepulchral chambers brought to light by Heinrich Schliemann; the intriguing circular, covered *peribolos* with a trilithon structure, formed of cleverly interlocking stone slabs; the palace of the Atridae, of which the entire central body and at least two floors have been identified; and the House of Columns, a fine example of an aristocratic dwelling.

The so-called Treasury of Atreus has all the defining characteristics of the imposing Mycenaean *tholos* tombs. It is approached from a *dromos*, 36 meters

long and 6 meters wide, open to the sky, flanked by sloping walls formed of enormous blocks of stone arranged in regular rows. Opening in the lofty facade of the *tholos* is a doorway, over 5 meters high and almost 3 meters wide. Its probable original decorative facing, with evidence of Minoan influence, has been entirely redone. Surmounting the lintel of the doorway is a relieving triangle.

The large circular chamber towers to a height of over 13 meters, with a diameter of 14 and a half. The concentric courses of overhanging blocks, shaped and stuccoed to make the curve of the false dome perfectly smooth, rise gently and regularly to the terminal slab that seals the structure; the huge pieces of stone are held in place by a system of interlocking blocks that allows their weight to be discharged over the entire curving structure.

The small side burial chamber is hewn out of the rock: only its dome—covered with earth, which also slopes down at the sides of the *dromos*—is visible from the exterior. In the so-called Tomb of Aegisthus, the access passageway is hewn from the rock as part of the circular chamber, instead of being built from huge blocks. From a technical standpoint the *tholos* tombs are among the most interesting Mycenaean architectural developments. In form and ideology, they stand at a somewhat hazy point of intersection between the long tradition of European (and Indo-European) megalithism and the gigantism of Near Eastern and Egyptian architecture. First experimented with in Crete in the 16th century BC in a distinctive local form, they reached the Peloponnese in the period following the Mycenaean conquest of the island of Minos.

188 top *The huge body of the most famous Mycenean* tholos *tomb, the so-called Treasury of Atreus, stands out with its false dome at the end of the long access* dromos.

188 bottom *The inside of Atreus'* tholos *contains a wall decoration stressing the regular curve of its walls.*

189 These two golden funeral masks are among six that were found in the wealthy tombs of Mycenae. Surprisingly they have no forerunners or derivatives, as if covering a dead person's face with a golden mask had been an exclusive ritual practice of Mycenean kings between the 16th and the 15th centuries BC.

EPIDAURUS, IN HONOR OF ASCLEPIUS

Another port of call of the Argolid is Epidaurus, home of the ancient sanctuary of Asclepius, which flourished from the late 5th century BC until the end of the Roman era. The town's magnificent amphitheater, still practically intact, stands in a wooded hollow on a hill not far from the archaeological museum. Beyond it are the vast ruins of the *xenon*, a hostelry with no fewer than 160 rooms on two floors, built in the 4th century BC to accommodate visitors to the sanctuary. Its four courts with peristyles and fountains can be identified. The nearby baths and gymnasium were constructed in the Hellenistic era. They were functionally related to the stadium, which was set in a natural dip in the terrain where the ground had been leveled to allow long seating tiers to be created. The remains of the North Propylaea also belong to the Hellenistic era.

The most interesting area brought to light by excavations is within the *temenos*

A Incubation Stoa
B Temple of Asclepius
C Tholos
D Temple of Artemis
E Propylaea
F Stadium
G Katagogion (inn)
H Theater

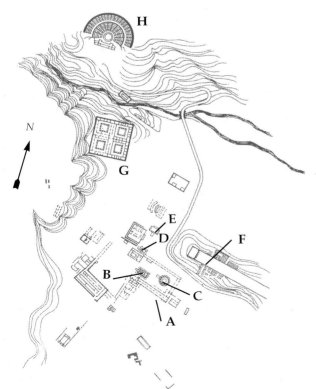

of the god, in the sacred wood where birth and death were strictly forbidden. Here a sloping ramp gives access to the temple of Asclepius. Built by Theodotus (380 BC), it offers a fairly conventional example of a Doric temple. Its pediments and acroteria were carved by the great Timotheus. (A few surviving fragments can now be seen in Athens.) A wide assortment of the finest quality materials—Pentelic marble, ivory, gold, exotic timbers, colored stones, etc.—was used in the construction of the building, which replaced an earlier temple, converted into *enkoimeterion*: a portico where patients slept and waited for divine cures, as attested by numerous votive inscriptions found here.

To the south are the few remains of a temple of Artemis (330 BC), a small Doric structure, enhanced internally by an Ionic colonnade. But the undisputed architectural masterpiece of Epidaurus is the Tholos, a small, circular temple that testifies to the genius of Polyclitus the Younger. (His only comparable earlier work is the sanctuary of Athena Pronoia at Delphi.) The Tholos at Epidaurus bears witness to one of the most important transitional phases in Greek art in the 4th century BC: the move toward rich, elegant ornamentation and graceful load-bearing structures, designed to create a luminous kind of beauty, as elusive as the fleeting, pictorial chiaroscuro effects of the carved surfaces. It was as though, through art, solid forms—manifestations of Being—were deprived of material substance and turned into semblances and shadows of a truth that, in that century of anguish and torment, seemed more and more to escape men's grasp.

190-191 *An aerial view of Asclepius' sanctuary shows its position in a region covered with pine woods, not far from the Aegean coasts of Argolis. An ancient Mycenaean bridge is* *still well preserved a few kilometers away. Epidaurus is the destination of a huge number of tourists, especially attracted by its theater and by the classical works that are still performed there.*

MESSENE, A SUPERB FORTIFIED CITY

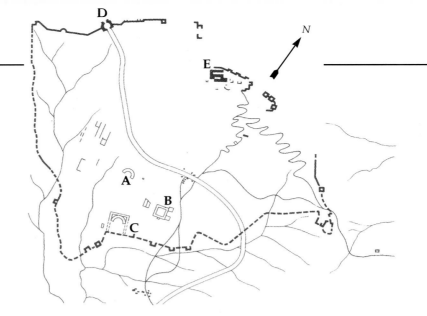

A Theater
B Temple of Asclepius
C Heroon
D Arcadia Gate
E Acropolis

In the region of Messenia the coastline is indented and the hills are rugged; only the confined plain of Pamisos, in the south, briefly interrupts the succession of spurs and ridges that eventually rise up to the sharp peaks of the legendary Taygetos range, on the border with Laconia. In the heart of the region, we come to the ancient city of Messene on the slopes of Mount Ithomi, close to the modern hamlet of Mavromati. Messene was built in 370 BC by Epaminondas, mastermind of the short-lived hegemony of Thebes, for centuries the luckless rival of Sparta. The city flourished until AD 395, when it was destroyed by the Goths.

Its ring of colossal walls is a truly impressive sight: built with regular blocks, the 9-kilometer circuit (2.5 meters thick, 4.5 meters high) is still entirely

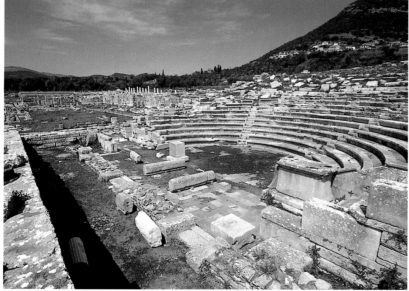

traceable, and much of its north side—with the Arcadia Gate—can still be walked along. This gate is the finest example of a fortified gateway offered by Greek architecture: flanked by two towers over 6 meters wide, its outer and inner portals open onto a perfectly circular courtyard almost 20 meters across! Placed at regular intervals along the circuit are semicircular and square towers; walkways once topped the embattled walls. In several parts of the huge urban area—where excavations are still in progress—there are well-preserved stretches of ancient paved roads, marked with the ruts of chariot wheels. Close to the agora is the spectacular sanctuary of Asclepius. Still visible are traces of the rectangular porticoed courtyard, opening onto numerous votive treasure houses of the late Classical, Hellenistic, and Roman periods, the delightful *odeion* and—in a prominent central position—the Doric temple dedicated to the god of healing and other deities associated with him (Hygieia, Macaone, Podalirio), and the huge open-air sacrificial altar right in front of it. There are further remains of temples on the summit of Mount Ithomi and east of Mavromati, while the ruins of the theater are closer to the Asklepieion.

192-193 Messene is a real novelty for many visitors to Greece: on the slopes of Mount Ithomi are visible the most beautiful enclosing walls of ancient times. Research in the wide sanctuary of Asclepius has uncovered a large temple, in the middle of a monumental site including a small covered theater **(top left).** *Do not miss a visit to the great Arcadia Gate* **(top right),** *with a forceps-shaped structure between its internal and external towers, nor a walk along the top of the 4th-century BC wall, bristling with square towers* **(next page).** *Stop to quench your thirst at Arsinoe's spring* **(bottom left).**

OLYMPIA, THE ANCIENT CAPITAL OF PEACE AND SPORTS

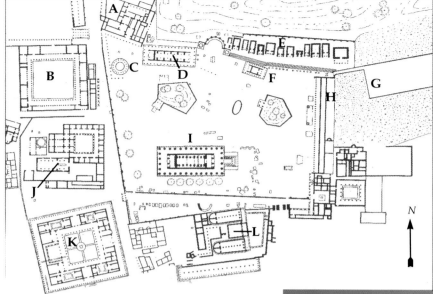

A Prytaneion
B Palaestra
C Philippieion
D Temple of Hera
E Treasuries
F Metroon
G Stadium
H Echo colonnade
I Temple of Zeus
J Workshop of Phidias
K Leonidaion
L Bouleuterion

N

194 left Seen from the air, the Olympia sanctuary appears deep among the ruins of the ancient Altis wood, at the foot of Mount Kronion.

194 right The starting posts at Olympia stadium, where the Olympic games in Zeus' honor took place from 776 BC to 395 BC. They were established— according to legend— by Heracles, on his return from the northernmost part of the world.

195 This wide, spectacular view of the sacred ring of Olympia highlights, in the forefront, the Leonidaion, a hotel with a wide inner courtyard with fountains, meant for athletes and distinguished guests (4th century BC). It lies on the boundary of the temenos and is served by training (gymnasium, sports ground) and relaxation facilities (thermal systems and rather well-equipped sanitary services, considering the era).

Deep in the heart of Elis, in a peaceful, luxuriant valley at the confluence of the rivers Alfios (Alpheus) and Kladhios, the vast archaeological site of Olympia stretches over the lower slopes of a hill covered with pines and bushes that fill the air with resinous fragrances on hot summer days. The ancient sanctuary of Zeus was the place where ideally all Greeks of antiquity abandoned the political rivalries of their city-states and were united in worship of their gods and in celebration of their common ethnic and cultural roots. Every four years, Greeks from all parts of the Greek world gathered in this nonoracular sanctuary to participate peacefully in the Olympiad. A sacred truce was kept during the period of the games, and attempts were made to settle wars and conflicts between the poleis on the basis of reasoning inspired by Zeus, rather than resort to the mystically equivocal oracular answers of Apollo, communicated by the Pythian priestess at Delphi.

The origins of Olympia as a cult center date back to the end of the second millennium BC, although the hill of Kronos and the Altis—the sacred grove that was the very earliest cultic precinct—have been permanently populated since 2800 BC. Because of its very ancient origins, Olympia is a point of convergence for cults and myths that center on Zeus but also involve other deities and heroes. It was reportedly Heracles who brought the sacred olive tree here from the mythical Hyperborean region and founded the Olympic games, to honor Zeus. They also commemorate the great feat of Pelops, who defeated the cruel king Oenomaus in a legendary chariot chase that enabled him to reinstate values of justice, humane behavior, and respect for divine laws. The entire region, the Peloponnese—meaning "island of Pelops"—is named after him. The part played by the river god Alpheus,

renowned for his love story with the nymph Arethusa, in Syracuse, testifies to an ideal link with the Western Greeks; the fact that Pelops came from the East emphasized the sanctuary's bonds with those far-off lands, which the Greeks colonized even before the coasts of Italy and Sicily.

Lastly there was Hera, wife of Zeus, to whom a temple was dedicated when, in keeping with protohistoric custom, the king of Olympus was still worshipped in the Altis, on an outdoor altar of which no trace now remains. The site itself—with its sacred buildings and surrounding complex of structures and facilities designed to host not only athletes but also visitors, pilgrims, and groups who came to the sanctuary at times other than during the Olympic games—had none of the scenic splendor of the sanctuary of Apollo at Delphi. Olympia's prestige stemmed instead from its vast dimensions and from the monumental features of its main buildings and works of art.

From the 7th through 4th centuries BC—when Emperor Theodosius I brought about the demise of Olympia by banning pagan cults and suspending

the games—countless votive treasuries and other structures were built all over the area. It is possible to get an immediate idea of their grandeur from the scale-relief models exhibited in the recently reorganized Archaeological Museum, near to which are ruins of the gymnasium, a huge rectangle enclosed by four porticoed wings where, as in the nearby *palaestra* (wrestling school), competitors did their pregame training.

Most important of all, a visit to Olympia is a chance to savor an exceptional, densely packed chronological review of art and architecture: the site's treasures extend from the Orientalizing phase of Archaism, through the Classical age—with magnificent works by Libon, architect of the temple of Zeus; Phidias, sculptor of the colossal statue of Olympic Zeus, which stood in the cella of the temple; Praxiteles and Paeonius, also preeminent sculptors—to Olympia's Hellenistic and, Roman period. To the onlooker, today as in ancient times, the most striking feature of the entire complex is the temple of Zeus (in spite of its totally mutilated structures). This Doric temple was built between 470 and 460 BC in stuccoed shell-limestone: decorating it were two celebrated pediments—masterpieces of Greek sculpture in the transitional phase from Severe style to Classical. Metopes above the pronaos and opisthodomos depicted the twelve labors of Heracles, all carved by the great anonymous Olympia Master.

In the centuries since the sanctuary was abandoned (early in the 5th century BC), numerous earthquakes have rocked the region, and flooding by the two rivers has also had devastating effects: the entablature and sturdy columns of the peristasis have collapsed, and their drums and capitals lie in crumbled pieces at the foot of the high steps of the stylobate.

The decorations on the pediment friezes, now preserved in the main room of the museum, are probably unmatched by any other temple in the Greek world for intensity of ethical/ religious content and richness of meaning, heightened by vibrant colors. On the east pediment, the legend of Pelops is portrayed at a fleeting

moment in which all the figures present evince the tension of approaching destiny, now in the hands of Zeus, who presides over the scene. (Pelops defeats Oenomaus, king of Pisa in Elis, weds his daughter Hippodameia, and deprives the king of his cruel reign.) Only the arrogant Oenomaus, blinded by hubris, is unaware of the drama unfolding. The poses of all the other figures only seem static at first glance: they in fact betray an almost tangible sense of disquiet (for example, the old soothsayer twists his beard as he stares at Oenomaus, already "seeing" his end), a presentiment inspired by the god (Hippodameia carries herself in a ritual

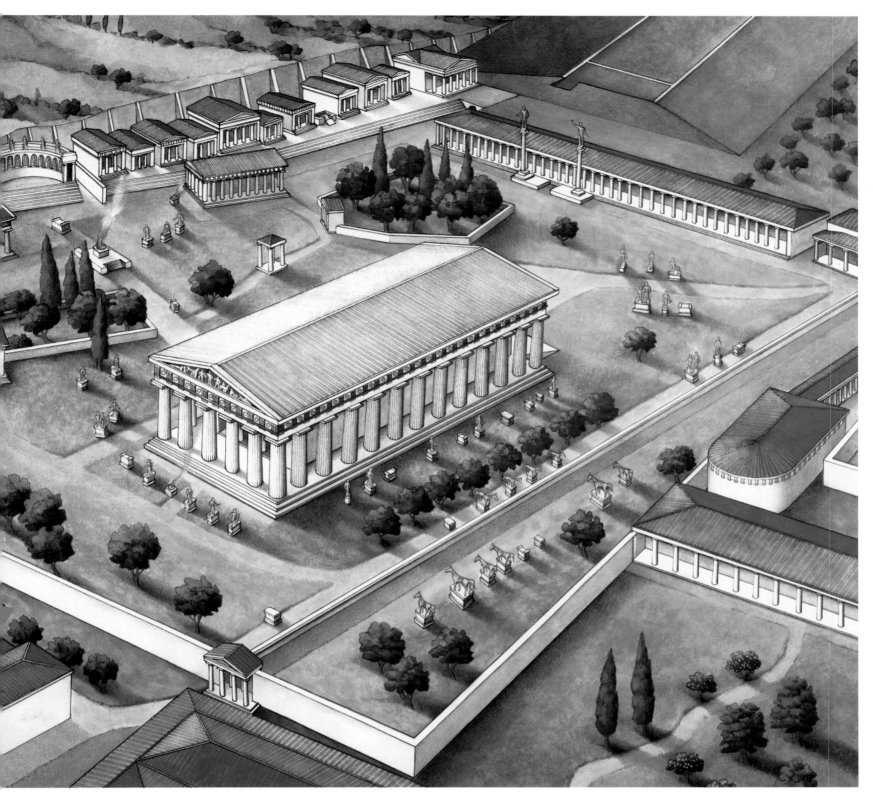

stance typical of the marriage ceremony), and a vague agitation (the young stableboy plays with his thumb without lifting his gaze).

A feeling of dynamism, by contrast, pervades the scene on the west pediment, where a fierce battle is being fought by Lapiths and Centaurs, observed by Apollo: an imposing symbolic representation of the eternal conflict between good and evil, justice and injustice, reason and basic instincts.

North of the temple of Zeus, the Doric temple of Hera was built according to a somewhat elongated plan, in the mid-7th century BC, and richly decorated with painted terracotta sculptures. It was

initially used to house precious votive offerings, but after the inauguration of the larger temple, it became a kind of museum of sacred art within the confines of the sanctuary, itself one huge and rich open-air museum. More and more statuary was installed on the site, as attested by numerous remains of stone bases from different periods: heroes, victorious athletes, deities, and political personages dotted the grounds in glorifying portrayals, halfway between exhibitionism and veneration. Among the statues found here—now preserved in the museum—is the famous group depicting Hermes with Dionysus as a child, attributed by some to

196-197 *This is how Zeus Olympios' sanctuary probably appeared during the Hellenistic age. Surrounded by a high temenos enclosing religious buildings and hundreds of works of art devoted to the god throughout the centuries, it was a veritable open-air museum. It was dominated by the huge temple of Zeus, with elegant arcades and the Treasury terrace in the background. Olympia* is one of the destinations no tourist should to skip during a trip to Greece. Along with its charming and evocative ruins, the renovated archaeological museum contains many extraordinarily important and beautiful works— especially the pediments of Zeus' temple and the beautiful Hermes with Dionysus, attributed to Praxiteles.*

198 *The beautiful image, unfortunately seriously damaged, of the Nike of Paeonius by Mende stood on a high column commemorating the victory of the Messenians and Naupactions over Sparta in 425 BC, during the Peloponnesian War.*

199 *This superb detail of Apollo's head, from the western pediment of Zeus' temple, is made of white Greek marble— and is one of the elements that replaced the originals, which were damaged by an earthquake, then reconstructed in the 1st century BC.*

Praxiteles, an absolute masterpiece of the late Classical period.

There were other outstanding buildings in the Altis. Still aligned on a fairly prominent terrace at the base of the Hill of Kronos are state treasuries, constructed by famous cities including Sicyon, Sybaris, Cyrene, Selinus, Megara, Gela, Byzantium, Metapontum, Syracuse, Epidamnus, and others not identified. Here, over the centuries, cities stored votive offerings to Zeus as lasting evidence of their gratitude. The "zanes," at the foot of the terrace, are a somewhat intriguing feature: this row of sixteen statues of Zeus—paid for using the heavy fines exacted by Olympia's judges from athletes guilty of attempts (successful or otherwise) to use bribery—served as direct warning, since they flanked the tunnel through which competitors and spectators reached the stadium (which had seating for 45,000 people on the low surrounding slopes).

A further highly interesting monument is the Philippeion, a small, elegant, circular temple built by Philip II after the Battle of Chaeronea (338 BC) and completed by Alexander the Great. Its exterior has an Ionic peristyle, while inside are Corinthian columns. The building once housed five gold-and-ivory statues of the Macedonian conqueror with his parents and ancestors—a lost masterpiece executed by Leochares. Perhaps a faint idea, at least, of this outstanding work of art can be obtained from five miniature heads, carved in ivory, found in Philip II's tomb at Vergina.

Other buildings at Olympia are worth mentioning for their functional attributes and elegance: the Leonidaion, a kind of luxurious hostel at the heart of the sanctuary, endowed with gardens and fountains; the numerous sports structures, including a wrestling school, gymnasium, and baths; and the spacious studio used by Phidias while working at Olympia.

PELLA, THE SPLENDID COURT OF MACEDONIAN RULERS

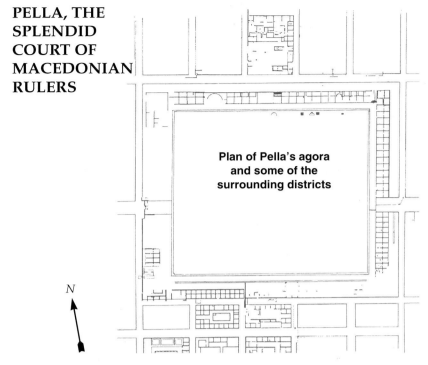

Plan of Pella's agora and some of the surrounding districts

N

200-201 *This exceptional stream-pebble mosaic (late 4th century BC), found at Pella, portrays Alexander and Hephaestion, a Macedonian officer and the king's friend, in the most dramatic moment of a lion hunt (an event told by the sovereign's official historians). The two men stand out, naked like Homer's heroes, against a black background neutralizing the atmospheric and environmental effects. Between them is the lion, with open growling jaws, unsure whether to jump on one or the other.*

A visit to Pella, capital of the Macedonian kingdom after 410-400 BC, is a must for anyone interested in the archaeological treasures of the region where the first universal empire—that of Alexander the Great—originated. Little is known about the history of the city before it became the capital; its palace was built where Euripides' tragedy *The Bacchae* was first performed. It is nonetheless certain that after the Roman conquest (168 BC) and Pella's relegation to mere chief town of a district, its prominent role was gradually taken over by Thessalonike, present-day Salonika.

Pella is a fine example of grid-based urban planning, and it was endowed with a sophisticated water supply and drainage system. It had blocks of well-appointed peristylar houses, probably duplexes, with mosaic-paved rooms on

the ground floor. Its finest building was the palace where archaeologists have uncovered pebble mosaics with black and white geometric patterns and colored figurative motifs (c. 300 BC), a few of which bear their designer's name. Particularly noteworthy are those of Alexander and Hephaestion hunting a lion, a deer hunt, the battle of the Amazons, and Dionysus riding a panther.

Definitely to be included on the visitors' itinerary are the monumental tombs of Vergina and the palace of Aegae, where the Macedonian monarchy instigated a renaissance of monumental palace architecture. The remains of the building—of truly impressive size (about 105 by 89 meters)—stand on the edge of a low hill overlooking the broad valley of the river Aliakmon, seemingly linking the citadel and the main body of the city. A huge, square arcaded court with sixteen Doric columns on each side was surrounded by structures protected externally by high walls; the wide gateway was probably the only point of entry. The building was divided into spacious rooms with varying characteristics and functions. The facade was a worthy complement to the building; it was also the first example in Macedonia of the spectacular architecture that was already seen in Kassope and Priene and eventually typical of Hellenistic Greek architecture generally. The fine-quality materials used in the palace—from the polychrome paving stones to fine multicolored pebble mosaics, true "stone carpets," to the hardwoods that, on the west side at least, made possible bold roofing designs—show a taste for luxury, as well as a

201 right *Many wealthy Pella houses were decorated with mosaics—indeed, these mosaics were "translations" of highly celebrated works by the greatest painters of the time, stone carpets perpetuating their fame.*

202-203 *The head of Hephaestion is vividly and realistically outlined in this detail of the stream-pebble mosaic showing the lion-hunting scene.*

predilection for spaciousness, color, and light. The plan of the palace of Aegae is a monumental version of central peristylar design, indicative of a rational use of space. From the 4th century onward, this layout was used in both luxury and standardized private dwellings in planned cities, as well as in large public complexes such as gymnasiums, *palaestrae,* and enclosed agorai.

204-205
This charming view of the theater conveys all the beauty of Dodona and its landscape, with the inaccessible Epirus Mountains looming over the green plateau, which hosted Zeus' sanctuary. Today the theater is still used for performances of classical comedies and tragedies.

204 bottom
The imposing external walls of the Dodona theater almost seem part of a fortress. It is an effect produced by the rustication, or rough surfaces on the blocks, which create a pleasant contrast with the regular harmony of the blocks' layout.

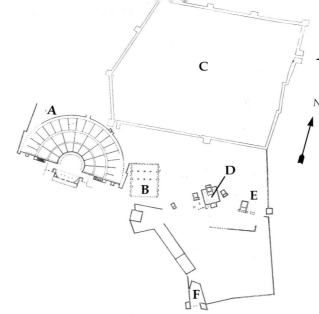

A Theater
B Bouleuterion (council house)
C Acropolis
D Temenos of Zeus
E Temple
F Propylaea

DODONA, WHERE THE OAKS WHISPERED TO MORTALS

Epirus has a varied landscape, from the peaks of the Pindus range to the rolling hills that slope down to the shores of the Ionian Sea and the sun-lit gulf of Amvrakikos. Sometimes the scenery is clad in lush green vegetation; elsewhere the land is stony and barren, its scant grass overgrazed by sheep for thousands of years and its trees extensively felled.

The logical point of departure for a journey through Epirus is the hillock at Dodona, on which stand the fascinating ruins of the oracle of Zeus.

The sanctuary, of extremely ancient origin, flourished in the 4th and 3rd centuries BC and was for a long time the most important religious center in this outlying region of Greece. The oracle spoke through the rustling leaves of the age-old sacred oak tree that grew in the sanctuary precinct. The utterances were interpreted by the temple's priests, mystics from a small group of families of ancient origin, who observed ancestral rites such as sleeping on the bare ground and—unhygienic as it may seem—never washing their feet! Rresponses to questions put to the oracle were based on divination: on the twittering and flight of sacred doves, the bubbling noise of a spring, the throw of the dice, and the ringing of a bronze gong.

Between the 7th century BC and the Roman age, the temple was destroyed many times and reconstructed with the same form, size, and orientation. Built of large stone blocks assembled in regular rows, the structure of the 219 BC version is still clearly visible. The *temenos* is reached through an Ionic propylaea, opposite which is a small temple, on a podiumlike structure, flanked by an Ionic colonnade.

What makes the journey to Dodona especially worthwhile is its splendid theater. It was constructed in its present monumental form by King Pyrrhus early in the 3rd century BC and was further enhanced by Philip V toward the end of the same century. Its enormous

semicircular cavea, hewn from the hillside just below the city's fortifications, is larger than that of the theater at Epidaurus. Divided horizontally by three corridors and vertically by ten stairways, it could seat 18,000 spectators. The massive retaining walls, made from local limestone, still stand to a height of over 20 meters; they were meticulously constructed from regular blocks. Beyond the few remains of the stone proscenium are the ruins of the stadium, partly adjoining the west *analemma* of the theater and surrounded by twenty tiers of seats, a further testimony of the religious significance attributed to sporting contests in the ancient world. On the opposite side are the disintegrated remains of the *bouleuterion,* or council house, comprised of a large hall with Ionic columns and a Doric portico.

205 top *The sacred ring of the sanctuary of Zeus at Dodona contained the holy oak, whose rustling branches were used to prophesy the god's will.*

205 bottom *The stage at the Dodona theater bears clear evidence of Hellenistic architecture. It has not been determined whether this theater—like the Megalopolis theater in Arcadia—was equipped with a system to change sets.*

206 top Apollo's temple at Delphi (seen here in its 373 BC version) had tall Doric columns made up of thick stacked cylindrical blocks. In its adyton, the Pythia expressed the god's will.

206-207 A real jewel of the first half of 380 BC is the famous Tholos of Delphi, a work by the Phocian architect Theodoros, in Athena Pronoia's sanctuary. Its elegance is enriched by its fine proportions, by the well-balanced color contrasts in the cella's materials, and by the architectural decoration, some traces of which still exist on the peristyle—a good example of a Doric frieze..

A Stadium
B Sacred Precinct
C Sacred Way
D Theater
E Temple of Apollo
F Castalian fountain
G Gymnasium
H Marmaria
I Tholos

DELPHI, THE NAVEL OF THE WORLD

Delphi stands high (at an elevation of 570 meters) on the slopes of Mount Parnassos, in the heart of Phocis, at the crossroads of important ancient trade routes. Seemingly suspended midway between the glittering Phaedriades cliffs and the massed olive groves that make the valley below gleam like silver, the site has enormous fascination and charm. The celebrated sanctuary of Pythian Apollo was built here in the Geometric period (10th-9th centuries BC), while the smaller temple of Athena Pronoia was added later, on an artificial terrace below.

The site had previously been used by the Mycenaeans for their chthonian cultic practices. Here, as in many other pre-Hellenic religious centers, the new preference for an Olympian god rather than earlier deities is a sign of the last massive migration of Indo-Europeans to Greece. But the legend at Delphi had deeper significance than others. According to the legend, Apollo defeated Python, serpent-son of Gea (the Great Mother Earth), who stood guard over a rock chasm whose vapors inebriated men and enabled them to make prophetic utterances. Apollo's triumph stemmed from a "necessary" act of violence over the primitiveness and ferocity symbolized by Python. Implicit in his deed was the determination to do away with the barbarities of the Dark Ages, and instead enforce civilized behavior and law and order, and establish reason, balance, knowledge, and creativity as the gods' prerogatives and gifts.

Apollo was the appointed protector of the mysterious, primordial natural force emitted by the chasm; likewise, he was endowed with its powers. To voice the oracular prophecies was the task of the Pythian priestess, whose utterances were interpreted by attendant priests. The reasons for Delphi's prominent role in religious and political matters, especially in the 7th and 6th centuries

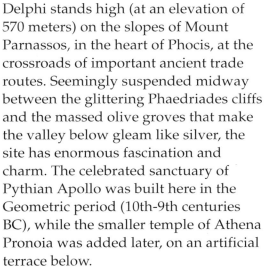

207 top *This 5th-century BC copy of the* omphalos, *the "umbilicus" enclosed in a sacred woollen net, reminds us that Delphi, according to legend, was the navel of the world. The stone was the funeral symbol of Python, the son of Gea, murdered by Apollo, who inherited his precious oracle.*

BC, are thus not hard to imagine: here, at the navel of the world, all initiatives of the Greeks—from founding colonies to waging wars—were condoned or vetoed by the deity, through the prophecies and replies of the oracle.

Evidence of the importance of Delphi lies in the impressive ruins of the sanctuaries of Apollo and Athena, with their imposing buildings (stadium, theater, gymnasion, hostelries) for the celebration of the Pythian festival, or "championships" of arts and sport held in honor of the god. But of still greater significance is the plethora of purely ornamental structures, works of art, and altars, especially the treasuries. Built here by many cities of the Greek world,

207 bottom
An unusual view of the Athenian Treasury at Delphi shows the marked slope of the sanctuary's site, which was built on a preexisting Mycenaean cult site. Not only is Delphi spectacular and intriguing, but the Byzantine monastery of Osios Loukas is also close by.

208 left *The romantic rock-setting of the Castalian spring lies along the route from Athena's sanctuary to Apollo's sanctuary.*

208-209 *The well-preserved Delphi amphitheater still stands on top of the sanctuary's hill, not far from the stadium, as in other Greek sanctuaries.*

209 top left *The wide gymnasium, on a terrace east of Athena Pronoia's sanctuary, was where athletes taking part to the Pythian games in Apollo's honor were framed.*

209 top right *The Pythian games stadium seen from the starting posts is a grand structure bordered by high tiers of seats.*

from Asian Ionia to the Cyclades, from the colonies to Attica and the Peloponnese, these treasuries were intended as temples to house votive offerings and as propagandistic show-places of opulence and prestige.

No Greek archaeological sites better preserve their architectural and artistic history in horizontal stratigraphic sequence than sanctuaries. From the 6th through 4th centuries BC, at the instigation of governments and tyrannies, and later, monarchs and magistrates, hundreds of building projects were constructed in the huge *temenos* of Delphi, on either side of the Sacred Way, which zigzags up the hill. There is absolutely no evidence of planning: buildings of different—and sometimes far distant—time periods occupy adjoining areas, with no regard for existing orientations. At Delphi as at other sanctuaries, while new structures were added, none were demolished—those damaged by natural disasters or the ravages of time were repaired or faithfully rebuilt.

Constructed in the 6th and 5th centuries BC from huge stone blocks, the Sacred Precinct has nine gateways. The largest is on the southeast side, where there is an ancient Roman agora flanked by porticoes—now with shops selling votive offerings and souvenirs.

The Sacred Way begins here. All around are countless bases of statues erected by Greek cities in the 5th and 4th centuries BC as memorials to important events in their history. Today we can get only a faint idea of the once-stunning lineup of offerings, often in bronze, that embellished the precinct from the very first ramp. Again, this awe-inspiring sight did not stem from the coordinated efforts of talented architects and urban planners but was the outcome of chance affinities or—perhaps—contrasts between monuments designed to glorify one Greek polis or another.

Farther along the path is the first of the series of treasuries built in honor of Apollo by Sicyon, Thebes, Megara, Syracuse, Cnidos, Corinth, and many other city-states of the Greek world. Of these only scant traces now remain, with occasional fragments of sculpture and architectural ornamentation. The Siphnian Treasury and the Treasury of the Athenians are both exceptional examples of Archaic and Severe-style architecture and sculpture.

Only the foundations of the Siphnian Treasury are still visible (the remains of the building are housed in the nearby Archaeological Museum) it was an Ionic temple, with two elegant caryatids substituted for the columns between the side walls of the pronaos. Built in 530-525 BC, it is still one of the most eloquent examples of late Archaic art; especially noteworthy are the north and east sides of its frieze, on which a battle between the gods and giants and the council of the gods on Olympus are portrayed with outstanding vibrancy, and plasticity and with bold, innovative use of space.

The Treasury of the Athenians was built after the Battle of Marathon (490 BC) to display some of the spoils taken from the Persians; after its excellent restoration, it stands almost intact today in its original position. This temple is slightly larger than the Siphnian

210 *The statue of Agias of Pharsalus, almost intact, a masterpiece by Lysippus, stands out in pink Paros marble. The athlete stands on his long legs according to the antithetical rhythm typical of this artist. His look is faraway, and his beautiful face is free of stress—like an ancient mythical hero.*

211 left *A detail from the late Archaic Ionic frieze of the Siphnian Treasury shows a dramatic clash between gods and giants. It appears on the northern side, by the Sacred Way, traveled by pilgrims looking for guidance from the god of wisdom and arts.*

211 right
This top of a votive column over 13 meters high, offered by the Athenians in 335-325 BC, represents three charming dancing korai. The wide capital is decorated with acanthus leaves. It is one of the best expressions of late-4th-century BC Athenian art.

Treasury below it but is constructed in the Doric order: its most significant features are the simple harmony of its proportions and a frieze with alternating triglyphs and metopes depicting the battle between Greeks and Amazons, the adventures of Theseus, and the labors of Heracles, in a Severe style still permeated with late Archaic elements.

Regrettably, the overall visual effect of the area occupied by the treasuries can now only be imagined. These buildings once conveyed powerful political messages too: for example, after its crushing victory over the Athenians in the Peloponnesian War, Syracuse erected its Delphi treasury directly opposite the Athenian monument, which had become the symbol of Greek independence.

The most important building in the main sanctuary was, of course, the temple of Apollo. The remains visible today date from the sixth construction phase (373 BC), which respected the dimensions of the previous Archaic temple. It is a classic example of a Doric structure (about 60 by 23 meters), built from limestone and tufa with stuccoed tufa columns; resting on its substantial base was a cellular-type stylobate with three steps. Embellishing the cella, peristyle, pronaos, and opisthodomos were artworks and objects of cultic and historic significance: consequently, as is frequently the case with prominent Greek sanctuaries, the temple and its surroundings had a secondary role as a sacred art museum. The imposing masses of the temple must have dwarfed the surrounding buildings, attacting people's gaze to the "house of the god," significantly situated about halfway between the two springs and the chasm traditionally associated with the Pythian oracle.

High above the temple terrace is the theater, in an excellent state of preservation (only the stage building is gone). Following Greek custom, it was built on the mountain slope, and it completes the panorama of the sanctuary complex. It was entered through an elegant semicircle of frescoed porticoes, decorated with sculptures and offerings in gleaming bronze. (That of the tyrant Polyzelus of Gela, dated 475 BC, is particularly

famous: the splendid Charioteer is exhibited in the museum.)

Outside the *temenos* was the stadium, where athletic events and horse races of the Pythian games took place, watched by as many as 70,000 spectators. Cut from the hillside, it was about 180 meters long and encompassed tiered seating on a high podium, probably protected by fencing.

In a picturesque setting along the road leading to the sanctuary of Athena Pronoia are the barely recognizable remains of the sacred Castalian spring, were priests and pilgrims purified themselves before their encounter with Apollo. The smaller, lower sanctuary incorporates the ruins of the two Archaic temples of Athena: the earlier of the two, particularly valued as a milestone in the evolution of the Doric capital, still bears evidence of a disastrous landslide that destroyed much of the building.

A short way farther on, visitors should not miss the splendid molding on the high foundation plinth of the Treasury of Marseille (530 BC), built in the Ionic order but with rare Aeolic capitals (now exhibited in the museum).

The most fascinating building in the precinct is the Tholos (380-370 BC), a masterpiece designed by the Phocian architect Theodoros: the origins of its somewhat rare rotundalike form may well lie in prehistoric traditions.

An Attic influence is seen in the building's proportions, in compliance with mathematical ratios, amply demonstrated by the external *peribolos*, or external court, whose twenty Doric pillars follow the classical columniation coded by Ictinus, architect of the Parthenon. But the Tholos also had novel features: the innovative configuration of the limited internal

212 left *Among the most famous examples of Greek Archaic art are these statues of Cleobis and Biton, made by Polymedes of Argos around 580 BC. They are dedicated to the two twins, who devoutly sacrificed themselves in the Delphi sanctuary to help their mother, a priestess of Hera. The heavy forms and the sharp features of the Doric style are quite evident.*

212 right *A slight idea of the value of the gold-and-ivory statues widespread in ancient sanctuaries is provided by this superb gold-plated ivory head, dating to the 6th century BC. It was found, together with many other equally important and valuable artworks, in a sort of warehouse in front of the Arcade of the Athenians, along the Sacred Way, just below Apollo's temple.*

space and the application of the Corinthian order to the ten columns of the cella. These columns, touching the wall but not actually joined to it, rise from a high base of dark Eleusinian limestone, in striking contrast to their own white Pentelic marble. The Doric frieze (repeated on the outer wall of the cella), the peristyle ceiling with its original coffering, and the downspouts denote a modified approach to decoration, one that goes beyond sharply defined frames of reference to introduce the *koine* and an architectural and artistic eclecticism subsequently absorbed by Hellenism.

The works of art housed in Delphi's archaeological museum bear witness to almost three thousand years of history, brought to light by French archaeologists who started excavations here in 1892. Unfortunately, as is often the case in Greek museums, the exhibits tend to be grouped by type of finds or work of art rather than in strictly chronological order. The very earliest traces of human

presence in the region, for example, are found in Room 13 (the last one), together with pottery from various periods, grave goods, votive offerings, and domestic pieces.

Some of the rooms contain finds of outstanding interest. In Room 2 are several splendid bronze tripods, votive offerings to Apollo, richly decorated in Geometric or Orientalizing style. Room 3 is dominated by two huge *kouroi* representing Cleobis and Biton (590-580 BC); around its walls are the remains of the beautifully carved Archaic frieze (560 BC) from the Sicyonian Treasury. All the surviving decorations from the Siphnian Treasury are to be found in Room 5, together with the Archaic sphinx dedicated to Apollo by the Naxians (570-560 BC), which once stood atop a pillar over 12 meters high. Exhibited in Room 6 are the 24 metopes from the Athenian Treasury. The statues from the late Archaic pediment of the

temple of Apollo (510 BC) in Room 7, attributed to Antenor, are undoubtedly among the great Athenian sculptor's finest works. In solitary splendor in Room 12—a discreet but precious kylix painted by Douris—is the celebrated Charioteer. This undisputed masterpiece of the Severe style, possibly by Pythagoras of Reggio or Critius of Athens, depicts a young man in the tunic typically worn for chariot races, his eyes—made of ivory and *pâté de verre*—still glowing with success.

Farther on is the last artistic masterpiece of the sanctuary of Delphi: a series of statues comprising the offering of Daochos II, probably contemporary copies of bronze originals by Lysippus (c. 360 BC), which once occupied a prominent place northwest of the temple.

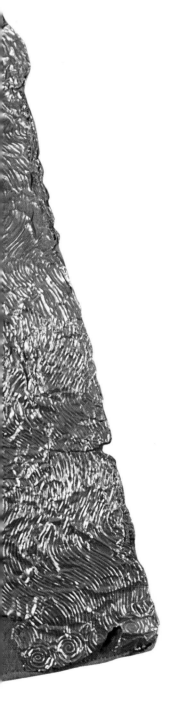

213 *The disquieting sphinx offered by the citizens of Naxos (in the Cyclades) to Apollo around 570-560 BC is marked by the typical iconographic and stylistic features of early Archaic art. It stood atop a votive column over 12 meters high, facing the god's temple. The supporting top was the abacus of a huge Ionic capital.*

Naxos was an important sculptural center during the 7th and 6th centuries BC, and works by Naxian artists may be found all around the Cyclades, thus demonstrating the political and economic power wielded by this island over the central Aegean sea.

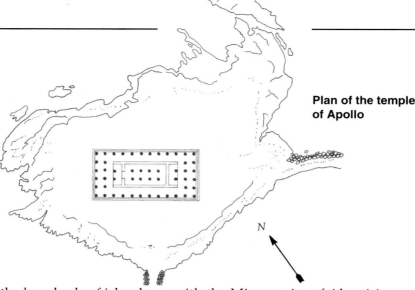

Plan of the temple of Apollo

N

214 *Tourists traveling from Naxos to Apollonas, a picturesque village jutting out on the sea, are surprised by a 10-meter-high* kouros, *an unfinished work of the second half of the 6th century BC, lying in a marble quarry used in ancient times.*

214-215 *This marble portal of the cella of Apollo's Ionic temple, an unfinished work of the 6th century BC, is almost the symbol of ancient Naxos. It stands on a small rock island facing the harbor of the modern Naxos village, the island's main center.*

A great many of the hundreds of islands that dot the Aegean were inhabited in ancient times, and excavations have revealed traces—sometimes of great significance—of the civilizations that came and went between prehistory and the end of antiquity. Some islands are sites of towns or religious centers of such archaeological importance as to make them de rigueur on the itinerary of every self-respecting cultural tourist. Only a few, however, can be included in our imaginary journey across Homer's "wine-dark sea," whose purple reflections enhance Greece's vivid dawns and splendid sunsets and do full justice to the poets' descriptions. We must regrettably and unjustly skip over Euboea, with Eretria; Chios; Thassos; Samothrace, former home of the celebrated Nike now in the Louvre (its base still stands in a splendid sanctuary); Syros, stupendous island of the Aegeans; Milos, with ancient Phylakopi; Thera, with the Minoan city of Akrotiri, some of whose splendid wall paintings are illustrated in this book.

The heart of the Cyclades is Naxos, its largest island, mythic place of exile of Ariadne who, abandoned by Theseus, was consoled by Dionysus. It was the birthplace of enlightened tyrants like Lygdamis and talented sculptors who made their own versions of insular-Ionic Archaic art, doubtless aided by the fine-quality local marble. The site of the ancient city is not far from the modern town of Naxos. A number of eloquent examples of Classical statuary discovered here are now exhibited in the archaeological museum, which also has excellent collections of Cycladic "idols" and Mycenaean pottery.

Situated on the islet of Strongyli—site of a Cycladic settlement in the third and second millennia BC and linked to Naxos by a narrow causeway—was the island's most important monumental structure: the unfinished Archaic Ionic temple of Apollo (540-530 BC), one of the very oldest of this architectural order. Among its characterizing features are a cella containing two rows of four columns, a two-columned pronaos and opisthodomos, and a chamber on the west side, between the cella and the opisthodomos. Still standing intact is the huge marble portal, its frame decorated with typical insular-Ionic motifs; beyond it the deep-blue waters of the Aegean stretch as far as the eye can see. At Apollonas it is possible to visit the abandoned marble quarries: lying in one of them is a colossal (10-meters-high) unfinished *kouros* statue, dated to the second half of the 6th century BC.

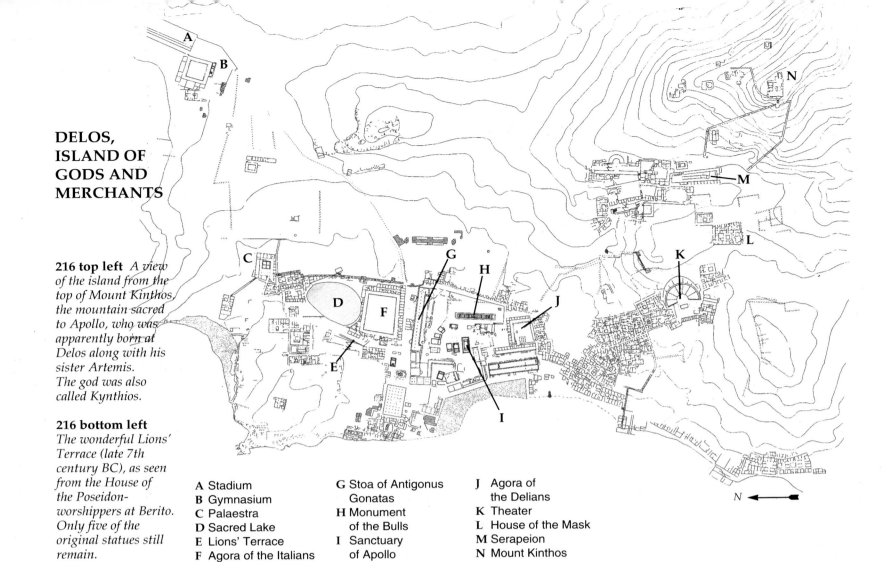

DELOS, ISLAND OF GODS AND MERCHANTS

216 top left *A view of the island from the top of Mount Kinthos, the mountain sacred to Apollo, who was apparently born at Delos along with his sister Artemis. The god was also called Kynthios.*

216 bottom left *The wonderful Lions' Terrace (late 7th century BC), as seen from the House of the Poseidon-worshippers at Berito. Only five of the original statues still remain.*

A Stadium
B Gymnasium
C Palaestra
D Sacred Lake
E Lions' Terrace
F Agora of the Italians
G Stoa of Antigonus Gonatas
H Monument of the Bulls
I Sanctuary of Apollo
J Agora of the Delians
K Theater
L House of the Mask
M Serapeion
N Mount Kinthos

N ⟵

216 right *Two huge phalluses—the symbols of Dionysus—stand on the sides of the god's Hellenistic votive chapel: a few Dionysian themes are also found on the sides of the tall bases of the phalluses.*

217 *In the Lions' Terrace, the animals are all looking toward the place where Apollo was born, the Sacred Lake (now drained for environmental security reasons).*

The religious heart of the Cyclades and one of the greatest sanctuaries in Greece was Delos. This tiny island, a few miles from Mykonos, is the legendary birthplace of Apollo, who was worshipped here for centuries, even in Roman times. (It was the Romans who turned Delos into a thriving Mediterranean "free port," after 168 BC.) The archaeological site is divided into four distinct areas: the sanctuary; the city, with residential and commercial quarters; the terrace, occupied by temples of the foreign gods; and the sports center (gymnasium, *palaestra*, and stadium). Several days would be needed for a thorough, unhurried visit. Behind the ancient port and a late Hellenistic/Roman agora, used by guilds of merchants, begins the Sacred Way. Nearby are the remains of the stoa built by the Attalids around the mid-3rd century BC and those of the portico that Philip V of Macedon had constructed in 210 BC and that was duplicated on the seaward side a few years later; in front of them are numerous bases of monumental statues.

Another agora nearby—the so-called Agora of the Delians—attests to the efficient organization of nonreligious activities on the island sacred to Apollo. Standing in the sacred precinct, behind the grand propylaea (2nd century BC), was the unfinished temple of the god, a small Doric structure (the only one on Delos) dated to the second quarter of the 5th century BC with finishings added,

218-219 *This spectacular aerial view of the expanse of Apollo's island and its uneven coasts shows the muddled layout of the town built around the god's ancient sanctuary. Here the Delian League (478-456 BC) and, under Athens' lead, the Ionian League were based.*

220-221 *This wide graphic reproduction suggests what Delos looked like during its greatest period, between the 3rd and the 1st centuries BC, when the Macedonians and Romans brought about its economic fortune.*

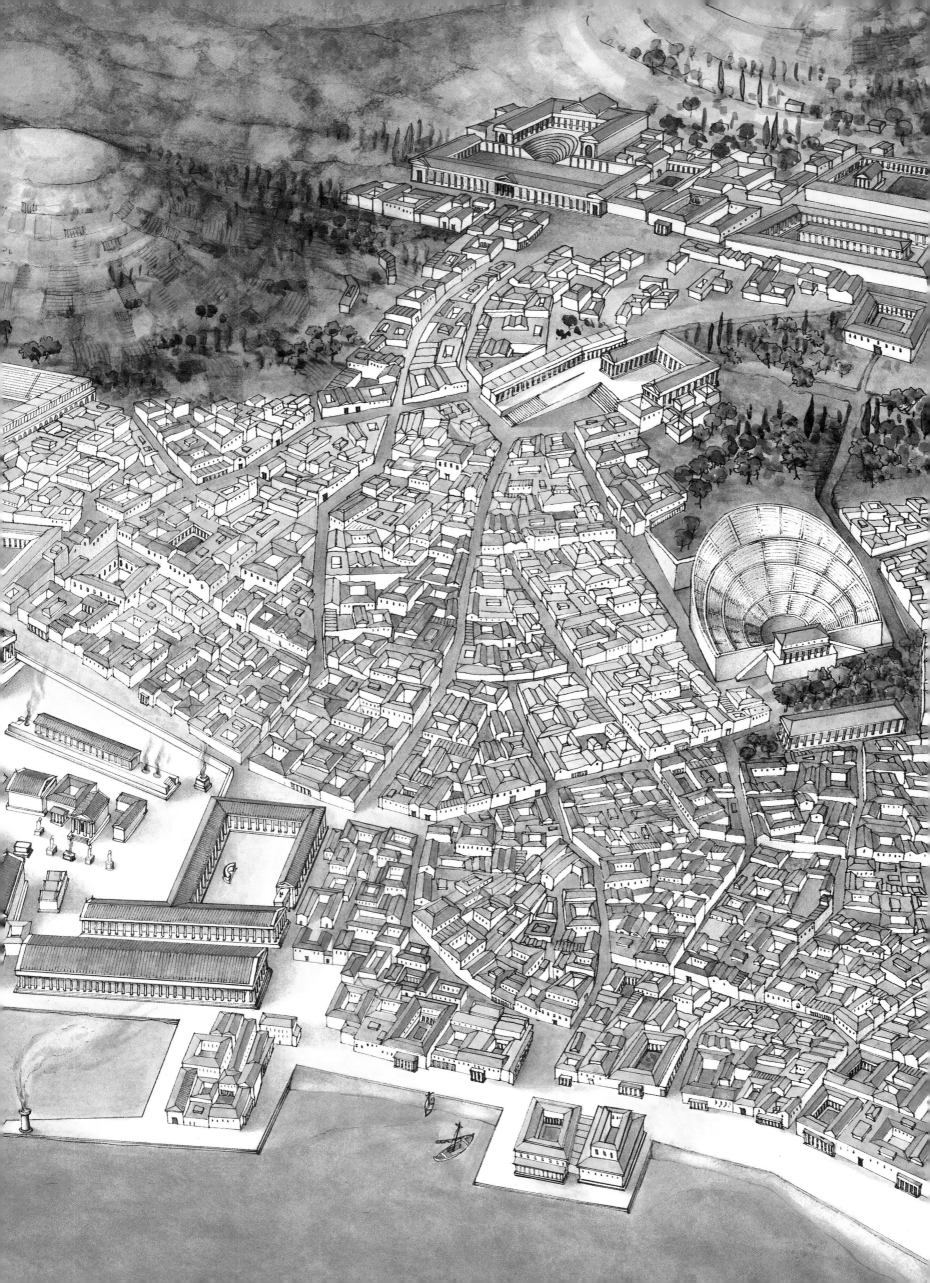

222 top left *One of the most beautiful Delian Hellenistic houses is this peristyle mansion, the Trident's House, in the elegant Theater Quarter, inhabited by rich merchants whose shops are still visible.*

222 center left
The wonderful Hermes' House, with its double row of columns around the peristyle, was probably a representative residence of a merchant trust operating between the 3rd and the 1st century BC.

222 bottom left
The Trident's House peristyle was supported by slender Doric columns. The Romans derived their own domestic building art from such Hellenistic houses in Delos and in other towns.

222 right *A famous Hellenistic mosaic representing a siren decorated a room of the beautiful Skardana House, overlooking a picturesque bay, not far from the Sacred Lake region.*

223 *A wonderful general view of the archaeological heart of Delos emphasizes its charm. The intriguing view is possible only during the few hours granted by the wind and by the strong sea currents between Mykonos and Apollo's island.*

rather poorly, in the 4th. Around it are the foundations of numerous treasuries and several Archaic and Classical temples, all of modest dimensions. Among them is the celebrated *oikos* of the Naxians, a rare example of an Archaic temple (7th century BC) with a bipartite cella and a four-columned pronaos. Still distinguishable near the portico close by are fragments of a gigantic *kouros,* probably portraying Apollo, a votive offering from the Naxians dated to the 6th century BC, and the Archaic "Porinos Naos," in which the cult state of the god was housed.

Beyond the minor sanctuaries of Artemis and Dionysus are remains of a huge, spectacular stoa (124 meters long, with 48 Doric columns) built by Antigonus Gonatas of Macedon in the 3rd century BC; it exemplifies the predilection for gigantism and scenic architecture characteristic of the Hellenistic period. Amid these remains are some curious stone phalluses dedicated to Dionysus and the even more intriguing Monument of the Bulls, named after a decorative feature. The monument was a long, narrow corridor, complete with basin, probably used to display a warship brought here as a votive offering by a Hellenistic king after a victory. The nearby Minoe spring is a fine example of a monumental Hellenistic fountain.

Along the shores, north of the sanctuary of Apollo, is another series of Hellenistic monuments: particularly prominent is the vast Exchange Chamber, once supported by a forest of Doric and Ionic columns and illuminated by a skylight. East of the sanctuary of Poseidon is the celebrated Agora of the Italians (2nd century BC), a grandiose precursor of modern shopping centers and malls. Here we are close to the oval Sacred Lake (drained in 1924), where swans and geese sacred to Apollo once swam. To the west of the lake is one of the best-known spots on the island: the Lions' Terrace, named after its five marble lions, survivors of

the original nine displayed in this open-air gallery—superb pieces of Orientalizing statuary (7th century BC).

Farther on is the Hellenistic residential quarter, with the imposing remains of sumptuously appointed homes, featuring central courts surrounded by columns, mosaic floors, and painted walls. Also located here are prestigious houses, such as the celebrated House of the Poseidon-worshippers of Berito, erected in the 2nd century BC by Syrian merchants from Beirut. They commissioned a famous group of marble figures, unearthed here, showing Aphrodite lifting a sandal to chase away Pan. South of the sanctuary of Apollo is the residential area known as the Theater Quarter; the amphitheater seated 5,500 spectators and is extremely well preserved. In the 2nd and 1st centuries BC dozens of dwellings with central courts, similar to those in the quarter to the north, were built here on a grid plan. Lastly, awaiting visitors who climb the steep path to the summit of the legendary Mount Kinthos is a fine view of numerous religious buildings, culminating in the reconstructed proto-Hellenistic sanctuary of Zeus and Athena.

224 left *The temple of Isis, partly restored, stands at the foot of Mount Kinthos, in the area sacred to several eastern deities. It was rebuilt in 135 BC by the Athenians. A statue of the goddess is visible in the temple.*

224-225 *The theater of Delos was built in the late 4th century BC in a picturesque depression by the harbor. The stage building, which had columns on all four sides, is the only ancient example of this kind.*

225 top left *By the landing dock for modern caiques is the wide Agora of the Hermes-worshippers of Delos, a group of Roman merchants that operated on the island with their own trade and religious center.*

225 top right *In the rich Theater Quarter are these statues of the owners of the House of Cleopatra and the Dioscurides, another good example of a Hellenistic mansion.*

226-227 *This was probably what Athena's sanctuary in Lindos looked like. It stands on the most spectacular site on Rhodes, on a sort of natural acropolis from which one of the best views of Greece may be enjoyed. The monumental complex, built between the 3rd and the 2nd centuries BC, exemplifies the scenic architecture of the Hellenistic age in Ionia and the Dodecanese islands.*

226 bottom *From the giddy, rocky cliffs of Lindos, still surrounded by Byzantine walls that were enlarged in the 15th century, Athena Lindia's temple overlooks the city below.*

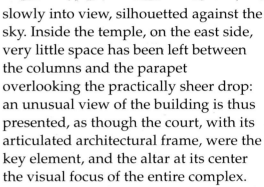

LINDOS, THE SANCTUARY OF ATHENA IN THE BLUE

A Temple
  of Athena Lindia
B Great Stoa
C Propylaea
D Ionic Stoa
E Ship of
  Hagesandros

Rhodes, the largest island of the Dodecanese group, is endowed with many archaeological areas of great interest—among them the ancient cities of Rhodes, Ialyssos, and Kameiros. But the island's biggest attraction is found in Lindos. Spectacularly situated on an ancient acropolis, high above one of the loveliest beaches in Greece, and encircled by the ruins of fortifications and a castle built over Byzantine defensive structures, is the proto-Hellenistic sanctuary of Athena Lindia. The cult site is of truly ancient origin: in the first half of the 6th century BC a Doric temple was built on the very edge of the bluff, above a grotto where the first cultic rites were held. Between the lake 4th and early 2nd centuries BC, after the buildings on the acropolis had been destroyed by fire, the entire area was replanned and rebuilt.

The new plan emphasized the scenic associations of stairways and colonnades characteristic of Hellenistic architecture, particularly in Asia Minor. The terraces of the acropolis were so designed that visitors would direct their steps spontaneously toward the temple through a series of breathtakingly spectacular structures. First they encountered the immense facade of the large p-shaped stoa, then a magnificent stairway leading up to the propylaea, and finally an arcaded court with the Doric temple, positioned off to one side. the altar. Even today visitors to the remains of the propylaea are struck by the simple series of five doorways, each coinciding visually with a pair of the ten columns of the facade, visible from the terrace below, where a long portico adds to the overall grandeur of the structures. On each side of the propylaea is an unmistakable reference to Mnesicles' design for the Athenian Acropolis—rooms with a columnar porch. As the visitor climbs the magnificent stairway, the surviving columns of the arcaded court surrounding the temple come

slowly into view, silhouetted against the sky. Inside the temple, on the east side, very little space has been left between the columns and the parapet overlooking the practically sheer drop: an unusual view of the building is thus presented, as though the court, with its articulated architectural frame, were the key element, and the altar at its center the visual focus of the entire complex.

Further enhancements made in the late 3rd or early 2nd century BC allowed the lower terraces to become more effectively part of the scenic whole. For the overall plan was clearly geared to molding man's activities to suit the landscape, to fuse nature and architecture in a multiform and constantly surprising ensemble. The sanctuary was also embellished with many works of art.

There were votive offerings to Athena Lindia between the colonnades, in the vast open spaces, and along the steep Sacred Way: still visible along this path is a large votive sculpture in the form of a ship, carved from the rock to form the base for the statue of one Hagesandros, a follower of the cult of Poseidon.

227 right *These columns from the pronaos and arcades of Athena Lindia's temple in Rhodes were restored at the beginning of this century. They stand in a highly charming spot, close to wonderful beaches.*

SAMOS, HERA'S CRADLE

A Northern Stoa
B Great Temple of Hera
C Temple of Hermes
D Temple of Apollo
   and Artemis
E Altar
F Temple of Hermes
   and Aphrodite

228-229 *Another view of Geneleos' votive offering highlights its location along the Sacred Way that led into Hera's sanctuary, where architectural structures alternated with works of art.*

229 top left *The only surviving column of Hera's temple is a part of the reconstruction carried out by Rhoikos and Theodoros after fire destroyed it in 525 BC. The work was never completed.*

228 top *A general view of Hera's sanctuary in Samos. The goddess's temple was repeatedly reconstructed between the 7th and the 4th centuries BC. Here and at Artemis' sanctuary at Ephesus, the Ionic style underwent its decisive development.*

228 bottom *Copies of a few statues from the votive offering made by Geneleos of Samos (approximately 560 BC) are still visible on the site where they were placed to decorate Hera's sanctuary.*

The island of Hera—for legend has it that here the goddess was born and wedded to Zeus—is a lush patch of green, emerging from the Aegean just two kilometers off the coast of Asia Minor. Like many Greek islands, Samos has a very ancient history: the first settlements, established in the third millennium BC, soon became prosperous and even more so in the following millennium. In the Dark Ages Samos—like all the islands and coasts of Asia Minor—was occupied by the Ionians, and an important polis was founded here. After a long aristocratic oligarchy, the tyrant Polycrates (540-522 BC) led the thriving island, famous for its wine and pottery, to exceptional wealth. The archaeological appeal of Samos is mainly in the remains of the Heraion, built in the 9th and 8th centuries BC on the banks of the

Imbrasos, a small river. Initially erected on this site were an altar, shrines, and a temple about 40 meters long. Its entrance faced east, and its long cella was divided into two sections. Nearby was a sacred pool, used for ritual bathing of the ancient wooden cult image of the goddess. The temple building was enhanced in the mid-8th and mid-7th century BC.

The sanctuary experienced its finest hour around 560 BC, when two local architects, Rhoikos and Theodoros, were commissioned to build a colossal new Heraion. Its orientation was to be changed, so that it would be placed on the same axis with the imposing altar, within a complex that included long colonnades and was embellished by prestigious works of art (like the celebrated Hera of Samos, now in the Louvre). Here the Ionic order was experimented with and some of its essential characteristics defined, in forms of a grandeur close to gigantism. The large temple (105 by 52.50 meters) was surrounded by a double peristyle comprising 104 columns approximately 18 meters tall.

In front of the vast cella was a deep pronaos divided into three sections, without capitals; the pillars, constructed from squat drums over a meter and a half in diameter, with no fluting, created the effect of a authentic "forest of stone." The mathematical order of their close-set arrangement nonetheless allowed for refined proportions and balanced the overall perspective. The reconstruction, started during the tyranny of Polycrates, was never completed: a terrible fire destroyed Rhoikos' and Theodoros' masterpiece within only a few years of its inauguration.

One solitary column is still standing amid the ruins of the temple. But the many capitals and bases give an idea of what the pillars must have looked like in the Archaic age, before Ionic volutes were introduced.

229 top right *This detail of one of the Archaic capitals of Hera's Ionic temple shows the variety of column-decorating elements in the mid-6th century BC.*

230 top *The Pergamum acropolis contains a fascinating group of monuments built between the age of the Attalids and the Roman Empire. The white colonnade in the background belongs to Trajan's temple.*

PERGAMUM, THE ACROPOLIS OF THE WIND

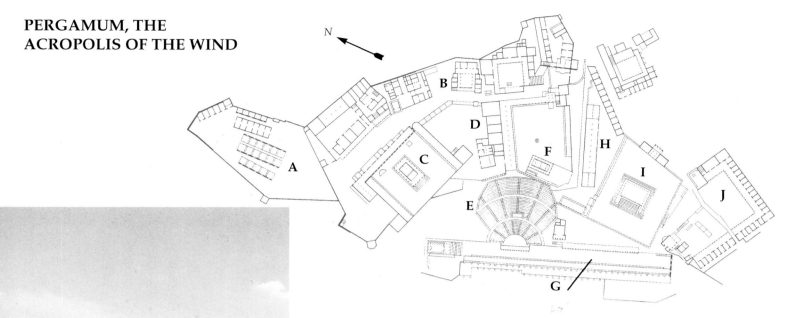

A Arsenal
B Palace
C Temple of Trajan
D Library
E Theater

F Temple of Athena
G Great Terrace
H Stoa
I Great Altar of Zeus
J Upper Agora

Many ancient Greek cities are located in what is now Turkey. Listing and describing them would be a hard task; it would be harder still to include all those—from Sardis to Halicarnassus—that, although of predominantly Asian culture, assimilated some aspects of Greek civilization. We therefore describe only two of the most important ancient cities in Asia Minor: Pergamum and Priene. The reader is nonetheless urged not to forget the outstanding assets of many others—Miletus, Smyrna, Assos, Phocaea, Teos, Cnidus, Didyma, Ephesus, Cyme, Clazomenae, Colophon, Claros—practically all of them on or close to the shores of the Aegean.

Pergamum, the great capital of the prosperous Hellenistic kingdom of the Attalids, is the perfect starting point for a journey back in time to the very roots of Greekness in Asia Minor. Its whole urban setting, which stems from a vast monumentalization program instigated by the ruling dynasty, makes it the most typical example of a Hellenistic city. Its layout is defined entirely by its division into an acropolis, a lower city, and a sanctuary of Asclepius, an approach designed to create a spectacular and emotive ensemble, which was also in keeping with the lush emotionalism expressed in figurative art (known as "Pergamene baroque"). The upper city, encircled by substantial multitowered walls from different periods, comprises royal palaces—sumptuous houses with peristyles, built in the aristocratic tradition—and temples dedicated to the cult of heroized deceased kings.

The system used to supply water to the acropolis from the surrounding higher areas was based on amazingly

230-231 *The wide view from the Pergamum acropolis includes the giddily steep cavea of the great theater, which faces an extraordinary view opening onto the esplanade below.*

231 *This cistern, on the Pergamum acropolis, provided the water supply to the royal palaces of the Attalids, but a huge waterworks supplied the town as a whole with water.*

232 *This detail of the battle of the giants on Zeus' altar in Pergamum shows the expressive power of Pergamene art, whose vigorous and deep emotionalism has been called "baroque."*

233 *One whole hall of the Berlin State Museum contains the reconstructed front of the large frieze of Zeus' altar, where the ancient theme of the battle between gods and giants received its highest expression.*

*The images shown in these two pages are from one of the best-preserved sections of the northeast side of the frieze. Scholars usually identify the following mythological characters **(from left to right):** Klytios, Hekates, Otos, Aigaion, and Artemis.*

234-235 *This is what the Pergamum acropolis probably looked like during the Roman age, after centuries of improvements apparently searching for majestic scenic effects.*

advanced engineering works, perfected in Roman times. Several cylindrical cisterns and long stretches of pipes have survived. Still visible on the acropolis are the splendid, picturesque ruins of the sanctuary of Asclepius, with its "miraculous" springs, covered walkways, porticoes to accommodate patients, theaters, and hostelries, all extensively altered in Roman times. Now the most prominent feature seen from the plain below is Trajan's magnificent marble temple, currently undergoing restoration.

But most important in terms of the history of Greek architecture and urban planning are the modest remnants of the once-imposing late Classical temple of Athena. Erected on a terrace above the dizzily steep slope from which a huge theater was hewn, the sanctuary complex was trapezoid-shaped. Three stoas with a double order of columns, Doric and Ionic, one of which served as a propylaea, framed the open space on which stood the temple, a classic Doric building.

At the foot of the theater, the great ensemble was completed by a spectacular series of colonnades.

Prominent on one side—and reached by means of unusually steep flights of steps—were the Ionic temple and sanctuary of Dionysus. Little is left here of the great altar of Zeus, which once stood on a terrace over 70 meters long and was decorated with friezes depicting the battle of the giants and the legend of Telephos; most of it constitutes one of the main attractions of the State Museum in Berlin. Still visible nearby are remains of the agora of the acropolis, while the imposing ruins of the sanctuary of Demeter are on a lower level.

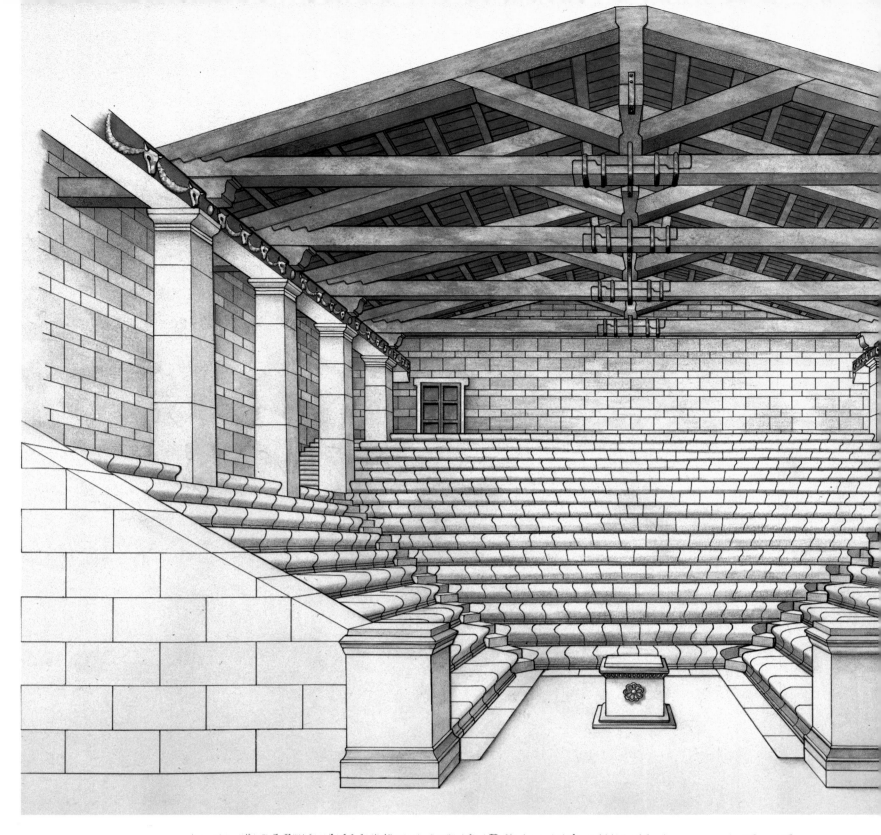

A Sanctuary
of Demeter
B Theater
C Sanctuary of Athena
D Upper Gymnasium
E Stoa
F Agora
G Sanctuary
of Asclepius
H Lower Sanctuary
I Stadium

N

PRIENE, AN OUTSTANDING URBAN PLAN

The small, ancient polis of Priene, in the region of Caria, was refounded by its 5,000 or so inhabitants in the mid-4th century, to escape the devastation caused by a flood of the Meander River. Their chosen site was on the slopes of Micale hill (almost 400 meters high): here four parallel terraces were constructed at the approximately 300-meter elevation between bluffs immediately above the river valley and those nearly inaccessible ones closer to the acropolis.

Late 19th-century excavations revealed a rectilinear grid layout in the Hippodamean tradition: set between the streets, of widths between 4 and 7 meters, are elongated rectangular apartment blocks measuring 120 by 160 Greek feet (35.40 by 47.20 meters), in a harmonious proportional ratio of 3:4. As in Olynthus and Kassope, the residential quarters encircle the city center, whose agora is flanked by monumental colonnades, shops, and a sanctuary of Zeus. The four terraces are connected by a series of parallel north-south paths, almost always stepped and therefore usable only on foot or with beasts of burden—unlike the east-west streets. The agora is physically connected to the temple of Athena above it by a long monumental stairway, which accentuates the temple's lofty position.

Dominating the layout is the theater, one of the best-preserved in the Greek world; its tiers climb up from the last terrace, where the hillside becomes even steeper. Not, to be overlooked is the stadium and other sports infrastructure, intelligently positioned on the edge of the first artificial terrace. Like the theater, they are in an out-of-the-way part of town, to make for smooth, noncongested movement by the thousands of spectators arriving and leaving.

The most interesting aspect of the city, however, is its entire urban ensemble, a spectacle clearly enhanced by the almost exclusive use of stone for its monumental and private buildings. Priene preceded the scenic Hellenistic cities of Asia Minor, with their bold "stacking" of quarters and monuments, by over half a century.

236-237 This reconstruction of the original appearance of Priene's bouleuterion *or* ekklesiasterion *shows the wide meeting hall, its long rows of seats divided by access staircases at the diagonals. The scheduled speakers sat by the altar. The roof was probably supported by imposing wooden beams.*

237 top This is the current appearance of the ekklesiasterion *of Priene, whose layout is also found in other Greek towns in Asia Minor.*

237 bottom A few columns of Athena's majestic temple in Priene still exist, with their elegant Ionic capitals. The temple was built in the 4th century BC by the great architect Pythius.

238-239 Priene probably looked like other Greek towns in Asia Minor that had been improved, rebuilt, or newly founded. Its regular layout, with monumental blocks located in outstanding sites, was scenically integrated with the natural environment.

KNOSSOS, THE LABYRINTH WITHOUT MINOTAUR

N

A Theater
B North Entrance
C Hypostyke Hall
D Storerooms
E Throne Room
F Central Court
G Grand Staircase
H King's Megaron
I South Propylaea
J High Priest's House
K Southwest House

The jewel of Cretan archaeology is undoubtedly Knossos, which boasts the island's largest and most important palace-settlement. During excavations in Knossos over a period of thirty years (1903-31), under the supervision of Arthur J. Evans, the palace-settlement underwent a disastrous "restoration." The result may be to the liking of tourists in search of picturesque views, but absurd and anachronistic concessions to undiscerning "lovers of ruins" turned several pieces of the complex—"reconstructed" using painted reinforced concrete—into backdrops for picture postcards. Nevertheless, thanks to comparisons with the palace-settlement of Festos, which was excavated with far different scientific criteria and respect by the Italian School of Archaeology in Athens, it has been possible to determine the fundamental scheme and technical solutions used by Cretan architects.

The surviving parts of the great palace of Knossos—for the most part rebuilt in the 17th century BC—point to outstanding skills in design and organization. With over a thousand rooms, often built two or three stories high, the amenities included staircases, corridors, porticoes, and ramps suitable for vehicles, arranged around a huge rectangular central court. Among their most significant features are the absence of fortifications, the combined use of wood and stone for load-bearing structures, and the logical distribution of facilities among the various wings of the palace, in spite of the apparent chaos and an overabundance of rooms. The rational aspects of the plan are seen in the positioning of storerooms and the grouping of workshops used by craftsmen in the service of the *minos*. Particularly striking is the elegant architectural and pictorial ornamentation in the porticoes, living quarters, throne rooms, and reception rooms, whose vibrant colors attest to the pleasure-loving lifestyle of the Cretans, who had no time for mysticism.

240 top left and center *The Knossos palace-settlement in Crete is world famous. Every year tourists charmed by the royal palace of the legendary* minos *wander in the peristyles of its residences (**top**) as well as along its spectacular paved staircases (**center**).*

240 bottom left *The "restoration" reproduced the complex layout of rooms, courtyards, and entrance halls, which promoted diffused lighting and fresh air in the elegant residential quarters of Knossos.*

240 right *This picturesque view of the Knossos royal palace shows concrete reproductions of the original painted-wood columns, a typical element of Cretan architecture.*

241 *The northern entrance to the Knossos palace-settlement is one of the most fascinating sites of the whole Minoan complex. But all of Crete deserves a thorough archaeological visit.*

The splendid paved Royal Road leads
to the theater, identified as such thanks
to its extremely well-preserved seating-
tiers and its "royal box." Another paved
road leads to the west entrance, starting-
point of the so-called Processional
Corridor, where copies of unearthed
frescoes are displayed. Here visitors get
their first intimation of what lies within
the multistory palace (its floors varied in
number, from two to four), built on the
irregular terrain of a low hill not far
from the sea. Its main structures lead off
a huge central court. This is entered by
passing through the Great Propylaea,
supported by imposing pillars originally
made of painted wood, and ascending
the grand stairway to the floor above.
Here, as in other such palaces, the cultic
altar is opposite the luxurious royal
apartments, which are organized on
several levels and fitted with remarkable
facilities and decorated with wall
paintings (including the celebrated
Dolphin Frieze). They are within easy
reach of the stupendous frescoed Throne
Room, where the alabaster throne of
King Minos is still intact. Amazing
construction technologies were used to
bring plenty of natural light and fresh
air into the rooms, chambers, and
corridors, most evident in this area.
Along the west side of the building are
storerooms, containing *pithoi* (huge clay
jars) in which foodstuffs were kept; on
the opposite side are the workshops of
potters and goldsmiths.

244 top *A "light pit" brightened up the guard rooms at Knossos palace, three levels below the royal apartments, by the Central Court.*

244 bottom left *The Queen's Apartment is where the famous fresco showing realistic dolphins darting among the waves was found; its jambs and lintels are decorated with colorful flower patterns.*

244-245 *The picturesque Throne Room still contains the intact alabaster throne on which the king sat, surrounded by frescoes with images of griffin vultures and exotic flowers.*

245 top *This outside view of the palace shows the sequence of its different levels, linked by means of stone staircases.*

246-247 *This is probably how the Knossos palace appeared when it was rebuilt after being destroyed around 1700 BC.*

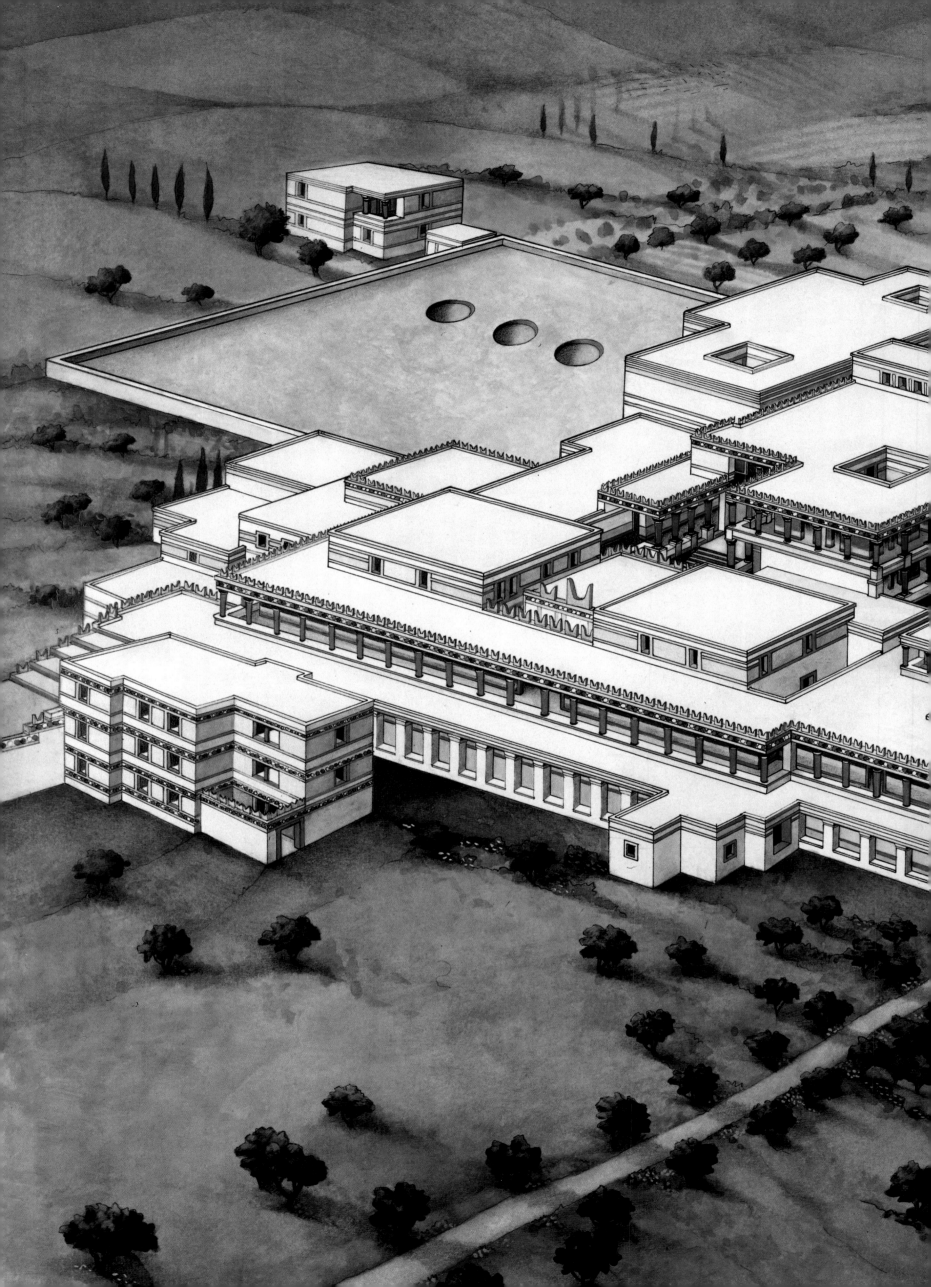

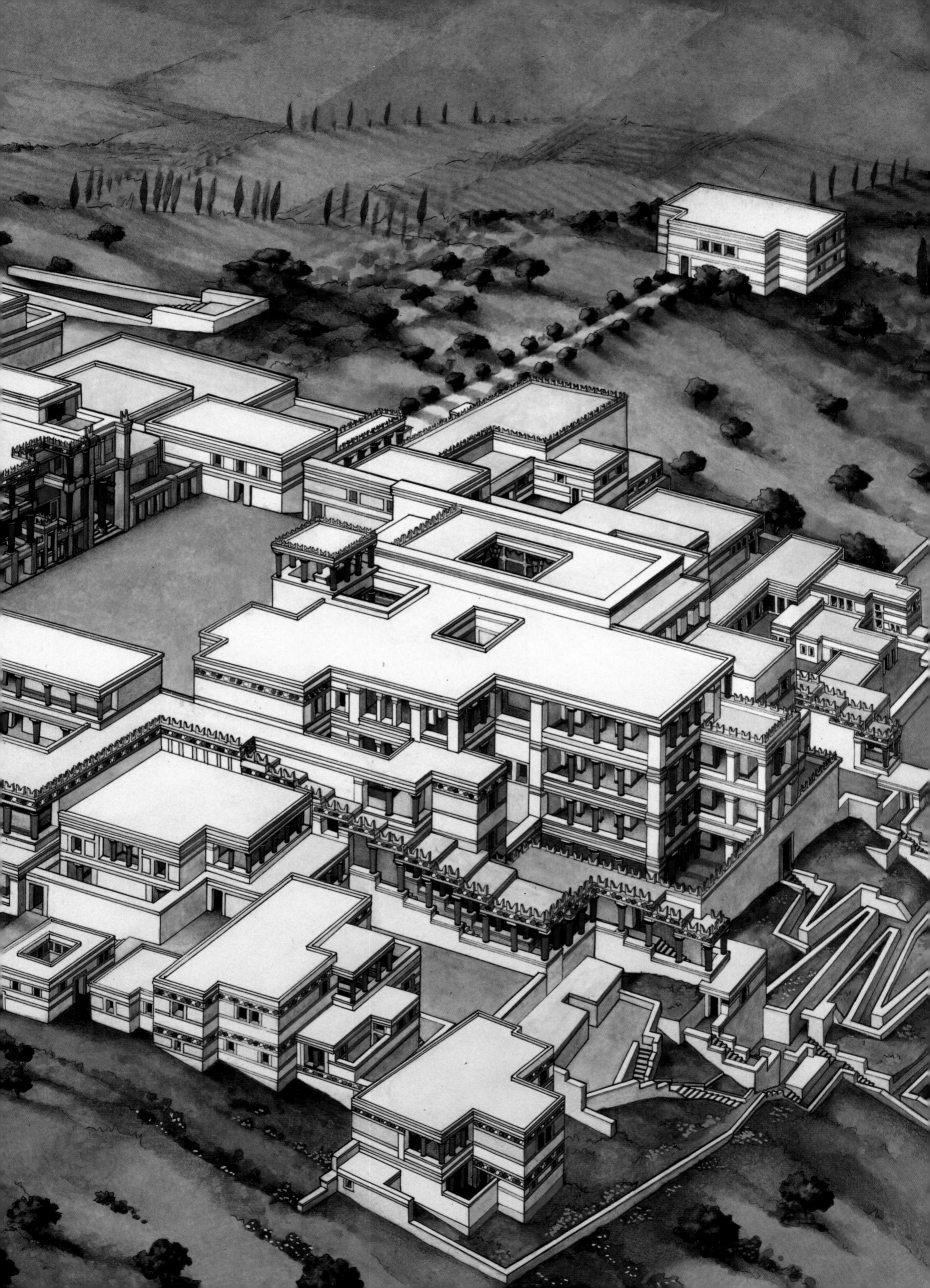

ARCHAEOLOGICAL ITINERARIES IN *MAGNA GRAECIA*

248-249 *This painting taken from a tomb in Ruvo di Puglia, dating to the second half of the 5th century BC, shows a* choros *of dancing women. Their expressive natural faces, reproduced with confident and quick brushstrokes, closely resemble those portrayed on contemporary pots of a local origin or imported from Attica.*

THE GREEKS IN ITALY: FOUNDATION OF A NEW WESTERN SPIRIT

No corner of southern Italy and Sicily—from Cumae to the Strait of Messina, from Selinus to Syracuse, from Metapontum to Tarentum—is without direct or indirect traces of the ancient Greeks and their centuries-long civilization. From desolate, windy Daunia to the deep valleys of Lucania, from luxuriant Sila to the fertile lands of the Elymians, in many thousands of ways—thanks to colonists, through trade, through economic and political interaction—Greek culture was transplanted to the ancient heart of Italy that beats beneath the silent wooded peaks of the Apennines, the sound half-lost amid the bleating of sheep moving to new pastures along tracks white with worn or crumbling limestone. Now-silent Greeks once scanned the shores of the Adriatic from Leuca to the Po delta—a coastline with few safe anchorages, myriad rocks, and unforeseen sandbanks—where Mycenaean merchants had already come laden with pottery, fabrics, and colored beads (the usual offerings for natives), in the emporia of Adria, Spina, and Mantua, among Etruscans, Venetics, and Celts.

Others journeyed across the Tyrrhenian Sea: here their routes crossed with those of merchants and pirates, Phoenicians and Etruscans. They experienced risky encounters with Ligurians—reputedly untrustworthy, they gave names to headlands and bays; they even traded with the Sardinians, buying and selling, selling and buying. They founded Cyrene, Massilia (Marseilles), Ampurias, and hundreds of emporia in the Mediterranean's far west, venturing farther and farther afield, sometimes never to return.

Mythology and philosophy, fact and legend, abstract theory at its most sublime and practical efficiency at its most concrete: the West—and especially Italy—owes everything to the Greeks. To the nymph Arethusa and to Alpheus,

250 *The surviving columns of a supposed temple to Hera from the late 6th century BC, named the Palatine Tables, stand out against the bright blue sky of Lucania.*

1 Pithecusa (Ischia)	8 Himera
2 Paestum	9 Segesta
3 Metapontum	10 Selinus
4 Tarentum	11 Agrigentum
5 Sibari	12 Gela
6 Croton	13 Syracuse
7 Locri	14 Megara Ityblaea

250-251 *Fifteen columns of the Palatine Tables temple are still standing, after twenty-five centuries. The* entasis, *their slightly swelled profile, and their expanded capitals are a few* typical elements of Archaic Doric architecture. **Magna Graecia** *colonies were a laboratory for architectural and town-planning experiments. Sometimes great* advances were made over the towns of actual Greece. Metapontum was a blooming agricultural colony and an exchange center on the Lucanian coast of the Ionian sea.

251 bottom *The so-called Temple of Neptune, actually dedicated to Hera, stands almost intact at Poseidonia, better known as Paestum. The local limestone used for building has* been coated with a warm golden color, enhancing the elegant traits of Doric architecture and the fine relations between full and empty spaces in the colonnade.

252-253 *One of the most fascinating archaeological sites in Syracuse and in all of Sicily is the fortifications of the Eurialo castle, an amazing system established for the protection of the town in the 4th century BC,* *under the tyrant Agathocles. His military engineers created such a well-contrived complex that it was both virtually impregnable and adaptable to different defense and counterattack requirements.*

252 bottom *The galleries of the Eurialo castle allowed the defenders to act without being seen by the enemies, one of a variety of solutions adopted by the builders.*

for instance, we owe a tale of invincible love beneath the sea near Syracuse; to Pythagoras, a mathematician and guru who made Italy his home, we owe the pleasure of numbers and the mystic harmony of a temple or a musical score; to Parmenides and Zeno of the Eleatic school, the certainty that Being is one and unique, delight in paradox as a means of guarding against excessive wisdom, hatred of tyrants, even on pain of death; to the tyrants of Sicily, deliverance from orientalization (as deplorable as the westernization of the Orient!); to the Greeks at large, an alphabet, countless words, dreams, projects, technologies and markets, the desire to read, the courage to risk and write, and always to face up to stormy seas—whether those of the mind or of life itself; the inevitability of doubt and the willpower to be bold and innovative.

This is what our itinerary in Western *Magna Graecia*—however brief—is all about. But before setting out to explore the temples and houses of Paestum, Segesta, Syracuse, Selinus, and Agrigentum, we must at least pay tribute to other outstanding sites of *Magna Graecia:* Pithekoussai, on the island of Ischia; the acropolis of Cumae; Pozzuoli, once called Dikearchia, in Naples, with its wonderful National Museum; Velia (Elea), with the philosophers Parmenides and Zeno, and its splendid Pink Gate; the colonies of Calabria and Basilicata—Metapontum and Locri Epizephyrii; Reggio, with the Riace bronzes; Sybaris, renowned for its affluent lifestyle; the spectacular and solitary sanctuaries of coasts and inland regions (have you never seen Capo Colonna?); Greekness mingled with Italic roots in Apulia, from Salento to Gargano; and lastly Sicily, with colonies both forgotten and recently rediscovered—Gela, dominated by powerful tyrants and impressive fortifications, Megara Hyblaea and Thapsos, Leontini and Catania, Himera and the Hellenized towns of the interior. Underlying this immense archaeological heritage are the very roots of Western spirit and culture, which we must on no account lose touch with.

For to do so would mean losing our last opportunity to rediscover ourselves.

253 top *Temple E in Selinus, from the first half of the 5th century BC, is generally believed to be a Heraion, a temple dedicated to Hera, widely worshipped in* the poleis of Magna Graecia. *A particular feature of its construction is the floor of the adyton, which is raised with respect the cella.*

253 center *In the Syracuse theater, performances still take place during a festival of Classical tragic and comic drama. The wide cavea is much flatter than others in the Greek world, and is mostly dug from the white limestone rock that characterizes Syracuse's soil.*

253 bottom *Temple E at Selinus is a highly striking site for first-time visitors to this powerful Greek colony in western Sicily.*

254 top Magna Graecia *produced abundant art and handicraft works. This clay plaque bearing a horrible face of Medusa suggests the considerable development of pottery in Tarentum, where this item comes (late 6th century BC). The models on which such products were based—cast from molds—indicate the close links between the colonies and their communities of origin. In this case, all of the* expressive power and toughness of the Doric style is preserved. Tarentum, a powerful Spartan colony founded in 702 BC on the Ionian Sea, soon turned into a blooming center for the diffusion of the Greek culture.

254 bottom *Another effective example of Magna Graecia's pottery may be found in this clay* pinax *from Locri Epizephyrii, a bas-relief tablet made by a craftsman of the early 5th century BC. It is still bound to late Archaic schemes in the depiction of Hades and Kore sitting on a throne, perhaps by customer request or out of ritual tradition.*

255 top *This clay lion's head was a gargoyle along the edge of a building roof. Such creations allowed rainwater to drip off the architectural structure, at the same time producing outstanding aesthetic effects.*

255 bottom *This clay statue representing one of the Dioscuri riding a horse, atop a sphinx with rather human traits, was an acroterium, or eave ornament, on a 470-450 BC temple. It was found at Locri Epizephyrii, and anticipates in a clumsier and stiffer manner two beautiful acroterial statues of the Dioscuri belonging to a temple of the second half of the 5th century BC, in this case made of marble and found at Contrada Marasa, still within the wide territory of the powerful colony.*

256 top *The richness of Italian pottery production took inspiration from Attic pottery and even exceeded it in quality after the 4th century BC. Production in Apulia, Campania, Lucania, and a few centers in Greek Sicily attained a high level, as shown by this beautiful Apulian lekythos with red figures and overpainted colors, with a Dionysian theme.*

256 bottom left *Themes referring to Dionysus, his myths, and his cult are often portrayed in the decoration of* Magna Graecia *pots, as in this richly painted spiraled* krater *(350-325 BC).*

256 bottom right *From approximately 340 BC, this bellied* lekythos *is painted in the typical style of the Apulian town of Gnathia (Egnazia). It probably contained ointments, as suggested by the sensual position of the female figure.*

257 *This beautiful 1st-century BC head from Tarentum is probably a copy of a Classical or Hellenistic original, made with the fine white marble from Paros.*

257

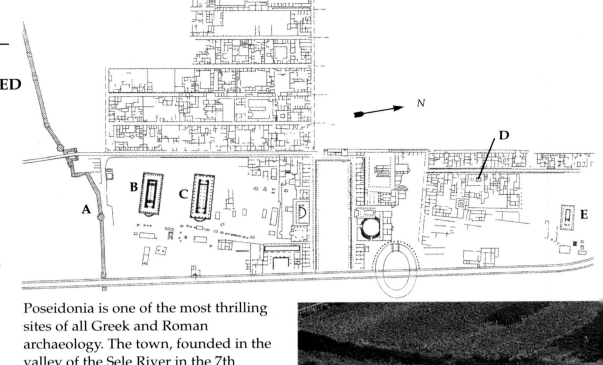

POSEIDONIA (PAESTUM), SACRED TO POSEIDON

A Wall
B Temple of Hera I (Basilica)
C Temple of Hera II ("Temple of Neptune")
D Heroon
E Temple of Athena ("Temple of Ceres")

258 left *This small clay statue of a female deity, probably dating to the second half of the 6th century BC, was found in the southern sanctuary and is kept in the Paestum National Museum.*

258-259 *This aerial view of the Paestum archaeological site highlights the sacred area with Hera's temples I (the "Basilica") and II ("Temple of Neptune"), still in excellent condition.*

259 top left *The two Doric temples known as the "Basilica" (left) and "Neptune's Temple" (right) have different layouts and structures. The former, with nine frontal columns, dates to around 550 BC; the latter is one century younger.*

259 top right *In the northern sacred area, the temple of Athena (known as the "Temple of Ceres"), was built around 510 BC in airy and harmonic forms. The Ionic columns in the pronaos are an interesting novelty.*

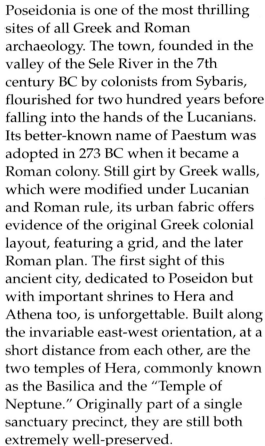

Poseidonia is one of the most thrilling sites of all Greek and Roman archaeology. The town, founded in the valley of the Sele River in the 7th century BC by colonists from Sybaris, flourished for two hundred years before falling into the hands of the Lucanians. Its better-known name of Paestum was adopted in 273 BC when it became a Roman colony. Still girt by Greek walls, which were modified under Lucanian and Roman rule, its urban fabric offers evidence of the original Greek colonial layout, featuring a grid, and the later Roman plan. The first sight of this ancient city, dedicated to Poseidon but with important shrines to Hera and Athena too, is unforgettable. Built along the invariable east-west orientation, at a short distance from each other, are the two temples of Hera, commonly known as the Basilica and the "Temple of Neptune." Originally part of a single sanctuary precinct, they are still both extremely well-preserved.

The Basilica is the oldest religious building in Paestum (c. 550 BC). Its masses of brownish local limestone, once stuccoed, rise from an ample stylobate (54 by 24 meters), with a peristyle of 9 by 18 columns: a rare example of a Doric temple in such a configuration. Traditional Archaic elements, such as the division of the cella into two naves, the massive profile of the load-bearing elements, and the heaviness of the ensemble, appear to be mixed with an unexpected predilection for bulkiness of Ionian/Asian derivation.

The so-called Temple of Neptune is the largest and best-preserved sacred building in Paestum, constructed c. 540 BC from local limestone that, with the passage of time, has taken on intense, dark blond nuances. Its proportional harmony reveals similarities with the Artemision of Corcyra (present-day Corfu) and several contemporary examples in eastern Sicily (Syracuse).

Just slightly larger than the Basilica, it

260-261 *Hera's Temple II, with its harmonious limestone body, was originally plastered and painted. It is representative of the Severe style in architecture.*

is a classic structure of the Doric order with six frontal columns. The chiaroscuro effects produced by its peristyle soften the sharp edges of the fluting and the traditional bulkiness of the column shafts: they elicit an overwhelming sensation of exploding, gravity-opposed forces and appear to lighten the masses, dimensions, and perspective of the ensemble.

The canonical decoration of the entablature and the classical layout of the cella make the temple an eloquent example of the autonomy of interpretation and elaboration typical of the colonial world. Taking the ancient Sacred Way and continuing past the forum and the noteworthy remains of republican and imperial Paestum, we are greeted by the splendid "Temple of Ceres" (in fact dedicated to Athena). It was erected around 500 BC using the classic Archaic measurements but the Doric order (in the peristyle) is already intermingled with the Ionic order (in the pronaos).

In the richness and importance of its collection, Paestum's archaeological museum is one of the finest in Italy. The exhibitions it offers are impressive indeed: artifacts from "Thesauros I" and the greater temple of the sanctuary of Hera beside the Sele River, famous for a series of carved metopes, of fundamental importance for a full appreciation of Archaic art in the western colonies; votive and ornamental ceramic objects; statuary; imported pottery; and several beautifully crafted bronze vases.

But the highlight of the museum is a group of painted slabs of limestone, unearthed in numerous 5th-and-4th centuries BC tombs. They are rare and precious testimony to the Greeks' great wall paintings, which for the most part are lost. The most important piece is undoubtedly the figured painting

discovered in the southern cemetery in 1968, in the so-called Tomb of the Diver. This traditional stone coffin had limestone wall and "ceiling" slabs that were decorated with paintings that are still extremely well-preserved. Grave goods have made it possible to date the tomb to about 480 BC, a date confirmed by a stylistic analysis of the paintings. Executed on plaster, on which the artist had first drawn sketches using the drypoint technique, the wall frescoes portrayed a festive, aristocratic symposium, while the "ceiling" presented the unusual theme of a naked youth diving from a board into a pool of water.

Included in the symposium scene, on the two long sides, are ten seminaked male figures, wearing wreaths of leaves and reclining on *klinai*—as was then the custom—beside low garlanded tables. On the two short sides are a young cup-bearer pouring wine from an *oinochoe* and a female flute player leading two men. Depicted on the northern long side

260 bottom left
Harmony is found in the fluid rhythm of the peristyle, in the profiles of capitals and columns, and in the sequence of the triglyphs on the columns' axes and between them, as well as in the lightness of the tympanums with their deep frames.

260 bottom right
The inside of the so-called "Temple of Neptune" is organized into a three-nave cella with a two-column pronaos and opisthodomos in front. The ridged roof was supported by a double row of lean Doric columns, like the temple of Athena Aphaea in Aegina.

261 *The double row of columns splitting the cella into three aisles, in Hera's Temple II, is a clear reference to the cella model in the temple of Aphaea at Aegina.*

are two men reclining on a *kline* in an affectionate pose: their intense looks, caressing movements, and seemingly whispered words are conveyed with simplicity and elegance. There is another pair of men in the center: the one on the right is looking at the two lovers and seems to be saying something to them; in his hand is a *kylix*, identical to one his companion is using to throw wine toward a single figure on the left-hand *kline*. (The game is *kottabos*, played at

262 top left *On one of the two short slabs of the Tomb of the Diver (c. 480 BC) is a scene recalling the Etrusean style. Two guests, preceded by a female flute player, are setting out to the symposium, or leaving it— symbolically hinting a farewell to life by the deceased.*

262 center left *On the other short slab, a servant pours wine from a huge krater standing on a table decorated with garlands.*

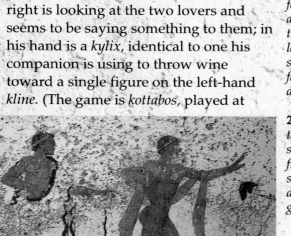

262 and 263 bottom *The two drawings show the original positions of the slabs of The Tomb of the Diver. Each slab on the long sides shows five men lying on klinai facing* low tables. Some of them are playing an instrument, while others seem to be listening to the performances. Still others are toasting each other with wine.

262-263 Barbyton music has just stopped: the instrument is set aside, the plectrum is still in the musician's hand. The young bearded man wearing a laurel crown seems to be turning toward the two men on his left, bearing wide flared wine cups, or kylikes.

263 top right
A fascinating enigma, this diving scene shows a young naked man jumping from a board into somewhat turbulent water, in a natural setting depicted with great simplicity. Is this a purifying dive toward the next world and reincarnation, or an athletic practice?

aristocratic banquets.) With freshness and realism the anonymous artist captured the moment of the last toast of the banquet that—in this funerary context—does not merely celebrate the traditional aristocratic symposium, or a drinking party, where the friendship uniting the guests was festively ritualized with wine, a refined and costly product; it is also clearly a metaphor for life on earth, a kind of melancholy elegy to pleasure and *joie de vivre*, which are inexorably swallowed up by death. The theme on the "ceiling" slab is important for a full understanding of the profound philosophical message contained in these paintings and their sophisticated cultural level. The diver is realistically portrayed "in flight" between the diving board and the water, in a natural setting defined by two stylized trees. The suggestion that the figure represents the deceased has been rejected. It is almost certain, rather, that the dive symbolizes the soul's journey to the next world: a dive into the unknown, satisfying a longing for purification that relates to the mystical/religious aspects of Pythagoras' teachings and his doctrine of the eternal reincarnation of souls.

264-265 *The splendid west facade of the so-called Temple of Neptune exemplifies the building's harmonious proportions. The fact that it belongs to the Severe period is evident from a number of Archaic features, such as the twenty-four grooves on the columns instead of the twenty that soon became canonical, and the fourteen columns on the long sides instead of thirteen or twelve.*

265 *Two exquisite bronze hydriai and a celebrated black-figured Attica amphora depicting the apotheosis of Heracles were discovered in the Heraion, an underground sanctuary in the agora of Paestum where, in 510-500 BC, they were part of a votive offering. One of the amphora's feet was broken off in ancient times and was reattached with bronze pins.*

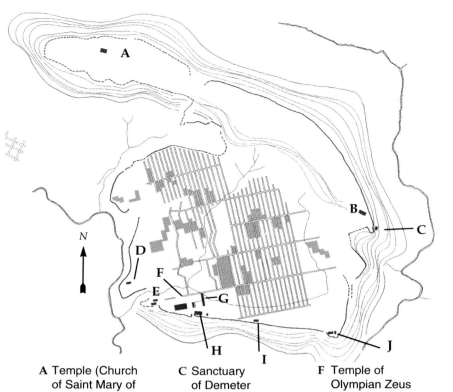

A Temple (Church
   of Saint Mary of
   the Greeks)
B Temple of Demeter
   (Church of
   Saint Biagio)

C Sanctuary
   of Demeter
D Temple of
   Hephaestus
E Sanctuary of the
   Chthonian Gods

F Temple of
   Olympian Zeus
G Agora
H Temple of Heracles
I Temple of Concord
J Temple of Hera

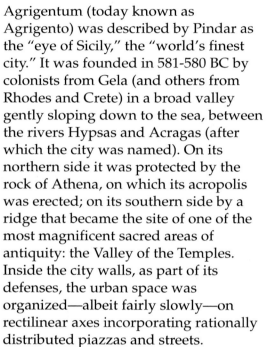

AGRIGENTUM, IN THE VALLEY OF THE GODS

Agrigentum (today known as Agrigento) was described by Pindar as the "eye of Sicily," the "world's finest city." It was founded in 581-580 BC by colonists from Gela (and others from Rhodes and Crete) in a broad valley gently sloping down to the sea, between the rivers Hypsas and Acragas (after which the city was named). On its northern side it was protected by the rock of Athena, on which its acropolis was erected; on its southern side by a ridge that became the site of one of the most magnificent sacred areas of antiquity: the Valley of the Temples. Inside the city walls, as part of its defenses, the urban space was organized—albeit fairly slowly—on rectilinear axes incorporating rationally distributed piazzas and streets.

The city had an essentially agricultural economy, based on meticulously parceled-out tracts of farmland and maximum use of every cultivable area (to the extent that the gods were "confined" to temples situated on the less fertile, stonier hillocks). Within a matter of decades the wealth and political prestige acquired under the tyrant Phalaris made Agrigentum one of the leading powers of Greek Sicily. In the dramatic upheavals in the region toward the end of the 5th century BC, the city was destroyed by the Carthaginians; it was resettled, twice, in the late Classical and Hellenistic periods, and enjoyed a long period of prosperity under Roman rule before its eventual decline in late antiquity.

Surprising as it may seem, the best-preserved quarter of the ancient city is the one built in the Hellenistic/Roman age, where the rational arrangement of urban space is more evident and where different building types of Greek and Italian origin can be seen. This quarter has to be crossed to reach the Oratory of

266 left *On a high ridge jutting out into the valley lie the imposing ruins of the temple of Hera; in the classical Doric style (450-430 BC) and based on the proportions of the Parthenon. The ruins of the huge altar facing the entrance are visible.*

266 right *This Archaic* kouros-*shaped mirror handle is a typical product of the small bronze pieces from Greek Sicily.*

267 *A masterpiece of* Magna Graecia *architecture, the temple of Concord (450-430 BC), probably dedicated to Castor and Pollux and showing perfect proportions, is the symbol of Agrigentum.*

268 top *This is the surviving corner of the peristyle of the temple of Concord, built in elegant classical Doric forms but modified during the Roman age.*

268-269 *The temple of Concord, the most beautiful building in the superb Valley of the Temples, unfortunately shamefully abused*

for many years. Yet this architectural jewel is the Parthenon of **Magna Graecia**. *No visitor to Sicily can help but admire it.*

269 top *A huge capital from the temple of Olympian Zeus (480 BC), a building whose magnificent forms reflect the extravagance of Agrigentum tyrants.*

269 bottom *The only surviving* telamon, *or male caryatid, that helped support the powerful beams of the huge Doric temple of Olympian Zeus lies on the ground nearby.*

Phalaris, a sacred structure of the Hellenistic period, underlying which are remains of a kind of rock-cut theater.

The renowned Archaeological Route leading to the Valley of the Temples and the remains of the ancient city is dotted with outstanding architectural evidence about life in Agrigentum, on which the rich collections of the regional archaeological museum shed further light. The city's most archaic and mysterious past is evoked by the sanctuary of Demeter and Persephone (Kore). Comprised of a double chamber hewn from rock, accessed through a vestibule, it is surrounded by fountains, its visual impact heightened by the terracing of the surrounding terrain. Not far away, near Gate I, are remnants of a defensive bastion with tenaille outworks and a reinforcing tower.

The visitor's first encounter in the Valley of the Temples is with remnants of the colossal temple of Olympian Zeus (112 by 56 meters), one of the largest ever built by Greek architects, erected c. 480 BC and completely destroyed by earthquakes. It was a Doric temple with half-columns interspaced with gigantic *telamones,* or male caryatids, 8 meters high. Scattered around it are remains of minor shrines and treasuries—the whole area was built up with monuments in the Classical and Hellenistic periods, with canonical embellishments such as porticoes and piazzas. A sanctuary precinct dedicated to the chthonian divinities Demeter and Persephone—their cult obviously linked with the colony's agricultural activity— still contains four elegant columns of the so-called temple of Castor and Pollux, from the 5th century BC but altered in Roman times. Partial reconstruction has restored dignity to the temple of Heracles (c. 510 BC) and facilitates understanding the dimensions and proportions of this Doric structure of the Classical type which may have had an

open-air cella. The most splendid of Agrigentum's gems is the celebrated temple of Concord—in actual fact probably dedicated to Castor and Pollux—still perfectly preserved. The meticulously designed, harmonious proportions of the building are part of what had become standard for temple architecture: seemingly developed around 450 BC, it was doubtless influenced by Callicrates' stylistic experiments, which reached their apogee with the Parthenon and the nearly contemporary Theseion, in the Agora of Athens. Less well preserved— but chronologically and stylistically practically a clone of the temple of Concord—is the temple of Hera Lacinia, notable for the elegant columns in its surviving peristyle.

270-271 *Another view of the temple of Concord, with modern Agrigento in the background shows that in the Gela subcolony deities were undoubtedly granted beautiful areas, but bristling with rocks.*

270 bottom
The temple of Hera Lacinia has a spectacular position, almost anticipating the scenic and spectacular architecture of the Hellenistic age.

272-273 *The blue Sicilian sky and the warm color of stone: a perfect combination that makes the powerful and elegant temple of Concord even more beautiful.*

271 top *In the surviving structures of the temple of Hera Lacinia, the anonymous designers found ways to create marked light and shade effects.*

271 bottom *The columns of the temple of Heracles, a six-column Doric building of the Archaic age, are still characterized by the swelling and clumsiness typical of that time.*

274-275 *Standing alone on the hill, beautiful although unfinished, the Doric temple at Segesta is surrounded by indefinable mystery in the wonderful natural setting of the green neighboring hills, once inhabited in the past by the ancient Elymians.*

274 bottom *Until fairly recently the remains of the Greek theater in Segesta were the city's only really significant archaeological asset. But excavations now in progress are throwing new light on Segesta's history and on its urban fabric and architecture.*

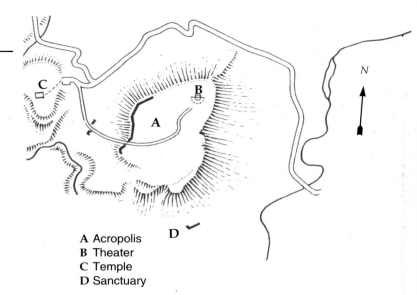

SEGESTA, THE GOD UNDER THE STARS

A Acropolis
B Theater
C Temple
D Sanctuary

Capital of the Elymians, rival of Selinus, and faithful ally of Rome, Segesta is one of the best-known archaeological sites of ancient Sicily but one of the least explored and studied of the Greek world as a whole. The town did not belong to the Greek world exclusively but assimilated various forms of civilization. This synthesis is most effectively illustrated by two buildings: the temple at Contrada Mango and the theater.

The temple, dedicated to an unknown deity, was erected in Classical Doric style during the last thirty years of the 5th century BC, and its peristyle—of voluminous proportions, with 6 by 14 smooth-shaft columns—and entablature are still perfectly preserved. The absence of any traces of a cella may have been due to a sudden interruption of building work because of the upheavals in the last decade of the century; but it may also have been a unique case in Greek architecture, perhaps stemming from the specific religious requirements of the Elymians. That is, the temple could have been an open-air cultic courtyard, used to celebrate sacred rites on movable altars or ones made from nondurable materials under the "concave vault of the heavens"—as Homer would have said—rather than in the smoky gloom of the *naos*.

The proportions and dimensions of the temple's travertine masses are of Attic derivation and may reflect the political links between the two cities at the end of the century, when Segesta had growing ambitions, manifest in this building. Although the monument is of evident propagandistic and political importance, its design points not to the gigantism of the late Archaic age and Severe style but to the dominant architectural criteria of the second half of the 5th century BC. It has, however, been pointed out that the form of the columns and capitals and the detailing of the decorative elements reveal a waning inventive force.

Segesta's theater, commonly dated to the 3rd century BC, is—in its lower part—well preserved. An important feature, typical of Sicilian theatre architecture, is the stage building with projecting wings.

275 *The famous Segesta Doric temple, dedicated to an unknown deity, was built according to Classical models. It has classical proportions, but it also shows many signs of waning creativity on the part of the architects and sculptors who worked on it during the last three decades of the 5th century BC. During this period Segesta was an ally of Athens and even ended up participating in a catastrophic military action against Syracuse in order to protect it (Peloponnesian War).*

278 *Perseus brutally digs his sword into the neck of the gorgon Medusa, whose blood gives life to the winged horse Pegasus: it is one of the famous metopes of the Doric frieze of Temple C, dating to 575-550 BC and one of the best examples of Sicily's Archaic style.*

283 *This fragmented island-marble head representing a goddess came from a metope of Temple E at Selinus (470 BC).*

279-282 *This is probably what Selinus looked like in the mid-5th century BC, at its peak, before the disputes with Segesta and Carthage began its early decline. Note the harbor's location at the mouth of the river Selino.*

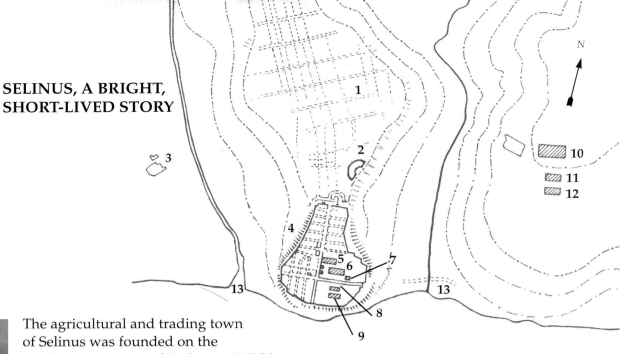

The agricultural and trading town of Selinus was founded on the southwestern coast of Sicily in 628 BC by colonists from Megara Hyblaea. Initially governed by an oligarchic regime, in the 5th century BC it was ruled by a tyranny, like many other Sicilian cities. The sack of the city by the Carthaginians in 409 BC marked the start of its inexorable decline; a period of modest recovery was followed by further destruction (250 BC) and the definitive end of its history.

The acropolis, accommodating the most ancient of its temples and probably some residential buildings, is situated on a vast low-lying plateau at a point where a spur juts into the sea; the residential quarters occupied the gently sloping land to the north. The almost perfect gridlike layout of roads and streets are part of an urban planning scheme developed in the first quarter of the 6th century BC: among its most interesting features are the rational arrangement of the residential areas, separate from the sacred enclave; close relations between the residential quarters, acropolis, and harbor, and the orientation of the sanctuaries, outside the city walls. As documented primarily by remains of its rich Archaic temple architecture, the urban space and the monuments within the landscape were clearly configured by both rational and scenic considerations. Temples C and D and the vast southeastern area of the acropolis, reserved for worship, were spectacularly located within sight of the sea, at exactly the right distance from the main thoroughfares. Prominent on the acropolis site was monumental Temple C (64 by 24 meters), built in 540-530 BC and dedicated to an unidentified deity. It is an elongated Doric building; its peristyle (6 by 17 columns), like the ensemble of its structural elements, appears to be airy and filled with light.

1 Site of the ancient city	7 Temple B
2 Theater	8 Temple A
3 Sanctuary of	9 Temple O
Demeter Malophoros	10 Temple G
4 Acropolis	11 Temple F
5 Temple D	12 Temple E
6 Temple C	13 Ancient harbor

276 top left *Temple C at Selinus is the only sacred building of the acropolis of which a few columns of the peristyle still exist. In the Doric style, its sculptured metopes are of the high Archaic style.*

276 top right *Temple E at Selinus belonged to the sacred area of the eastern hill outside the walls. Its peristyle has remained intact thanks to a reconstruction.*

276-277 *Temple C dominates the ruins of the Selinus acropolis, in which traces of the town's occupation by Carthage after the siege and conquest of 409 BC are kept.*

277 *The colossal Temple G at Selinus is now a bunch of ruins from which one single broken-up column stands out— the only witness to the huge building, which was started around 510 BC but never completed.*

The cella had a vestibule and adyton. All these factors indicate that Ionic influences—generally fruitful in the eclectic world of the Western Greeks—were here fused with traditional Doric forms: although not exceedingly elegant, the results are at least original.

Of interest in the vicinity of Temple D are remains of Punic dwellings from the 4th and 3rd centuries BC, evidence of occupation of the city by the Carthaginians. The colossal Temple G, in a visually stunning position on the east hill and probably dedicated to Apollo, dates to the last quarter of the 6th century BC. Its large size (110 by 50 meters) may have been one reason why its construction was so slow. (It took at least half a century to complete.) The

building is of the Doric order, and its pronaos was preceded by a projecting part with six columns. From here, three doorways gave access to three naves of the cella, whose columns guided the gaze of the faithful to the small adyton, or inner shrine, where the oracle must once have been located. On the opposite side, the opisthodomos is consistently executed from a typical Doric blueprint.

The voluminousness of the building is, by contrast, definitely Ionic, reflecting a predilection for gigantism typical of tyrants, who also came to power in Selinus. Part of a crowded ensemble of sacred buildings on a hillock east of the city (following a model common to other western colonies), Temple G is to be interpreted as an expression—even more eloquent than Temple C—of the tyrants' desire to extol the prosperity and prestige of their city by deference to the revered deity and cult, a practice followed by contemporary tyrants in Athens and Asia Minor. In these monumental schemes, propaganda, demogoguery, and a touch of parochialism mixed and mingled with the traditional cultural and spiritual values of Greekness.

Also of notable visual impact is Temple E, dating from the Severe period, with unadulterated Doric forms from which magnificent carved metopes have been recovered; much of the peristyle and cella of the temple has been reconstructed. Before reaching the extramural sanctuary (5th century BC) of Demeter Malophoros (cultic archetype of the Christian "Madonna of the Pomegranate Tree") and the cemetery, which are outside the city's walls, it is worth stopping to admire the substantial fortifications north of the acropolis, including a long, covered gallery, a defensive ditch with towers, and protected ramparts.

284 top *The Doric columns of Temple E seen against the background of the sky, a tribute to the Greeks' constant search for a link between buildings and nature.*

284 bottom *The skill of the designer of Temple E also appears in the accurate layout of triglyphs and corner columns on the same axis.*

284-285 and 285 bottom *Temple E, built around 480 BC, fine harmonic proportions in its powerful but slender peristyle.*

286-287 *Temple E is attributed by consensus to Hera, the goddess who protected married couples and ensured fertility.*

GLOSSARY

ABACUS: *a slab-shaped element, either square (Doric) or rectangular (Ionic), placed between the capital and the architrave.*

ACROPOLIS: *the upper part of a city, often fortified with walls and embellished with temples.*

ACROTERION: *a decorative architectural element placed at the top or on both sides of the pediment.*

AGORA: *the main part of a city; also a marketplace, where public meetings were held.*

BOULEUTERION: *a building in which the boule, the council of representatives of the polis, gathered.*

CANON: *a body of established rules that govern the proportions of statues, according to a standardized ideal of beauty.*

CHRYSELEPHANTINE: *made of gold and ivory, relating in particular to statues.*

DEMO: *the smallest administrative territorial unit.*

DIPTERAL: *a temple surrounded by a double order of columns.*

DROMOS: *a corridor leading to the entrance of a monumental tomb.*

ECHINUS: *the rounded element of a Doric or Ionic capital, placed under the abacus.*

ENTASIS: *the bulge of the column at a third of its height, used as an optical adjustment.*

GYMNASIUM: *a place devoted to the moral and intellectual education of young people.*

HEXASTYLE: *a temple having six columns on its short sides.*

HOPLITE: *an infantry soldier equipped with heavy armor, made up of a shield, spear, sword, helmet, cuirass, and shin guards.*

HYDRIA: *a ceramic or bronze vase used for water, having a bellied body, a foot, a high, narrow neck, and three handles.*

IN ANTIS: *said of a temple that shows two central columns in the front and two pillars at the end of the side walls.*

KOINE: *the commonly spoken Greek language, based on the Attic dialect, that became widespread from the 4th century BC on in the central-eastern Mediterranean area.*

KORE: *a votive statue having the shape of a young woman, dressed; typical of Archaic Greek sculpture.*

KRATER: *a large vase with a wide mouth, fitted with a foot and two handles, in which water and wine were usually mixed.*

KOUROS: *a votive statue portraying a young naked youth, standing; typical of Archaic Greek sculpture.*

MEGARON: *the largest and most sumptuous room in palaces of the Mycenaean period; later, any large room.*

METOPE: *in the Doric order, the square space between two triglyphs, filled with sculptures in bas-relief of marble or terracotta, floral patterns, or rounded shields.*

NAOS: *in a temple, the cella in which the image of the god was kept.*

OINOCHOE: *a jar-shaped vase with a single handle, used for drawing and pouring wine.*

OPISTHODOMOS: *the back part of a temple, opposite the pronaos, used for storing treasure.*

PALAESTRA: *usually an outdoor space, used by young pupils for physical exercise, generally located next to a gymnasium.*

PEDIMENT: *a triangular architectural part, placed on the front as a gable on a temple or other monumental building.*

PERIBOLOS: *an area surrounded by a wall around a temple, often adorned with statues, altars, and votive monuments.*

PERISTYLE: *in Greek houses and also in sanctuaries, a court surrounded by a colonnade.*

PRONAOS: *in a temple, the space between the cella and the front colonnade.*

PRYTANEOS: *originally a public building where the archons, the magistrates ruling a city, each for the tenth part of the year, gathered.*

RHYTON: *a vessel used for drinking, made of metal or ceramic, molded in the shape of a curved horn, often topped with the head of an animal.*

SCOTIA: *a concave molding in the base of a column or pillar. It has two convex moldings.*

SKYPHOS: *a vase shaped like an upside-down truncated cone, with a foot and two horizontal handles level with the lip.*

STYLOBATE: *the base of a temple on which the columns rest.*

STOA: *a portico with a colonnade and usually a blind wall in back, used as a gathering place.*

TEMENOS: *a sacred enclosure, usually delimited by a wall or by boundary stones.*

THALASSOCRACY: *a state founded on maritime supremacy.*

THOLOS: *a temple, building, or part of a building having a circular plan, delimited by an order of columns, and usually topped with a dome or a cone-shaped roof.*

TORUS: *a molding of semicircular convex profile, forming a sort of ring at the base of a column.*

TRABEATION: *in classical architectural, the frame resting on the columns, composed of the architrave, the frieze, and the cornice.*

TRIGLYPH: *in the Doric order, an ornament of the frieze between two metopes, similar to a square tablet of stone or terracotta, with two vertical central channels of triangular section and two half channels on the sides.*

TYMPANUS: *in a temple, the triangular face of the front, limited by two sloping sides and by the architrave, usually decorated with sculptures.*

BIBLIOGRAPHY

HISTORY AND CIVILIZATION

Albini, U., *Nel nome di Dioniso. Vita teatrale nell'Atene classica*, Milan 1994.

Bérard, J., *La Magna Grecia*, Turin 1963.

Bengtson, H., *Griechische Geschichte* (II ed.), Munich 1960.

Beye, C.R. (edited by), *La tragedia greca. Guida storica e critica*, Rome-Bari 1994.

Bianchi Bandinelli, R. (edited by), *Storia e civiltà dei Greci*, Milan 1979.

Casson L., *Ships and Seamanship in the Ancient World*, Princeton 1986.

Coulton J.J., *Greek Architects at Work*, London 1977.

Glotz, G., *The Greek City and Its Institutions*, New York 1930.

Guthrie, W. K. C., *The Greeks and Their Gods*, Boston 1950.

Maddoli G., *La civiltà micenea. Guida storica e critica*, Rome-Bari 1992.

Musti, D. (edited by), *Le origini dei Greci. Dori e mondo egeo*, Rome-Bari 1990.

Musti, D., *Storia greca*, Rome-Bari 1989.

Snodgrass, A. M., *Un'archeologia della Grecia*, Turin 1994.

Various Authors, *Magna Grecia. Il Mediterraneo, le metropoleis e la fondazione delle colonie*, 1985.

Vernant, J.-P., *L'uomo greco*, Rome-Bari 1991.

ART AND ARCHITECTURE

Adam, J.-P., *L'architecture militaire grecque*, Paris 1982.

Becatti, G., *L'arte dell'età classica*, Florence 1971.

Bianchi Bandinelli, R., *La pittura greca*, Rome 1980.

Bianchi Bandinelli, R., *L'arte classica*, Rome 1984.

Boardman, J., *Athenian Black Figure Vases*, London 1974.

Boardman, J., *Athenian Red Figure Vases. The Archaic Period*, London 1975.

Boardman, J., *Greek Sculpture. The Archaic Period*, London 1978.

Boardman, J., *Athenian Red Figure Vases. The Classical Period*, London 1989.

Boardman, J., *I Greci sui mari. Traffici e colonie*, Florence 1986.

Charbonneaux, J., Martin, R., and Villard, F., *La Grecia arcaica*, Milan 1971.

Charbonneaux, J., Martin R., and Villard, F., *La Grecia classica*, Milan 1971.

Charbonneaux, J., Martin R., and Villard, F., *La Grecia ellenistica*, Milan 1971.

Coldstream, J.N., *Geometric Greece*, London 1977.

De Franciscis, A., *Considerazioni sull'architettura greca arcaica*, Naples 1973.

Demargne, P., *Arte egea*, Milan 1971.

De Polignac, F., *La nascita della città greca*, Milan 1991.

Fuchs, W., *Scultura greca*, Milan 1982.

Immerwahr, S.A., *Aegean Painting in the Bronze Age*, London 1990.

La Rocca, E., *L'esperimento della perfezione. Arte e società nell'Atene di Pericle*, Milan 1988.

Lauter, H., *Die Architektur des Hellenismus*, Darmstadt 1986.

Martin, R., *La Grecia e il mondo greco*, Turin 1984.

Moreno, P., *Pittura greca*, Milan 1987.

Pesando, F., *La casa dei Greci*, Milan 1989.

Various Authors, *Megale Hellas*, Milan 1983.

Various Authors, *Sikanie*, Milan 1985.

Various Authors, *L'oro dei Greci*, Novara 1992.

Various Authors, *I Greci in Occidente*, Milan 1996.

ARCHAEOLOGICAL SITES

Andronikos, M., *Vergina. The Royal Tombs and the Ancient City*, Athens 1987.

De Miro, E., *La Valle dei Templi*, Palermo 1994.

Greco, E., *Magna Grecia*, Rome-Bari 1980.

Greco, E., and Theodorescu, D., *Poseidonia-Paestum I*, Rome 1980.

Greco, E., and Theodorescu, D., *Poseidonia-Paestum II*, Rome 1983.

Mallwitz, A., *Olympia und seine Bauten*, Munich 1972.

Mertens, D., *Der Tempel von Segesta*, Mainz 1984.

Mertens, D., *Der alte Heratempel in Paestum und die archaische baukunst in Unteritalien*, Mainz 1993.

Petrakos, V., *Delfi*, Athens 1977.

Ridgway, D., *L'alba della Magna Grecia*, Milan 1984.

Schede, M., *Die Ruinen von Priene*, Berlin 1964.

Thompson, H.A., and Wycherley, R.E., *The Agora of Athens*, Princeton 1972.

Various Authros, *Guide de Délos*, Athens 1965.

Von Gerkan, A., and Mueller Wiener, W., *Das Theater von Epidauros*, Stuttgart 1961.

Yalouris, A., and Yalouris, N., *Olimpia. Guida del Museo e del Santuario*, Athens 1986.

Zafiropoulou, F., *Delos*, Athens 1983.

ILLUSTRATION CREDITS

INDEX